THE MANY FACES OF GLOBAL PENTECOSTALISM

THE MANY FACES OF
GLOBAL PENTECOSTALISM

EDITED BY

HAROLD D. HUNTER
NEIL ORMEROD

CPT Press
Cleveland, Tennessee

The Many Faces of Global Pentecostalism

Published by CPT Press
900 Walker ST NE
Cleveland, TN 37311
USA
email: cptpress@pentecostaltheology.org
website: www.cptpress.com

Library of Congress Control Number: 2013951568

ISBN-10: 1935931393
ISBN-13: 9781935931393

Scripture taken from the NEW AMERICAN STANDARD BIBLE®, Copyright © 1960, 1962, 1963, 1968, 1971, 1972, 1973, 1975, 1977, 1995 by The Lockman Foundation. Used by permission.

CONTENTS

SECTION III
THE GLOBAL NORTH

This book seeks to the the reader in a greater understanding of Pentecostalism within various religions and _____ cultures.

I was Elevated, & enlightened & challenged by various authors in the book. The many faces of Pentecostalism The Book

EDITORS' PREFACE

In the summer of 2010, Dr Billy Wilson approached Dr Harold D. Hunter about pulling together a group of scholars from 11 geographical regions of the world. This was in anticipation of a global conference to be sponsored by Empowered 21 in 2015.

Dr Hunter was able to expand the team by including not only Pentecostal scholars but also Roman Catholic, Eastern Orthodox, and a representative from the World Council of Churches. Hunter made a site visit to Oxford, England, and put out a call for a consultation to be hosted at the Oxford Centre for Mission Studies.

Hunter sent letters of invitation to a wide range of scholars and in addition, invitations were extended to three scholars resident in Oxford. These were Metropolitan Professor Dr Kallistos Ware, Professor Paul S. Fiddes, and Dr Wonsuk Ma. The event was billed as a Consultation on Global Pentecostalism.

A team of 15 persons convened at the Oxford Centre for Mission Studies from June 7-9, 2012. Funding from Empowered 21 covered local expenses while the team was in Oxford. Dr Billy Wilson came to the meeting and made a presentation on behalf of Empowered 21 and Jerusalem 2015 in particular.

Given the remote places from which many scholars came, it was no small undertaking for them to locate funding to pay for their travel expense. Hunter wrote not a few letters of appeal and all who promised to come were able to make it to Oxford as planned.

Each participant had been asked to make a presentation about Pentecostalism in their part of the world. After all the papers were read, the group decided that these papers should be revised and published in a single volume. Thus the contents of the volume in hand which however does not include a paper read at Oxford 2012 by Dr Tamara Grdzelidze regarding relations between the World Council of Churches and Pentecostals.

Hunter asked distinguished Roman Catholic scholar Dr Neil Ormerod to serve as co-editor. The editing process has been handled by scholars separated by 14 hours, but the shared work has gone well and we were able to adhere to a tight schedule to meet all the relevant deadlines.

Oxford 2012 illustrated that a definition of Pentecostalism is not possible. This does not imply that Pentecostal theology is wanting, as should be apparent in the pages of this volume. The contents of this volume should also put to rest some stereotypes that still survive about the texture of Pentecostalism.

Here now are summaries of the contents of this important contribution toward trying to understand global Pentecostalism.

The impenetrable question is posed yet again by the Orthodox to Roman Catholics. Where are we on the question of papal primacy? This extraordinary study tries to move the discussion forward, while exhorting all to ecumenical patience. His Eminence Metropolitan Kallistos Ware addresses all the major topics that have conflicted the Orthodox and Roman Catholics in the past century.

A forward model in ecumenical matters for many Pentecostals will be found in the journey of some Baptist theologians' remarkable record. Paul S. Fiddes's starting point is that ecumenism is now done 'from the bottom up' and that 'full communion' with an emphasis on diversity has replaced any notion of an emerging 'one world Church'.

Wonsuk Ma states categorically that Pentecostalism in the twenty-first century will be known as it develops in the Global South, with the Global North little more than a distant memory. Trends from the two millennia of Christendom are outlined, which then are foundational to projections for the next millennia.

A delicate narrative is moderated by Connie Au, who wishes not to inflict more suffering on those Chinese House Churches that continue to be persecuted in mainland China. Their kinship with Pentecostalism is mostly phenomenological, which would be at the periphery of their journey as they seek to survive but not spurn martyrdom.

Yohanna Katanacho represents Arab speaking Christians, particularly those in Palestine. He reminds us of the long history of Arabic involvement with God's plan of salvation in the Old and New Testaments and their leading lights is the life of the early

Church. He reminds us that they were 'pioneers in theological thinking and sharing Christ at the cost of martyrdom from the very beginning'.

Highlighting the challenges faced by Pentecostals in Latin America, Elizabeth Salazar-Sanzana raises questions about the widespread 'pentecostalization' that is occurring across the various churches there through evangelical churches and reaching as far as the Catholic Church. She is particularly critical of the influence of 'neo-Pentecostal' groups who risk turning religion into a commodity, while paying scant attention to the basic doctrine of justification by faith. She gives particular attention to the challenges faced by theological education and the need to preserve the distinctive character of the different national Pentecostal communities.

Agustina Luvis-Núñez speaks of the Caribbean experience of Pentecostalism and its lively interaction with the various religious traditions in the islands. Out of this experience Caribbean theologians are seeking to respond to a context of violence, injustice, drug abuse, and suffering, which recognizes 'the praxis of Jesus Christ as one of justice in the social, political, and economic arena'.

J. Kwabena Asamoah-Gyadu draws parallels between primal religiosity in Africa and the Pentecostal movement in that continent. He argues that the world view of a biblical Pentecostalism is much closer to that of primal religions in Africa than to modern rational worldviews. These similarities help explain the uptake of Pentecostal Christianity within the African continent, noting that 'when people appropriate new faiths, they do so by drinking from familiar wells'.

Philippe Ouédraogo has provided us with an important account of the work of Pentecostal and evangelical missionaries in French speaking Africa, especially Burkina Faso. From small and difficult beginnings, the church in Burkina Faso has been able to send missionaries out to Côte D'Ivoire, Ghana, Togo, Benin, Niger, Mali, Guinea Conakry, Senegal, Tchad, Switzerland, Belgium, Luxembourg, and even the USA.

Clifton R. Clarke explores the situation in Britain, where black Pentecostalism combines traditions from both the Caribbean and Africa, particularly Nigeria. These two waves of migration have developed distinctive forms of church life with their own challenges. Clarke calls for a return to Pentecostal distinctives through mutual cooperation between these two communities to renew black Pentecostalism in Britain.

Lecturing in both Pentecostal and Russian Orthodox seminaries in Russia, Olga Zaprometova senses a reversal of fortunes with Russian Pentecostalism perhaps now faltering while Russian Orthodoxy reclaims biblical foundations to hold postmodernity in check. A common call is made for reflection on the Eastern patristic living tradition.

Laced with music from immigrant Oneness Pentecostals, David Ramírez lays bare the difficult life from the 'borderlands' that increasingly accounts for one of the fastest growing segments of Pentecostalism in the USA.

A colorful commentary with much insight into the matrix of Australian Pentecostalism is revealed by Mark Hutchinson as he assesses Pentecostalism's impact or lack thereof on the public square.

The future of Anglican–Pentecostal relations could be shaped by a series of talks that began in earnest in 2013. David Hilborn has himself been no small player in moving the Anglican community to the point where they must finally admit publically their need for engaging Pentecostals in formal conversations of international significance.

While most people would not view Pentecostalism and feminist thought as having comfortable relations, Pamela Holmes brings the two into dialogue to raise the question of the place of women within the Pentecostal movement in Canada. Drawing on insights from Elisabeth Schüssler Fiorenza, she finds parallels in the ways in which Pentecostals and feminist scholars read the Bible, seeking to know not just what the Bible meant to its original audience but what it means here and now in the light of the experience of liberation. In this she carefully distinguishes Pentecostal approaches from evangelicals and Fundamentalists.

Dr Harold D. Hunter
Dr Neil Ormerod

Consultation on Global Pentecostalism (Oxford, 2012) – Back row: Daniel Ramírez, J. Kwabena Asamoah-Gyadu,
Neil Ormerod, Harold D. Hunter, Clifton Clarke, David Hilborn, Olga Zaprometova. Front row: Agustina Luvis-Núñez, Connie Au,
Yohanna Katanacho, Elizabeth Salazar-Sanzana, Mark Hutchinson, Tamara Grdzelidze, Philippe Ouédraogo, Pamela M.S. Holmes

INTRODUCTION:
GLOBAL PENTECOSTALS ARE NOT
'PROTESTANTS' AND ARE NOT 'WESTERN'

HAROLD D. HUNTER[*]

Not unlike Anglican communions, Pentecostals around the world do not accept the generic label of being called Protestants nor as having risen solely from soil of the Global North. Negative perceptions of Pentecostalism are often skewed by what one sees from independents who communicate through television, radio, social media, and the web. A more accurate commentary would come from analyzing churches like the Yoido Full Gospel Church in Seoul, South Korea.[1]

The above paragraph attempts to summarize a 2010 course on Global Pentecostalism that I taught for Gordon-Conwell Theological Seminary in Asia then Africa. However, even at the first global conference for Pentecostal scholars known as *Brighton '91*, I tried to start a conversation between David Barrett and Mel Robeck. Unfortunately, Barrett declined my invitation, so the papers published

---

[*] Harold D. Hunter (PhD, Fuller Theological Seminary) is Director of the IPHC Archives & Research Center. Denominational executive positions, seminary teaching, and ecumenical dialogues have taken him to about 70 countries. Hunter actively engages the World Council of Churches, Eastern Orthodox Churches, the World Alliance of Reformed Churches (WARC), and the NCCCUSA Faith and Order Commission.
[1] A good place to start is Allan Anderson's *An Introduction to Pentecostalism* (Cambridge: Cambridge University Press, 2nd edn, 2013). Margaret Poloma and John C. Green, *The Assemblies of God: Godly Love and the Revitalization of American Pentecostalism* (New York: New York University Press, 2010), pp. 22, 32, document the growing number of European-American congregations in the USA – including Central Assembly in Springfield – that can be labelled 'Evangelical Assemblies of God'. This should challenge Grant Wacker and other scholars in the USA who consider the Assemblies of God (Springfield, Missouri) the axiomatic typology of global Pentecostalism.

under the title *All Together in One Place*[2] give the inaccurate impression that I endorse the concept that the Azusa Street Revival is the epicentre of Global Pentecostalism.

The largest organization of Pentecostals is the Pentecostal World Fellowship (PWF), which was formed in 1947. It currently consists of approximately 60 Pentecostal denominations or associations spread throughout the world. As of the 2010 Pentecostal World Conference, the chairman of the PWF is Rev. Dr Prince Guneratnam, Senior Pastor of Calvary Church and General Superintendent Emeritus of the Assemblies of God of Malaysia.

The PWF is a cooperative body that does not provide legislative or jurisdictional oversight to its member churches and associations. Instead, through a triennial conference, the PWF encourages the formation of partnerships and cooperation among Pentecostal bodies for the sake of common mission.

The PWF network extends deep into the Global South to embrace denominations like the Church of Pentecost in Ghana and the Indian Pentecostal Church in India with early ties to Syriac Orthodoxy. Although lacking a formal apparatus to engage sister Pentecostal churches, mutual cooperation takes many forms. This expands the reach of the PWF community to represent the majority of Pentecostals around the world. Not included, however, are African Instituted Churches, House Churches in China, autochthonous Pentecostal churches in Latin America, and like groupings.

The Pentecostal World Fellowship 2010 conference convened in Stockholm and welcomed Dr Olav Tveit, the WCC General Secretary, to bring greetings. One of the hosts for the 2013 WCC General Assembly in Korea will be the Yoido Full Gospel Church. Senior Pastor Rev. Dr Young-hoon Lee has chaired the National Council of Churches in Korea and recently hosted the Global Christian Forum. Previously, the Yoido Full Gospel hosted the World Alliance of Reformed Churches – Pentecostal Dialogue then the WCC – Pentecostal Joint Consultative Group and has extended an invitation to host future talks between Orthodox and Pentecostals.

---

[2] Harold D. Hunter and Peter D. Hocken (eds.), *All Together in One Place: Theological Papers from the Brighton Conference on World Evangelization* (JPTSup 4; Sheffield: Sheffield Academic Press, 1993).

We do not have anything comparable to a Pope, Ecumenical Patriarch, or Archbishop of Canterbury. Any attempt to impose foreign ecclesiastical structures on Pentecostals would be seen as betraying our ecclesiology as well as our pneumatology with an emphasis on gifting and calling. This pneumatic emphasis insists on accountability to the discernment of the community. At the same time, however, it has been suggested that some of our autocephalous ecclesial structures function in ways not unlike Patriarchs.

Apostolicity is frequently depicted by member churches of the PWF as continuity with the life, teachings, and practices of the early Church. This consciousness gave birth to names like the Apostolic Faith Movement, *The Apostolic Faith*, and the Apostolic Faith Church of South Africa. A search for 'apostolic' in the digital version of *Bridegroom's Messenger* turns up countless hits in this periodical started by G.B. Cashwell, a minister in the Pentecostal Holiness Church.[3] This practice gained momentum in the 21st Century as can be illustrated by the Pentecostal churches in Ghana that incorporate apostolic in their name.

Pentecostals have two primary sacraments: Water Baptism and the Eucharist. In addition, most Pentecostals practice Holy Unction, the anointing of persons (and of cloths in the absence of the person) with oil as part of the prayer for healing of the sick. Some Pentecostals also practice footwashing (John 13) as a post-baptismal cleansing from sin and thus sacramental in nature.

In January 2011, the International Pentecostal Holiness Church (IPHC) celebrated the centennial of the merger of the Fire-Baptized Holiness Church with the Pentecostal Holiness Church. The historic achievement of unity made visible on January 31, 1911, writes plainly the message that much Pentecostal theology has been done in the context of prayer and worship. It is this matrix that caused two churches to realize a common mission and vision. The older, larger church was the Fire-Baptized Holiness Church (FBHC), but a secure anchor was found in the Pentecostal Holiness Church

---

[3] See *Bridegroom's Messenger* 2.26 (November 15, 1908), p. 3, for an article about Beulah Home that refers to this being an apostolic town, with an apostolic Bible and literary school that will teach apostolic music and build an apostolic orphanage. There is an ad in *Bridegroom's Messenger* 1.18 (July 15, 1908), p. 14, about a meeting in Falcon, North Carolina that promises 'the restoration of Apostolic Gifts and Power to the Church, Mark 16:17, Acts 2:1, Acts 4:39, and the Healing of the Sick, According to James'.

(PHC). The group at the merger was small, but their vision was big as they sensed a calling to propel the emerging church to far flung parts of the world.

These saints imbibed a spirituality of the cross. They talked continually about being living sacrifices crucified unto Christ and lived that out through constant prayer, fasting, covenant-keeping, and non-stop church attendance. Their discipline and spirituality although remarkable were not particularly unusual in the early twentieth century and not exclusively owned by any particular group of Christians in the Global North.

With the fresh winds of the Spirit came the Pentecostal message with its empowering and liberating message of the resurrection. Some of these theological themes coalesce in J.H. King's 1914 *Passover to Pentecost*.[4] King wrote this influential thesis in Memphis, Tennessee, after returning to the USA from Asia, the Middle East, and Europe. At the time of the merger, King was in India making connections important to global Pentecostalism through those like Pandita Ramabai at the Mukti Orphanage with direct ties to a future IPHC affiliate, the Pentecostal Methodist Church of Chile.

Early Pentecostals had a passion for their faith that thought little about much of anything other than singing, praying, preaching, agonizing, confessing, seeking the anointing, testifying, episodes of ecstasy, studying and memorizing the Bible, while taking light to dark places. These early Pentecostals faced threats by people with guns, knives, fire, hangings, poison, whips, brute force, etc., yet they were quite literal about bringing in the 'poor, the crippled, the blind and the lame' (Lk. 14.21, NRSV) as well as going 'out into the roads and the country lanes and compel people to come in, so that my house may be filled' (Lk. 14.23, NRSV). Their version of social justice usually started with the individual which was in no small measure explained by Pentecostals often being the victims of discrimination or persecution. Pentecostals around the world still have martyrs, although it is possible that the first Pentecostal martyr in the

---

[4] J.H. King, *From Passover to Pentecost* (Franklin Springs, GA: Advocate Press, 4th edn, 1976).

USA was killed by police in 1918 due to his commitment to pacifism.[5]

In the context of this discussion those who surrender to the postmodern paradigm of post-denominationalism and care little about 'pre-denominational churches' should read the commentary on Jn 17.21 by J.H. King and G.F. Taylor. North Carolina Pentecostal Holiness Church Conference Superintendent A.H. Butler would call on this text during the November 21-23, 1911, PHC North Carolina convention as he looked back at recent events. The January 31, 1911, merger of the FBHC and PHC was the first instance of organic unity achieved by Classical Pentecostals in the USA.[6]

Dr Harold D. Hunter
Fall 2013

---

[5] See Paul Alexander, *Peace to War: Shifting Allegiances in the Assemblies of God* (Telford, PA: Cascadia Publishing House, 2009), pp. 136-37. Also, email (6/04/ 2010) from Jay Beaman.

[6] Harold D. Hunter, '"Full Communion": A Pentecostal Prayer', *Ecumenical Trends* 37.1 (January 2008), pp. 1-7, 15. See *Proceedings of the Twelfth Annual Convention of the Pentecostal Holiness Church of North Carolina, November 21, 22 and 23, 1911* (Goldsboro: Nash Brothers, 1911), p. 4; G.F. Taylor: 'Other Organizations', *Pentecostal Holiness Advocate* 1.24 (October 11, 1917), p. 9; *idem*, 'Perilous Times', *Pentecostal Holiness Advocate* 1.49 (April 4, 1918), p. 4; *idem*, 'Editorial Thoughts', *Pentecostal Holiness Advocate* 1.50 (April 11, 1918), p. 1; *idem*, 'Bear With Me', *Pentecostal Holiness Advocate* 1.50 (April 11, 1918), p. 8; J.H. King, 'A Word to the Ministry and Membership of the Pentecostal Holiness Church', *Pentecostal Holiness Advocate* 5.4 (May 26, 1921), p. 2-4.

SECTION I

GLOBAL VOICES FROM OXFORD

In chapter one

1

THE ORTHODOX CHURCH AND THE PRIMACY OF THE POPE: ARE WE ANY CLOSER TO A SOLUTION?

HIS EMINENCE METROPOLITAN KALLISTOS WARE[*]

Priorities: The Council of Florence and Today

On the last occasion when Catholics and Orthodox met together at the highest level – at the Council of Ferrara-Florence (1438-39) – the two sides occupied some ten months debating the Procession of the Holy Spirit and the addition of the *Filioque* to the Creed. They devoted about four months to the subject of purgatory and the blessedness of the saints. But on the question of the papal primacy, they spent no more than ten days, towards the very end of the Council.[1]

Ten months for the *Filioque,* ten days for the papal claims: such was the order of priorities in the fifteenth century. Our perspective in the twenty-first century is altogether different. In the eyes of most Orthodox and of most Catholics today, the crucial point at issue between our two Churches is not the theology of the Holy Spirit but the position of the Bishop of Rome within the universal

---

[*] His Eminence Metropolitan Kallistos (Ware) of Diokleia (DPhil, University of Oxford) is a titular metropolitan of the Ecumenical Patriarchate in Great Britain. From 1966-2001 he was Spalding Lecturer of Eastern Orthodox Studies at the University of Oxford, and he is known around the world as one of Orthodox Christianity's leading scholarly and learned voices.

[1] The discussions at the Council of Ferrara-Florence were not in fact continuous, and so allowance has also to be made for intervals when no meetings took place.

Church. In the words of Cardinal Walter Kasper, President of the Pontifical Council for Promoting Christian Unity and Co-Chairman of the Joint International Commission for the Theological Dialogue between the Orthodox Church and the Roman Catholic Church, 'For non-Catholic Christians, the papal ministry is the major hindrance on the path towards unity'.[2] 'The main theological problem we now face', he writes, 'is our shared and different understanding of *communio* (*koinonia*)'.[3] His counterpart, the Orthodox Co-Chairman of the Joint International Commission, Metropolitan John Zizioulas of Pergamon, is in full agreement here: 'Historically the question of the papal authority and primacy has been the main cause for the gradual estrangement between the West and the East[4] ... The question of primacy undoubtedly lies at the very heart of Roman Catholic–Orthodox relations'.[5] The Ecumenical Patriarch Bartholomew I is of the same opinion: 'We have different ecclesiologies, and the place of the Bishop of Rome in the Universal Church of Christ constitutes the principal obstacle'.[6]

It will be noticed that Cardinal Kasper, Metropolitan John Zizioulas, and the Ecumenical Patriarch all speak of papal primacy, rather than papal infallibility, as constituting the chief difficulty between Orthodoxy and Rome. Obviously the question of papal infallibility will also need to be discussed in the Orthodox–Catholic dialogue. But there seems to be general agreement on both sides that we should begin by first discussing the subject of primacy.

Even if papal primacy is indeed the 'principal obstacle' in our search for Orthodox–Catholic *rapprochement*, this does not mean that the other topics debated at the Council of Florence are devoid of significance; far from it. The most serious among these other topics,

---

[2] Walter Kasper (ed.), *The Petrine Ministry: Catholics and Orthodox in Dialogue* (New York/Mahwah, NJ: The Newman Press, 2006), p. 9.

[3] Walter Kasper, *That They May All Be One: The Call to Unity* (London/New York: Burns & Oates, 2004), p. 21.

[4] 'Primacy in the Church: An Orthodox Approach', in James F. Puglisi (ed.), *Petrine Ministry and the Unity of the Church: 'Towards a Patient and Fraternal Dialogue'* (Collegewille, MN: Michael Glazier/The Liturgical Press, 1999), p. 116.

[5] John Zizioulas, 'Recent Discussions on Primacy in Orthodox Theology', in Kasper, *The Petrine Ministry*, p. 231.

[6] Quoted in Adriano Garuti, *The Primacy of the Bishop of Rome and Ecumenical Dialogue* (San Francisco, CA: Ignatius Press, 2004), p. 29, n. 76. Although I do not always agree with Fr Garuti's conclusions, I have found his book a valuable source of information.

certainly, is still the question of the Procession of the Holy Spirit. There continues to exist a significant number of Orthodox, on Mount Athos and elsewhere, who regard this as the root cause of all the 'errors' of Rome. Yet there are other Orthodox (myself included) who see the Trinitarian theologies of the Greek East and the Latin West as complementary rather than contradictory. If the *Filioque* were to be omitted from the Western text of the Creed, then many of us Orthodox might be willing to accept the doctrine of the Spirit's Double Procession as a *theologoumenon,* although not as a dogma. It would be necessary, it is true, to safeguard the position of God the Father as the sole *principium* and fountain-head within the Trinity; but St Augustine and the Council of Florence were in fact careful to do precisely that.[7]

What of the remaining points at issue? Although the delegates at Florence gave lengthy consideration to the state of the departed, few of us today would regard this as an *impedimentum dirimens* between our two Churches. On the Orthodox side, we are greatly encouraged to note that Roman Catholic writers since Vatican II usually interpret purgatory in therapeutic rather than forensic and penal terms, that is to say, as a hospital rather than a prison.[8] This makes it much easier to effect a reconciliation between the Western and Eastern understandings of the afterlife.

In the realm of sacramental theology, many Catholics continue to be disturbed by the Orthodox practice of permitting remarriage after divorce. This was briefly mentioned at Florence but never properly discussed, and nothing was said about it in the final act of union.[9] If in the fifteenth century the two sides agreed to differ over

---

[7] See Augustine, *De Trinitate XV,* 29 (xvii); XV, 47 (xxvi): the Spirit proceeds from the Father *principaliter,* and from the Son solely *per donum Patris.* See also the decree of union at the Council of Florence, in Joseph Gill, *The Council of Florence* (Cambridge: Cambridge University Press, 1958), p. 413; and note also the statements by Montenero, in Gill, *The Council of Florence,* pp. 212-13, 221.

[8] For a typical example of this therapeutic approach, see Robert Ombres, 'Images of Healing: The Making of the Traditions concerning Purgatory', *Eastern Churches Review* 8.2 (1976), pp. 128-38, especially p. 138, n. 47: 'Purgatory is God's love healing us into freedom'. Such is precisely the viewpoint of, among others, Dante, St Catherine of Genoa, and Cardinal Newman, and it is an approach with which many Orthodox are deeply in sympathy.

[9] See Gill, *The Council of Florence,* p. 297: when Pope Eugenius IV raised the question of remarriage after divorce, 'the only answer forthcoming [from the Greeks] was — it is not allowed without reason'. It seems that the Latins did not press the matter further.

this matter, might they not likewise agree to differ here in the twenty-first century?

There are also two further problems not included in the agenda at Florence that will need to be discussed at some point in our present-day dialogue. The first is the distinction made by St Gregory Palamas, on the basis of earlier patristic tradition, between the essence and the energies of God. This was formally endorsed by three Councils of Constantinople (1341, 1347, 1351), which are accepted as authoritative throughout the Orthodox Church. There is an evident incompatibility here between Palamism and Thomism; the Palamite standpoint makes no sense in Thomistic terms, nor can the Thomist teaching be spelled out in Palamite categories. Yet surely what is at issue in this matter is not a fundamental dogmatic conflict but rather a divergence of theologies, each of which deserves to be assessed according to its own criteria. When this is done in the case of Palamism, many contemporary Catholic authorities see no reason to repudiate Palamas as a heretic. The succinct agreement reached on the essence–energies question by the Anglican–Orthodox Joint Doctrinal Discussions at Moscow in 1976 could well serve as a model when the matter comes to be considered by the ongoing Catholic–Orthodox dialogue.[10]

The second issue not raised at Florence, but often regarded as a serious difficulty by modern Orthodox theologians, is the doctrine of the Immaculate Conception of the Blessed Virgin Mary. Here, however, the point in dispute is not primarily our respective beliefs concerning the sanctity of the Mother of God, but rather our dif-

---

[10] For differing estimates of Palamite theology, see the articles in *Istina* 19.3 (1974), pp. 257-349, and in *Eastern Churches Review* 9.1-2 (1977), pp. 1-71; also A.N. Williams, *The Ground of Union: Deification in Aquinas and Palamas* (New York/Oxford: Oxford University Press, 1999), pp. 1-27.

As regards the acceptance of Palamas in Catholic circles, it is significant that the four-volume Ἀνθολόγιον τοῦ Ὅλου Ἐνιαυτοῦ, which commenced publication in 1967, printed at the Monastery of Grottaferrata with official endorsement from the Vatican, includes as an appendix (in the volume devoted to the Triodion) the service on the second Sunday in Lent in honor of St Gregory Palamas. Since the Grottaferrata Ἀνθολόγιον is not an academic reference work but a service-book intended for practical liturgical use, it follows that it is legitimate for Catholics of the Byzantine rite – and, by extension, for Catholics in general – to regard Palamas as a Saint and Father of the Church. I understand that Fr Irénée Hausherr, SJ, for many years Professor at the Pontifical Oriental Institute in Rome (May his memory be eternal!), when consulted about the service for Palamas, strongly supported its inclusion in the Ἀνθολόγιον.

ferent understandings of original sin; and this is a matter that the Greek East, at any rate, has never attempted to define as a dogma.[11]

Nevertheless, even if due weight is given to all these further matters – to the *Filioque,* purgatory, divorce, the essence energies distinction, the Immaculate Conception – yet all of them, with the possible exception of the *Filioque,* are surely to be considered secondary in comparison with the question of the papal claims. It is here, in our respective understandings of the *diakonia* of the Bishop of Rome in the universal Church that we must look for a fundamental and decisive solution in our quest for unity.

At the Council of Ferrara-Florence, the participants began by discussing the points of disagreement between Rome and Orthodoxy. When the current international dialogue between the Roman Catholic Church and the Orthodox Church was inaugurated at Patmos and Rhodes in 1980, a different approach was adopted. The members of the dialogue, to borrow a phrase later used by Pope John Paul II in his 1995 Encyclical *Ut Unum Sint,* desired to be 'open to a new situation'.[12] They feared that if they were to commence as at Florence with the points of disagreement, this would merely result in each party repeating well-worn arguments from the polemical arsenal of the past. They began, therefore, not by considering the familiar matters of the controversy, but by exploring possible areas of consensus between East and West.

In this spirit the delegates at the Joint International Commission have produced four 'convergence documents', adopted at Munich (1982), Ban (1987), Valamo (1988),[13] and most recently at Ravenna

---

For the Moscow Agreed Statement of 1976, see Kallistos Ware and Colin Davey (eds.), *Anglican–Orthodox Dialogue: The Moscow Statement Agreed by the Anglican–Orthodox Joint Doctrinal Commission 1976* (London: SPCK, 1977), §§ 1-3, pp. 82-83; and cf. pp. 45-50.

[11] See Kallistos [Ware] of Diokleia, 'The Sanctity and Glory of the Mother of God: Orthodox Approaches', *The Way,* Supplement 51, pp. 79-96; and *idem*, 'Mary in Christian Tradition', *The Way* (Autumn 1984), pp. 79-96, especially pp. 90-91.

[12] *Ut Unum Sint,* § 95.

[13] For these three statements, see Jeffrey Gros, Harding Meyer, and William G. Rusch (eds.), *Growth in Agreement II: Reports and Agreed Statements of Ecumenical Conversations on a World Level 1982-1998* (Geneva: WCC Publications; Grand Rapids, MI: Eerdmans, 2000), pp. 652-68, 671-79. A further statement by the Joint Commission was issued at Balamand in 1993, on 'Uniatism: Method of Union of the Past, and the Present Search for Full Communion' (in Gros, Meyer, and Rusch (eds.), *Growth in Agreement II,* pp. 680-85). This has been much criticized, es-

(2007). Underlying all of these agreed statements there are three master themes: the fundamental importance of the notion of communion or *koinonia* in our theology of the Church, the central significance of the local Church, and the integral connection between Church and Eucharist. It is only in the most recent of the four statements, that of Ravenna, that there is any direct consideration of papal primacy; and even here the document does no more than suggest, without entering into details, a possible way of making further progress. None the less, the Ravenna statement contains, in my opinion, three points that constitute deeply encouraging signs of hope for the future. What are they?

The Three Levels of Ecclesial Authority: An Outline Map

In order to answer that question, let us identify the fundamental perspective of the Ravenna statement. It is entitled 'Ecclesiological and Canonical Consequences of the Sacramental Nature of the Church: Ecclesial Communion, Conciliarity and Authority'.[14] As this somewhat ponderous title indicates, the ecclesiology of the Ravenna statement is fundamentally an ecclesiology of Eucharistic *koinonia*. This is made plain at the outset, when the Ravenna delegates ask: 'Since the Eucharist, in the light of the Trinitarian mystery, constitutes the criterion of ecclesial life as a whole, how do institutional structures visibly reflect the mystery of this *koinonia*'?[15] Speaking of 'the living Tradition received from the Apostles', the Ravenna statement then goes on to declare, citing 1 Cor. 10.16-17 and 11.23-26, 'At the heart of this Tradition is the Eucharist'.[16] In thus stressing the integral connection between Tradition, Eucharist, and ecclesial *koinonia,* the Joint Commission is following the teaching of (among others) its Orthodox Co-chairman, Metropolitan John Zizioulas.

This 'bond of communion', according to the Ravenna text, involves 'the very being of the Church'.[17] It is a bond that encom-

---

pecially by Eastern Catholics and is widely considered to stand on a different level from the statements of Munich, Ban, Valamo, and Ravenna.

[14] 'Ravenna Document', <http:// www.vatican.va/roman_curia/pontifical_councils/chrstuni/sub-index/index_orthodox-ch.htm>.

[15] 'Ravenna Document', §3.

[16] 'Ravenna Document', §15.

[17] 'Ravenna Document', §33.

passes the entire human family: 'Ecclesial *koinonia is* the gift by which all humankind is joined together, in the Spirit of the risen Lord'.[18] More specifically, every expression of authority and primacy within the Church is to be interpreted in the light of *koinonia:* 'This communion is the frame in which all ecclesial authority is exercised. Communion is the criterion for its exercise'.[19]

This ecclesial communion exists at three levels:

> The conciliar dimension of the Church is to be found at the three levels of ecclesial communion, the local, the regional and the universal: at the local level entrusted to the bishop; at the regional level of a group of local Churches with their bishops who 'recognize who is the first among themselves' (Apostolic Canon 34); and at the universal level, where those who are first (*protoi*) in the various regions, together with all the bishops, cooperate in that which concerns the totality of the Church. At this level also, the *protoi* must recognize who is the first among themselves.[20]

This threefold distinction – local, regional, universal – constitutes a *leitmotif* that recurs throughout the statement and gives it unity. It is, indeed, a distinction that is long-established and widely accepted. It is applied, for example, to the ministry of the pope by Leo Allatius (d. 1669), native of Chios, *alumnus* of the Greek College in Rome, and sometime Prefect of the Vatican Library, in his classic work *De Ecclesiae Occidentalis atque Orientalis Perpetua Consensione*:

> As even the Greeks concede, in the Roman pontiff there is a threefold power. The first is episcopal, whereby he is joined to the diocese of Rome; the second is patriarchal, whereby, occupying the patriarchal throne that is at Rome, he governs the provinces assigned to him and exercises authority over the bishops of those regions, in the same way as the other patriarchs; the third is apostolic, whereby he presides over the whole Church and rules it as Vicar of Christ, and this third power he has received from no one else than Christ, despite the objections raised by the innovators.[21] The Supreme Pontiff has, as bishop, everything in common with the other bishops; as patriarch, everything in

---

[18] 'Ravenna Document', §31.
[19] 'Ravenna Document', §18.
[20] 'Ravenna Document', §10.
[21] Probably Allatius is referring here to the Protestants, not the Orthodox.

common with the other patriarchs … But as Vicar of Christ, endowed by Christ with apostolic power, not only does he stand on a higher level than bishops and patriarchs, but he also wields authority over them, strengthening them, promoting them, and, if need be, deposing them.[22]

The Pontifical Council for Promoting Christian Unity, in a 'Working Document' issued in 2002, makes the same point somewhat more concisely: 'The Bishop of Rome acts simultaneously at once as bishop of a local diocese, as "patriarch" of the Western or Latin Church, and as the universal minister of unity'.[23] What, then, is the attitude of the Orthodox Church towards these three levels of papal authority? As regards the first level, that of the pope as bishop of the diocese of Rome, we Orthodox have here no problems, and so there is no need to speak further about this. As a diocesan bishop, presiding over a local Eucharistic community, the pope is sacramentally equal to all other diocesan bishops.

As regards the second level, that of the pope as first among the patriarchs,[24] again there is in principle no difficulty. As Patriarch of the West, the pope is essentially the elder brother within the worldwide Christian family, 'first among equals', *primus inter pares*. Just as, *qua* Bishop of Rome on the local diocesan level, he is equal to all other diocesan bishops, so *qua* Patriarch of the West he is equal to the other patriarchs, enjoying only certain rights of 'seniority' (πρεσβεία), but no power of jurisdiction over the other patriarchates. Between the Roman bishop as Patriarch of the West and the other patriarchs there does not exist a mother-daughter relationship; they are brothers or sisters. Such is the view of the Greek

---

[22] *De Ecclesiae Occidentalis atque Orientalis Perpetua Consensione* (Cologne: Jodocus Kalcovius, 1648), col. 158. A photographic reprint of this work, with an introduction by Kallistos Timothy Ware, was issued by Gregg International Publishers (Farnborough, Hants, UK) in 1970. On the life of Allatius, see Philip P. Argenti, *The Religious Minorities of Chios: Jews and Roman Catholics* (Cambridge: Cambridge University Press, 1970), pp. 233-69.

[23] 'Petrine Ministry: A Working Document', *Information Service* (Vatican City) 109.1-2 (2002), p. 34; cited by V. Nicolae Dură, in Kasper, *The Petrine Ministry*, pp. 163-64.

[24] On an intermediate level, between the position of the pope as diocesan bishop and his position as patriarch, there is also the lower-level regional primacy assigned to the pope as metropolitan of part or all of Italy. Here again, from an Orthodox standpoint, no problems arise. As metropolitan, the Bishop of Rome is equal to all other metropolitans.

Catholic Allatius, and we Orthodox have no reason to disagree with him over this.

It is only when we come to the third level, that of the pope's universal primacy as Vicar of Christ, that Catholics and Orthodox find themselves on more disputed territory. As the language of Allatius makes clear – 'on a higher level ... wields authority over them ... if need be, deposing them' – the pope in this context is no longer viewed as *primus inter pares* but is definitely superior to the rest of the episcopate. Some Orthodox, as we shall shortly have occasion to note, altogether deny the legitimacy of this third level. Others admit that there are strong grounds historically for allowing the pope an appellate jurisdiction over the Christian East, as stipulated by the Council of Sardica (c. 343), the canons of which form part of Orthodox church law. But this appellate jurisdiction manifestly falls far short of the 'supreme', 'ordinary', and 'immediate' power of jurisdiction ascribed to the pope by Vatican I, and confirmed by Vatican II. Other Orthodox are willing to attribute to the Bishop of Rome, not merely an appellate jurisdiction, but also a certain power of initiative, whereby he might intervene in all parts of the Christian world whenever urgent problems arise that call for his support and guidance. Yet once more this falls short of the provisions of Vatican I and II; for the Orthodox see this 'power of initiative' not as an exercise of 'immediate jurisdiction' but rather as a pastoral 'care for all the Churches', *sollicitudo omnium ecclesiarum,* to use the Pauline phrase (2 Cor. 11.28) applied by Innocent I (402-17) to his papal ministry.[25] Since the schism between East and West, we may add, the Ecumenical Patriarch of Constantinople has exercised *de facto* a certain degree of universal primacy within the worldwide Orthodox Church.[26] But, once again, the universal primacy assigned to the

---

[25] *Ep.* 30, 2 (*PL* 20: 590A; cf. *PL* 33: 784); E. Giles (ed.), *Documents Illustrating Papal Authority A.D. 96-454* (London: SPCK, 1952), §180, p. 202.

[26] While it is generally accepted throughout the Orthodox Church that the see of Constantinople occupies the first place among the patriarchates and Autocephalous Churches, there is considerable inter-Orthodox disagreement – especially between Constantinople and Moscow – concerning the precise powers and prerogatives implicit in this primacy. For the viewpoint of the Ecumenical Patriarchate (but citing also the opinions of Russian canonists), see the authoritative study of Metropolitan Maximos Christopoulos of Sardis, Τὸ Οἰκουμενικόν Πατριαρχεῖον ἐν τῇ Ὀρθοδόξῳ Ἐκκλησίᾳ. Ἱστορικοκανονικὴ Μελέτη (Thessaloniki: Patriarchal Institute for Patristic Studies, 1972): also available in English and French translations. See also Archimandrite Grigorios D. Papathomas, *Le Patriar-*

pope by Vatican I and II is obviously on an altogether different level from this.

Are we then, as Orthodox and Catholics, at a deadlock on this issue of papal primacy? Or does the Ravenna statement offer us some basis, however tentative, for future progress?

'Patriarch of the West'?

Something more, however, needs first to be said about the second level, that of regional primacy. We asserted earlier that, as regards the Orthodox–Catholic dialogue, there is *in principle* no problem here. But *in practice* a serious difficulty has indeed recently arisen. We Orthodox are puzzled and disturbed by the omission from the *Annuario Pontificio* for 2006 (and subsequently) of the traditional papal title 'Patriarch of the West'. Why was this done? No explanation is given for this innovation in the *Annuario Pontificio* itself, and it seems to have taken people by surprise. But in fact the decision to eliminate the patriarchal title did not happen altogether unexpectedly, like summer lightning from a cloudless sky. It has a prehistory. As long ago as 1990 a closely argued monograph appeared on the subject, written by Fr Adriano Garuti, who worked for twenty-seven years (1975-2002) in the Congregation for the Doctrine of the Faith. Here Garuti concludes that the title is inappropriate and should be abandoned:

> The title and role of Patriarch of the West, attributed to the Bishop of Rome, seem therefore to lack any sound basis, alike from the historical and from the doctrinal viewpoint. They originate from a defective ecclesiology, founded upon an exaggerated emphasis on the local aspect of the Church, at the expense of its universal dimension … In the light of Vatican I and Vatican II,

---

chat oecuménique de Constantinople (y compris la Politeia monastique du Mont Athos) dans L'Europe unie (Approche nomocanonique), Νομοκανονκή Βιβλοθήκη 1 (Katerini: Epektasis, 1998), especially pp. 92-137; idem, *Essai de bibliographie (ad hoc) pour l'Étude des questions de l'autocéphalie, de l'autonomie et de la diaspora (Contribution bibliographique à l'Étude des questions – Essai préliminaire)*, Νομοκανονκή Βιβλοθήκη 7 (Katerini: Epektasis, 2000).

it is impossible to make a distinction between the primatial and the patriarchal roles of the pope.[27]

Garuti goes on to conclude that it would be 'opportune' if the title Patriarch of the West 'were no longer to figure' in the *Annuario Pontificio*.[28] In this way, some sixteen years after the appearance of Garuti's book, with disquieting precision his proposal has now been carried into effect. Clearly much more is at stake than a mere title. In maintaining that 'it is impossible to make a distinction between the primatial and the patriarchal roles of the pope', Garuti in effect 'telescopes' the threefold scheme of the Ravenna statement into a twofold structure: instead of the triad 'episcopal body/patriarchs/pope', he affirms a dyad 'episcopal body/pope', with no intermediate level.

Garuti's conclusions have not gone unchallenged. Cardinal Kasper, for example, observes: 'The thesis of Garuti is to be considered a personal historical thesis, one which is vigorously disputed by reputable historians'.[29] In this connection Kasper mentions among others Fr W. de Vries, Fr Yves Congar, and Fr George Nedungatt, and he continues: 'So it is surprising that the Congregation for the Doctrine of [the] Faith props up its argument so one-sidedly with the historically disputed theses of one of its former members, without taking into account the more comprehensive current research'. According to Fr Nedungatt, so Kasper notes, 'such theses come from people who want to be more papist than the pope'.[30]

What, however, is the opinion of Pope Benedict XVI concerning Garuti's thesis? Since, as Cardinal Ratzinger, the present pope was head of the Congregation for the Doctrine of the Faith during much of the time that Garuti was working there, it follows that the pope must be well aware of the opinions of his former assistant. How far, then, does he actually agree with them? To judge from the books and articles that he wrote in the 1960s when he was a university professor, he does not in fact support Garuti in his attempt to

---

[27] Adriano Garuti, *Il papa patriarcha d'occidente? Studio storico dottrinale*, Collectio antoniana 2 (Bologna: Edizioni Francescane, 1990), p. 269.

[28] Garuti, *Il papa patriarcha d'occidente?*, pp. 269-70.

[29] Kasper, *That They May All be One*, p. 82.

[30] Kasper, *That They May All be One*, p. 93, n. 23. For an Orthodox discussion of the title, see Vlassios Phidas, 'Pariarche d'Occident et institution papale. Une approche orthodoxe', *Episkepsis* 660 (2006), pp. 14-24.

'telescope' the second and third levels of ecclesiastical authority. For in these early writings he speaks explicitly about the need to 'build up patriarchal spaces' in which 'the consciousness of reciprocal interconnections at the horizontal level' can develop.[31] Writing with particular reference to Canon VII of the Council of Nicaea (325), he speaks of the emergence in the early fourth century of two kinds of primacy: 'the primacies of Alexandria and Antioch are regional primacies; the Bishop of Rome possesses a regional primacy and, in addition, a "primacy" of another kind relating to the whole Church'. Difficulties have arisen, he continues, because in the subsequent history of the Latin West, this distinction – between the 'regional primacy' of the Bishop of Rome as first among the patriarchs and his 'primacy of another kind' as successor of Peter and universal minister of unity – was not properly maintained. 'The most tragic aspect of all', he writes, 'rests in the fact that Rome did not manage to differentiate between the apostolic responsibility and the essentially administrative idea of patriarchate, with the result that it has presented to the East a claim that in this form could not be, and ought not to be, necessarily accepted'. It is therefore important to reemphasize the difference between the 'Petrine office' that the pope exercises over the universal Church, and the 'patriarchal office' that he exercises only over the Latin West.[32] In other words, the kind of jurisdiction exercised by the pope over Latin Christianity as 'Patriarch of the West' is not to be extended unchanged and in its totality to the Christian East. There is a vital distinction of levels.

If in the 1960's such was the standpoint of Professor Ratzinger, as he then was, then evidently at that time he was not in agreement with the opinion advanced by Garuti, that 'it is impossible to make a distinction between the primatial and the patriarchal roles of the pope' and that the title 'Patriarch of the West' lacks 'any sound ba-

---

[31] Joseph Ratzinger, 'Konkrete Formen bischöflicher Kollegialität', in Johann Chr. Hampe (ed.), *Ende der Gegenreformation? Das Konzil, Dokumente und Deutung* (Stuttgart: Kreuz, 1964), pp. 159, 161; cited by Hermann J. Pottmeyer, 'Papacy in Communion: Perspectives on Vatican II, in Gerrard Mannion *et al., Readings in Church Authority: Gifts and Challenges for Contemporary Catholicism* (Aldershot, Hants: Ashgate, 2003), p. 262.

[32] Joseph Ratzinger, *Il nuovo popolo di Dio: questioni ecclesiologiche* (Brescia: Editrice Queriniana, 4th edn, 1992), pp. 144-56, especially pp. 144, 146, 156. This work originally appeared in German as *Das neue Volk Gottes: Entwürfe zur Ekklesiologie* (Düsseldorf: Patmos Verlag, 1969).

sis'. Does Pope Benedict still hold the views that he propounded forty years ago, or has he now shifted to the position of his erstwhile assistant at the Holy Office? Should the pope's views be indeed unchanged, then it will reassure us Orthodox if he will unambiguously reaffirm what he wrote in the 1960's.

On the Orthodox side, we certainly do not wish to see the threefold pattern 'episcopal body/patriarchs (and heads of Autocephalous Churches)/pope' collapsed into the dyad 'episcopal body/pope'. 'Patriarchal spaces' definitely need to be maintained. The pope's universal primacy is to be viewed as the top of a pyramid, below which there is to be distinguished the lower level of regional primacy. Only when proper allowance is made for this lower level can the universal primacy of the Bishop of Rome be correctly understood. In the words of the French Joint Roman Catholic–Orthodox Committee, 'The primacy of the Church of Rome and of its bishop is inscribed within a fabric of regional primacies, of "centres of communion", recognized as such by other Churches, both in the East and in the West'.[33]

During the past millennium, there has been little or no practical reason in the Latin West to differentiate between the patriarchal jurisdiction of the Bishop of Rome and his position as universal primate. For the Christian East, however, the distinction is crucial. That precisely is the reason why we Orthodox are deeply troubled by the recent elimination of the title 'Patriarch of the West'. It is disturbing, from the Orthodox standpoint, to observe how frequently in recent ecumenical discussions the level of regional primacy has been left out of account. For example, the Anglican–Roman Catholic International Commission (ARCIC I), in its statements on 'Authority in the Church', works with the dyadic scheme 'pope/episcopate', while making no more than vague allusions to the level of regional primacy.[34] Orthodox, who might have hoped to

---

[33] Quoted in Garuti, *The Primacy of the Bishop of Rome*, p. 40, n. 138.

[34] See *Anglican-Roman Catholic International Commission: The Final Report, Windsor, September 1981* (London: CTS/SPCK, 1982). The statement 'Authority in the Church I' (Venice, 1976) speaks only in very imprecise terms about 'bishops of prominent sees' (§ 10; *The Final Report*, p. 56). The 'Elucidation (1981)' notes that the Venice report has been criticized for saying little about regional primacy and, in particular, about patriarchates; in reply, the 'Elucidation' states (somewhat unhelpfully) that its avoidance of the terms 'patriarch' or 'metropolitan' was deliberate (§7; *The Final Report*, pp. 75-76). Finally, 'Authority in the Church II' (Wind-

use the ARCIC statements as a guideline for their own discussions with Rome, are naturally disappointed. Nowhere does ARCIC I directly confront the possibility that the pope's authority in the West, that is, within his own patriarchate, might be different from the authority he exercises as universal primate in the Christian East. Presumably it was felt that this question was not directly relevant to the Roman Catholic–Anglican dialogue, but it is certainly a matter of concern to Orthodoxy.

It is also disappointing that, in his 1995 Encyclical Letter *Ut Unum Sint*, Pope John Paul II likewise ignores the level of regional primacy, adhering almost entirely to the dyadic scheme 'pope/ episcopate'. Since the letter has in mind the Orthodox, among others, the omission is somewhat more serious. The bishops of the Church of England, in their 1997 response to *Ut Unum Sint*, rightly draw attention to the way in which the Pope overlooks regional primacy; and the 2006 Cyprus Agreed Statement issued by the Anglican–Orthodox Theological Dialogue repeats the same point.[35] So far as we Orthodox are concerned, encouraged though we are by the positive aspects of *Ut Unum Sint*, we cannot but express the same reservations.

For these reasons, we Orthodox are definitely encouraged that the Ravenna statement, for its part, seeks to 'build up patriarchal spaces', making a clear differentiation between the patriarchal and the papal levels of ecclesial authority. Here, then, is an agreed statement, adopted unanimously by both the Roman Catholic and the Orthodox delegates present at Ravenna, which deliberately and consciously adopts a threefold rather than a dyadic scheme, and which in this way distinguishes firmly between the 'apostolic responsibility' and the 'idea of patriarchate', to use the phraseology of Pope Benedict XVI.[36] It has of course to be remembered that the

---

sor, 1981), says merely, 'The jurisdictions associated with different levels of *episcope* (e.g. of primates, metropolitans and diocesan bishops) are not in all respects identical'; once more, nothing is said about patriarchs (§16; *The Final Report*, p. 88). To an Orthodox reader, such a remark is bound to appear inadequate.

[35] See *The Church of the Triune God: The Cyprus Statement Agreed by the International Commission for Anglican–Orthodox Theological Dialogue 2006* (London: The Anglican Communion Office, 2006), pp. 64-65 (citing the Church of England 1997 response).

[36] Can it be said that the Ravenna statement was actually unanimous, in view of the fact that, on the first day (9 October 2007) of the Ravenna meeting, the two-member delegation of the Russian Church, headed by Bishop Hilarion

clergy and laity at Ravenna who signed the agreed statement in October 2007 were acting only as delegates, and the statement has now been referred to the respective church authorities which they represent for endorsement and perhaps emendation. It needs to be received, moreover, not only by the higher authorities but by the main body of the faithful, by the People of God as a whole, on either side;[37] and in the case at any rate of the Orthodox, this process of reception may take a long time. Nevertheless, the firm insistence by the Ravenna delegates on the differentiation between regional and universal primacy is a positive development of major importance, especially in view of the recent tendency in some Roman Catholic circles to undervalue the patriarchal dimension of the ministry of the Bishop of Rome.

Alfeyev of Vienna and Austria, withdrew and took no further part in the deliberations? This withdrawal, however, was not because the Russian delegates disagreed with the other Orthodox representatives concerning Orthodox relations with the Catholics. They withdrew specifically because they objected to the presence on the Orthodox side of a delegation from the Church of Estonia, recognized as an Autonomous Church by Constantinople but not by Moscow. It should be emphasized that, when what eventually became the Ravenna statement was being discussed in draft form at the previous meeting of the Commission (Belgrade, 18-25 September 2006), Bishop Hilarion did not raise any substantive objections to it, except in regard to §39. Even here, his objections did not concern the papal primacy. He disagreed with the assertion that, as a result of the schism between Orthodoxy and Rome, it was impossible to hold 'ecumenical councils in the strict sense of the term', and also with the description of the Orthodox Church as 'the bishops of the local Churches in communion … with the See of Constantinople'.

It should also be noted that the delegates of the Church of Bulgaria were absent from the meetings at both Belgrade and Vienna; but this seems to have been for technical and not for theological reasons. Except for the representatives of the Russian and Bulgarian Churches, the delegates from all the other Orthodox Churches unanimously affirmed the Ravenna statement (Constantinople, Alexandria, Antioch, Jerusalem, Serbia, Romania, Georgia, Cyprus, Greece, Poland, Albania, the Czech lands and Slovakia, Finland, Estonia).

[37] Whether we adopt a triadic or a dyadic scheme in our ecclesiology, it is vital to allow also for the *charismata* conferred upon the total Body of the Church, that is to say, upon the entire *laos* or People of God, by virtue of the sacraments of baptism and Chrismation: 'You have an anointing (χρίσμα) from the Holy One, and all of you have knowledge' (1 Jn 2.20). Our theology of primacy will be gravely defective if it leaves out of account what the West terms the *sensus fidelium,* and what the East styles the 'general conscience' (γενική συνείδησις) of the Church. See Kallistos [Ware] of Diokleia, 'The Exercise of Authority in the Orthodox Church', *Εκκλησία και Θεολογία* 3 (1982), pp. 941-69, especially pp. 948-51; J.M.R. Tillard, 'The Ecumenical Kairos and the Primacy', in Puglisi, *Petrine Ministry and the Unity of the Church,* p. 192.

For me, then, this is the first of the three 'signs of hope' that I discern in the Ravenna document.

Supreme and universal pontiff?

Let us turn now to the third of the three levels of authority indicated in the Ravenna statement, that of universal primacy. Can the Orthodox Church find a place for such primacy, at any rate in *some* form? To this in the past many Orthodox have responded emphatically in the negative, and many would doubtless still so respond today. As a typical example of this negative viewpoint, we may take the *Answer of the Great Church of Constantinople,* sent in 1895 by the Ecumenical Patriarch Anthimos VII and the Holy Synod in response to the Papal Encyclical on union *Praeclara Gratulationis* issued by Pope Leo XIII in the preceding year. Here the Patriarch and the Holy Synod state:

> Having recourse to the fathers and the Ecumenical Councils of the Church of the first nine centuries, we are fully persuaded that the Bishop of Rome was never considered as the supreme authority and infallible head of the Church, and that every bishop is head and president of his own particular Church, subject only to the synodical ordinances and decisions of the Church universal as being alone infallible, the Bishop of Rome being in no wise excepted from this rule, as Church history shows. Our Lord Jesus Christ alone is the eternal Prince and immortal Head of the Church.[38]

This manifestly excludes the exercise of any universal primacy on the part of the pope. The negative standpoint of the 1895 *Answer* was reaffirmed in 1973 by the Ecumenical Patriarch Demetrios I, predecessor of the present Ecumenical Patriarch, when he said:

> No bishop in Christendom possesses the privilege, either divine or human, of universality over the One, Holy, Catholic and Apostolic Church of Christ. We are all purely and simply (fellow

---

[38] Ecumenical Patriarch Anthimos VII, *Answer of the Great Church of Constantinople to the Papal Enyclical on Union* (trans. Archimandrite Eustathius Metallinos; Manchester: The Orthodox Greek Community, n.d. [1896]), §14, p. 37; cf. I.N. Karmiris, *Τα Δογματικά και Συμβολικά Μνημεία της Ορθοδόξου Καθολικής Εκκλησίας* (Athens, 1953), II, p. 938.

bishops under the one supreme High-Priest and head of the Church, who is Jesus Christ'.[39]

A similar position was espoused by Professor Ioannis Karmiris, the leading academic theologian in Greece during the middle of the twentieth century, in his magisterial study *Orthodox Ecclesiology,* also dating from 1973. Here he maintains that the Bishop of Rome enjoys 'by human and not divine order *a simple primacy of honour and order,* as the first among equal presidents of the particular Churches'.[40] In Karmiris's opinion, the present-day structure of primacies, resulting originally from the Byzantine Pentarchy and later supplemented in the Christian East by the creation of newer patriarchates and Autocephalous Churches, is due primarily to historical circumstances, such as the political importance of the leading cities in the Roman Empire. In Rome's case, it is true, Karmiris allows also for the fact that the Apostles Peter and Paul were martyred there. But it is clear that, in his view, the Bishop of Rome is to be seen simply as the most senior of the patriarchs, the first among equals, and that as such he enjoys only a primacy of honor, and not of direct jurisdiction.

In this way, Orthodox spokesmen such as Patriarch Anthimos, Patriarch Demetrios, and Professor Karmiris seem to exclude altogether the third level of ecclesial authority, that of universal primacy. Such, however, is by no means the only view in the contemporary Orthodox Church. Fr Alexander Schmemann, for instance, in his influential essay 'The Idea of Primacy in Orthodox Ecclesiology', originally published in 1960, distinguishes three levels of primacy (not exactly identical with those adopted by Allatius and the Ravenna statement):

(1) *regional primacy* – within an ecclesiastical province or metropolitan district, i.e. in a group of dioceses (as defined, for example, in Apostolic Canon 33 [*sic*]);

---

[39] Address by Patriarch Dimitrios I to Cardinal Willebrands, 30 November 1973, in E.J. Stormon (ed.), *Ecumenical Documents III. Towards the Healing of Schism: the Sees of Rome and Constantinople. Public Statements and Correspondence between the Holy See and the Ecumenical Patriarchate 1958-1984* (New York/Mahwah: Paulist Press, 1987), §311, p. 260; cited in a slightly different form by Garuti, *The Primacy of the Bishop of Rome,* p. 16.

[40] Cited by Metropolitan John Zizioulas, 'Recent Discussions on Primacy in Orthodox Theology', p. 233 (emphasis original).

(2) primacy within the so-called *autocephalous churches:* the power of a patriarch or archbishop (e.g. the Patriarch of Moscow); and (3) *universal primacy:* that of Rome or Constantinople.[41]

In regard to the third of these levels, Schmemann states in trenchant terms:

> An age-long anti-Roman prejudice has led some Orthodox can-onists simply to deny the existence of such primacy in the past or the need for it in the present. But an objective study of the canonical tradition cannot fail to establish beyond any doubt that, along with local 'centres of agreement' or primacies, the Church has also known a universal primacy. The ecclesiological error of Rome lies not in the affirmation of her universal prima-cy. Rather, the error lies in her identification of this primacy with 'supreme power', which transforms Rome into the *principium, radix et origo* of the unity of the Church and of the Church herself. This ecclesiological distortion, however, must not force us into a simple rejection of universal primacy. On the contrary, it ought to encourage its genuinely Orthodox interpretation.[42]

Schmemann is followed here by his colleague at St Vladimir's Orthodox Seminary, Fr John Meyendorff, who likewise affirms the universal primacy of the Bishop of Rome:

> It is a fact, however, that there has never been a time when the Church did not recognize a certain 'order' among first the apos-tles, then the bishops, and that, in this order, one apostle, St Pe-ter, and later, one bishop, leading a particular church [*i.e.,* the Church of Rome], occupied the place of a 'primate' ... I would venture to affirm here that the universal primacy of one bishop ... was not simply a historical accident, reflecting 'pragmatic' re-

[41] A. Schmemann, 'The Idea of Primacy in Orthodox Ecclesiology', in John Meyendorff *et al., The Primacy of Peter* (London: The Faith Press, 1963), pp. 30-56; in the second edn (Crestwood, NY: St Vladimir's Seminary Press, 2nd edn, 1992), pp. 145-71. The passage quoted is on p. 30 (2nd edn, p. 145) (emphasis original). The original French edition was entitled *La primauté de Pierre dans l'Église orthodoxe* (Neuchâtel/Paris: Delachaux et Niestlè, 1960). The Apostolic Canon reckoned by Schmemann as 33 (following the enumeration of Mansi) is more usually num-bered 34.

[42] Schmemann, 'The Idea of Primacy', p. 48 (2nd edn., p. 163). The phrase *principium, radix et origo* comes from *Epistola S. Officii ad episcopos Angliae* (September 16, 1864), in H. Denzinger and A. Schönmetzer, *Enchiridion Symbolorum* (Barcelo-na: Herder, 1976), p. 574. I have corrected the misprint in Schmemann's text.

quirements ... The function of the 'first bishop' is *to serve* ... unity on the world scale, just as the function of a regional primate is to be the agent of unity on a regional scale.[43]

From the Greek side, Metropolitan John Zizioulas of Pergamon is in agreement with Schmemann and Meyendorff. Primacy, he argues, disagreeing here specifically with Karmiris, exists not merely by human but by divine order. It is rooted in the very essence of the Church as a Eucharistic organism.[44] At every concelebrated Eucharist there has to be a presiding officiant; and equally at every council – and a council is to be seen as *par excellence* a Eucharistic event – there has to be one among the bishops who acts as president:

Synodality cannot exist without primacy. There has never been and there can never be a synod or council without a *protos*. If, therefore, synodality exists *iure divino,* as the above theologians [*i.e.,* in particular, Karmiris] would (rightly) maintain, primacy must exist by the same right.[45]

Here Metropolitan John Zizioulas emphasizes the intrinsic reciprocity – what Fr Edward Farrugia terms the 'differentiated interdependence'[46] – between collegiality and primacy. We may appropriately take as our motto, *Never the one without the other.* In the words

---

[43] John Meyendorff, *The Byzantine Legacy in the Orthodox Church* (Crestwood, NY: St Vladimir's Seminary Press, 1982), pp. 244-45 (emphasis original). It is noteworthy that Meyendorff here regards the universal primacy of the Bishop of Rome as a specifically Petrine ministry. Even though many Orthodox ecclesiologists regard *all* bishops as in a sense successors of Peter (cf. St Cyprian, *De unitate* 4), yet most of them agree that the Bishop of Rome is Peter's successor in a more particular sense.

Orthodox exegetes today are also inclined to accept that the 'rock' in Mt. 16.18 denotes not only Peter's faith but also his person: see Dumitru Popescu, 'Papal Primacy in Eastern and Western Patristic Theology: Its Interpretation in the Light of Contemporary Culture', in Puglisi, *Petrine Ministry and the Unity of the Councils,* pp. 99-113; Theodore Stylianopoulos, 'Concerning the Biblical Foundation of Primacy', in Kasper, *The Petrine Ministy,* pp. 37-64, esp. pp. 42-53.

[44] For a masterly analysis of Zizioulas's Eucharistic ecclesiology, see Paul McPartlan, *The Eucharist Makes the Church: Henri de Lubac and John Zizioulas in dialogue* (Edinburgh: T&T Clark, 2nd edn, 1993).

[45] Zizioulas, 'Recent Discussions on Primacy in Orthodox Theology', in Kasper, *The Petrine Ministry,* p. 237 (italics in original).

[46] Edward Farrugia, 'The Ongoing Debate on the Chair of Peter: East Side Story', in *Jesuits in Dialogue: Christian Ecumenism Forty Years after 'Unitatis Redintegratio',* 18th International Congress of Jesuit Ecumenists, Dublin, 12-18 July 2005 (Rome: Secretariat for Interreligious Dialogue, nd.), p. 35.

of the Cyprus Agreed Statement between the Anglicans and the Orthodox, 'Primacy and conciliarity are inseparable'.[47] Developing this point, Metropolitan John Zizioulas insists:

> Synods without primates never existed in the Orthodox Church, and this indicates clearly that if synodality is an ecclesiological, that is, a dogmatic necessity, so must be primacy. The fact that *all* synods have a primate as an ecclesiological necessity means that ecumenical synods should also have a *primus*. This automatically implies universal primacy. The logic of synodality leads to primacy, and the logic of the ecumenical council to universal primacy … Primacy, like everything else in the Church, even in God's being (the Trinity) is *relational*. There is no such thing as individual ministry, understood and functioning outside a reality of *communion* … The reciprocal conditioning between primacy and synodality has profound theological implications. It means that primacy is not a legalistic notion implying the investment of a certain individual with power, but a form of *diakonia,* that is, of ministry in the strict sense of the term.[48]

Primacy, Metropolitan John Zizioulas observes in this connection, since it involves 'ministry' or *diakonia,* can never be a mere 'primacy of honor'.[49] Many Orthodox, when discussing papal primacy, express reservations about the notion 'primacy of jurisdiction'. But, bearing in mind the fundamental meaning of 'jurisdiction', one wonders how far these reservations are justified. As was pointed out in the discussion following the paper of Metropolitan John Zizioulas from which we have been quoting, 'Jurisdiction basically means the necessary authority given to someone in order that he may be able to fulfill his ministry in the Church'.[50] If, then, papal

---

[47] *The Church of the Triune God,* §5.20, p. 64.

[48] Zizioulas, 'Recent Discussions on Primacy in Orthodox Theology', pp. 242-43 (emphasis original).

[49] Zizioulas, 'Recent Discussions on Primacy in Orthodox Theology', pp. 234-35.

[50] Kasper, *The Petrine Ministry,* p. 247. Elsewhere, when speaking about papal primacy, Zizioulas asserts: 'The primacy should not be *primacy* of jurisdiction' ('Primacy in the Church: An Orthodox Approach', in Puglisi, *Petrine Ministry and the Unity of the Church,* p. 124 [emphasis original]). But the logic of Zizioulas's argument, as set forth in his other article from which we have been quoting, 'Recent Discussions on Primacy in Orthodox Theology', inevitably signifies that the

primacy signifies the performance of a ministry (*diakonia*), then it must surely be a primacy not just of honor but of jurisdiction.

In signing the Ravenna agreed statement of 2007, the Orthodox delegates endorsed the standpoint of Schmemann, Meyendorff, and Zizioulas concerning universal primacy and not that of Patriarchs Anthimos VII and Demetrios I and of Karmiris. For, cautiously yet unambiguously, the Ravenna statement does indeed affirm that the pope exercises a universal primacy: 'The fact of primacy at the universal level is accepted by both East and West'.[51] It is this affirmation, accepted by all the Ravenna delegates without any exceptions, that constitutes precisely the second of my three 'signs of hope'.

At once this leads us to a further question: *What kind* of primacy is to be attributed to the pope? The Ravenna statement does not answer this question directly and in detail, but it does offer a significant guideline. And this brings us to the third of my 'signs of hope'.

Trinitarian primacy

In its discussion of the meaning of universal primacy, the Ravenna statement begins by noting areas of agreement and disagreement:

> Both sides agree that [there was a] canonical *taxis* ... recognized by all in the era of the undivided Church. Further, they agree that Rome, as the Church that 'presides in love' according to the phrase of St Ignatius of Antioch (*To the Romans,* Prologue), occupied the first place in the *taxis,* and that the bishop of Rome was therefore *protos* among the patriarchs. They disagree, however, on the interpretation of the historical evidence from this era regarding the prerogatives of the bishop of Rome as *protos,* a matter that was already understood in different ways in the first millennium.[52]

In the ancient Church, so the Ravenna statement continues, the role of the Bishop of Rome as *protos* among the bishops of the major sees was definitely an 'active role'. Although he did not convene the Ecumenical Councils and did not personally preside over them,

---

implementation of primacy, whether at the regional or at the universal level, always presupposes *some kind* of jurisdiction.

[51] 'Ravenna Document', §43.

[52] 'Ravenna Document', §41.

'he nevertheless was closely involved in the process of decision-making by the councils'.[53] Summing up their conclusions, the Ravenna delegates state that they are agreed on the *fact* of primacy at the universal level, but they have *not yet agreed upon the manner of its exercise:*

> 1. Primacy at all levels is a practice firmly grounded in the canonical tradition of the Church.
> 2. While the fact of primacy at the universal level is accepted by both East and West, there are differences of understanding with regard to the manner in which it is to be exercised, and also with regard to its scriptural and theological foundations.[54]

Outlining their future programme, the Ravenna delegates declare:

> It remains for the question of the role of the bishop of Rome in the communion of all the Churches to be studied in greater depth. What is the specific function of the bishop of the 'first see' in an ecclesiology of *koinonia* and in view of what we have said on conciliarity and authority in the present text? How should the teaching of the first and second Vatican councils on the universal primacy be understood and lived in the light of the ecclesial practice of the first millennium? These are crucial questions.[55]

Although on their own admission the Ravenna delegates did not address these 'crucial questions', it does not follow that the meeting during October 2007 was in any sense a failure. The agreed statement they issued makes no claim to finality. It is merely a progress report, providing a foundation for the next stage of the continuing dialogue. Yet the agreement of the delegates, both Orthodox and Catholic, upon *the fact* of the universal primacy vested in the Bishop of Rome is in itself no mean achievement, if we bear in mind the diversity of viewpoints that has existed in this matter among Orthodox theologians in the past.

Nor is this all. Even though the Ravenna statement does not claim to provide detailed answer concerning the nature and scope

---

[53] 'Ravenna Document', §42.
[54] 'Ravenna Document', §43.
[55] 'Ravenna Document', §45.

of the pope's universal primacy, yet it supplies a vital clue regarding the general spirit in which that primacy is to be understood. This the delegates do by emphasizing the significance of Apostolic Canon 34. In its original context this canon refers not to universal but to regional primacy. The Ravenna text, however, hints at the possibility of applying the canon also to the universal level. If papal primacy is indeed to be interpreted according to the spirit of this canon, then this will make it incomparably easier for the Orthodox to accept and welcome such primacy.

The Apostolic Canons are usually assigned to the late fourth century,[56] although it is possible that, at any rate in part, they may date from the third century.[57] As they were confirmed by Canon 2 of the Council in Trullo (692), they possess within the Orthodox Church an ecumenical authority. In particular, Apostolic Canon 34 constitutes for Orthodoxy nothing less than 'the golden rule of the theology of primacy', to quote Metropolitan John Zizioulas.[58] In the canon law of the Christian West, however, the influence of the Apostolic Canons has been much more limited.[59]

As cited in the Ravenna text, Apostolic Canon 34 reads:

> The bishops of each province (*ethnos*) must recognise the one who is first (*protos*) amongst them, and consider him to be their head (*kephale*), and not do anything important without his consent (*gnome*); each bishop may only do what concerns his own diocese (*paroikia*) and its dependent territories. But the first (*protos*) cannot do anything without the consent of all. For in this way concord (*homonoia*) will prevail, and God will be praised through the Lord in the Holy Spirit.[60]

---

[56] Kasper, *That They May All Be One,* p. 80.

[57] Vittorio Peri holds that Apostolic Canon 34 can be 'documented as far back as the end of the third century': 'The Role of the Bishop of Rome in the Ecumenical Councils', in Kasper, *The Petrine Ministry*, p. 136.

[58] Zizioulas, 'Recent Discussions on Primacy in Orthodox Theology', p. 243. On the significance of this canon, see also Archpriest Evgraph Kovalevsky (Mgr Jean de Saint-Dénis), *Organisation de l'Eglise: XXXIVe Canon Apostolique* (Paris: Cahiers Saint-Irénée, 1961).

[59] As is pointed out by Garuti, *The Primary of the Bishop of Rome,* pp. 73-74.

[60] 'Ravenna Document' §24; for the text (Greek and Latin), see P.-P. Joannou, *Discipline générale antique (IVe-IXe s.),* vol. 1. Part 2, *Les canons des Synodes Particuliers* (Grottaferrata [Rome]: Tipografia Italo-Orientale 'S. Nilo', 1962), p. 24. In place of the phrase 'the first cannot do anything', a more exact translation would be 'Let not the first do anything'. In its version of the last sentence, the Ravenna

It would be a grave error to dismiss the concluding clause of this canon, referring to the Holy Trinity, as nothing more than a decorative *coda*. On the contrary, a vital ecclesiological principle is being underlined. The *homonoia* that unites the local bishops and the *protoi* to one another is nothing less than a reflection of the eternal *perichoresis* that holds sway within the very heart of God. The Church is a living icon of the Trinity. This is rightly emphasized by the Cyprus Agreed Statement, adopted in 2006 by the Anglican–Orthodox International Commission:

> The fellowship or communion (*koinonia*) of life in the Church reflects the communion that is the divine life itself, the life of the Trinity … It is within and by the Church that we come to know the Trinity and by the Trinity we come to understand the Church because 'the Church is full of Trinity' (Origen, Fragment on Psalm 23.1, *PG* 12, 1265).[61]

As Jesus affirmed in his High Priestly Prayer on the eve of his Passion, 'May they all be one: even as you, Father, are in me and I in you, may they also be one in us' (Jn 17.21). One of the leading 'elders' on the Holy Mountain today, Archimandrite Vasileios of Iviron (formerly of Stavronikita), claims with good reason: 'This holy Trinitarian "even as" … is the one thing which is needful … There is no other way of authentic and fruitful living'.[62] Miroslav Volf draws out the ecclesiological implications of Christ's prayer:

> 'As' underscores the fact that the unity of the divine 'we', lived out as the mutual interiority of the Father and the Son, provides the model for the unity of the ecclesial 'we'. The nature of [the] ecclesial unity for which Jesus prayed is trinitarian.[63]

---

statement follows the Latin version; the Greek runs, 'For in this way concord will prevail, and glory will be given to Father, Son, and Holy Spirit'.

[61] *The Church of the Triune God*, § 1.3, p. 13.

[62] Archimandrite Vasileios, *Hymn of Entry: Liturgy and Life in the Orthodox Church* (Crestwood, NY: St Vladimir's Seminary Press, 1984), p. 43.

[63] Miroslav Volf, 'Trinity, Unity, Primacy on [*sic*] the Trinitarian Nature of Unity and Its Implications for the Question of Primacy', in Puglisi, *Petrine Ministry and the Unity of the Church*, p. 175. In this connection, Volf draws attention to the fact that Vatican I – which most of us would not immediately associate with an ecclesiology of communion – in fact refers to this very biblical text, Jn 17.20-21, in the preamble to the Dogmatic Constitution *Pastor aeternus* on the primacy and infallibility of the pope. As Farrugia shrewdly comments, 'We need a relecture of

Coming now to the main substance of Apostolic Canon 34, we find that in the Ravenna statement it is initially cited in the section dealing with 'regional synodality';[64] and this is to be expected, since in its original historical context the canon does indeed refer specifically to primacy at the regional level. However, when the Ravenna statement then goes on to consider the universal embodiment of primacy and collegiality, without explicitly quoting Apostolic Canon 34 it employs language – in particular the terms *protos* and *kephale* – that inevitably calls the canon to mind. Thus, towards the end of the section entitled 'The Universal Level', we read:

> In the history of the East and of the West, at least until the ninth century, a series of prerogatives was recognized, always in the context of conciliarity, according to the conditions of the times, for the *protos* or *kephale* at each of the established ecclesiastical levels: locally for the bishop as *protos* of his diocese with regard to his presbyters and people; regionally, for the *protos* of each metropolis with regard to the bishops of his province, and for the *protos* of each of the patriarchates, with regard to the metropolitans of each circumscription; and universally, for the bishop of Rome as *protos* among the patriarchs. This distinction of levels does not diminish the sacramental equality of every bishop or the catholicity of each local Church.[65]

If, then, by implication – albeit not explicitly – the Ravenna statement applies the principles of Apostolic Canon 34 not only to the regional but also to the universal level of primacy, that is to say, to the primacy of the pope, what do these principles presuppose? Fundamental to the canon is the notion of reciprocity and mutual concord. At the regional level, the bishops of a province are to 'recognize the one who is first amongst them' and 'not to do anything important without his consent'; but equally the *protos* should not do anything 'without the consent of all'. The Ravenna statement encourages us to extend this pattern of 'differentiated interdepend-

Vatican I to break the ice in the Orthodox–Catholic dialogue' ('The Ongoing Debate on the Chair of Peter', p. 36). Compare Hermann J. Pottmeyer, 'Recent Discussions on Primacy in Relation to Vatican I', in Kasper, *The Petrine Ministry*, pp. 210-30, especially pp. 212, 215.

[64] 'Ravenna Document', §24. There is also an earlier allusion to the canon in §10, where again it is noted that it refers to regional primacy.

[65] 'Ravenna Document', §44.

ence' likewise to the Bishop of Rome as *protos* within the universal Church. At this level also there is to be reciprocity. It is not a question of one-sided domination, with the pope as the supreme ruler who issues ordinances, while the regional primates – from the Orthodox standpoint, this means the patriarchs and heads of the Autocephalous Churches – are submissively obedient. On the contrary, there is to be mutuality and co-responsibility. The regional primates cannot function without the pope, but neither can he fulfil his ministry without them: 'Let not the *protos* do anything without the consent of all'. All is to be governed by the principle of concord and consensus (*homonoia*), in the spirit of Eucharistic concelebration and according to the image and likeness of God the Holy Trinity.

I am not sure how far the Roman Catholic members of the Joint International Commission will share my understanding here of the intention of the Ravenna statement. If, however, I am indeed correct in my interpretation, then in a far reaching fashion the Ravenna statement modifies and qualifies many earlier affirmations of the Roman Catholic Church. At Vatican II, for example, in the Dogmatic Constitution on the Church *Lumen Gentium*, it is asserted that the college of bishops cannot act without its head, the pope, while the pope can very well act without the college. As the *Prefatory Note of Explanation* states, 'As supreme pastor of the Church, the Sovereign Pontiff can always exercise his authority as he chooses', whereas the college acts only 'at intervals' and 'with the consent of its head'.[66] This does not seem to signify the kind of reciprocity envisaged by Apostolic Canon 34 and the Ravenna statement. Here is a matter that will require further clarification in our future discussions.

Obviously the Ravenna statement constitutes merely an initial prelude or overture, doing no more than opening up the whole question of papal primacy. The real problems are going to arise when the two sides in the Catholic–Orthodox dialogue come to discuss matters of detail. But if Apostolic Canon 34 can be taken as a guideline for understanding the ministry of the Bishop of Rome, we have here an approach to papal primacy that may in time prove

---

[66] 'Nota Explicativa Praevia', in W.J. Abbott (ed.), *The Documents of Vatican II* (London/Dublin: Geoffrey Chapman, 1966), §4, p. 100; cf. Vatican II, 'Lumen Gentium 22', in Abbott (ed.) *The Documents of Vatican II*, pp. 42-44).

acceptable to the Orthodox. That, then, is the third of my major 'signs of hope'.

Because of these three 'signs of hope' in the Ravenna statement – the firm distinction between the patriarchal and the primatial office of the pope, the recognition by the Orthodox members of the joint Commission that the pope possesses universal primacy, and the suggestion that this universal primacy is to be interpreted in terms of Apostolic Canon 34 – there is good reason to accept the claim made in the final paragraph of the Ravenna text: 'The above statement on ecclesial communion, conciliarity and authority represents positive and significant progress in our dialogue, and … it provides a firm basis for future discussion of the question of primacy at the universal level in the Church'.[67] So, if we are asked, 'Are we any closer to a solution?', with sober hope we can answer, 'By God's grace and under his mercy – yes, we are'. But we still have a long way to go. In the words of that great pioneer in the work for Christian unity, Fr Georges Florovsky, 'The greatest ecumenical virtue is patience'. Perhaps we should add: an *impatient patience, a patient impatience.*

[67] 'Ravenna Document', §46.

2

THE CHURCH'S ECUMENICAL CALLING: A CHALLENGE TO BAPTISTS AND PENTECOSTALS

PAUL S. FIDDES[*]

1. The Present Form of the Call[1]

Some while ago my predecessor as Principal at my college in Oxford felt the need for a couple of days' spiritual retreat, and booked himself into a house run by the Carmelite Order. He was made to feel very welcome, but during a discussion period on the second day, a nun turned to him with an air of anxious enquiry. She knew he was a distinguished Baptist historian, so she thought he could answer a question that had often troubled her: could he please explain why Baptists were followers of John the Baptist rather than Jesus?

I wonder if Pentecostals ever face the same kind of misunderstanding. Are Pentecostalists ever asked, for instance, why they celebrate Pentecost rather than Christmas and Easter? Such misinformed challenges as that by our nun can be dealt with easily, but not so easy is the real ecumenical challenge facing us. How shall we hear the call to be 'one', first issued by Jesus himself in John chapter

---

[*] Paul S. Fiddes (DPhil, University of Oxford) is Professor of Systematic Theology in the University of Oxford and was formerly Principal of Regent's Park College and Chairman of the Theology Faculty.
[1] This essay is an abbreviated and extensively revised form of chapter 9 in my book *Tracks and Traces: Baptist Identity in Church and Theology* (Milton Keynes: Paternoster, 2003; Eugene: Wipf and Stock, 2007), pp. 193-227, used by kind permission of both publishers.

17 and now re-issued in our world today? That is the theme I am taking for this essay. How can Baptists, among whom I am numbered, respond to the call to unity, given our particular understanding of the Church? And how far – I am venturing to enquire – might this also apply globally to Pentecostals?

My impression, as a sympathetic observer, is that Pentecostal ecclesiology has tended to begin from the experience of Spirit baptism, thinking of the Church as local assemblies of people who are individually filled with the spirit, but who are exercising spiritual gifts with a communal love and a passion for mission prompted by this baptism. As the Pentecostal theologian Steven Land puts it, 'Christian affections of the heart', shaped by Pentecostal biblical and eschatological beliefs, generate the making of witness and a concern for the Kingdom of God.[2] An individual experience thus leads to an increasingly expanding community. Evidence has been brought, using careful sociological methods, for a link between charismatic experience and church growth by Margaret Poloma in the USA and by William Kay in the UK.[3] However, while not losing the significance of this dynamic, I also notice that in recent years several Pentecostal theologians have thought about the church from a more ecumenical perspective,[4] and I intend to make reference to some of them in this essay.

Through my involvement in a range of ecumenical conversations over the past 30 years, I detect three general trends in the way that churches are hearing God's call to unity.

First, it is a unity which begins *from the bottom up* rather than from the top down. The story of the Cistercian nun shows perhaps that mutual understanding *has* to begin on the ground. Whatever fine things have been happening in the airy heights of theological commissions, such as the dialogue between the Baptist World Alliance

---

[2] Steven J. Land, *Pentecostal Spirituality: A Passion for the Kingdom* (JPTSup 1; Sheffield: Sheffield Academic Press, 1993), p. 66.

[3] Margaret M. Poloma, *The Assemblies of God at the Crossroads* (Knoxville: University of Tennessee Press, 1989), summary p. 232; William K. Kay, *Pentecostals in Britain* (Carlisle: Paternoster, 2000), pp. 253-64.

[4] A similar observation has been made by Andy Lord, *Network Church: A Pentecostal Ecclesiology* (Leiden: Brill, 2012), pp. 63-87, to which I am indebted for insights into Pentecostal ecclesiology.

and the Roman Catholic Church,[5] it is another thing for this to trickle down to the roots. It is better for unity to grow at grass-roots level in the first place, in a sharing of resources for worship and witness at local and regional levels.

This was a central point in the creation of the present ecumenical movement in England, Scotland, Wales, and Ireland called 'Churches Together'. Replacing a former British Council of Churches, the aim was to create lighter ecumenical instruments, designed not to join existing church structures together but to serve the churches in their actually working together *as they are*.[6] The hope was that these new forums and assemblies would assist cooperation to turn into commitment and so enable a growing into unity. The new ecumenical pattern made it possible, for example, for the Roman Catholic Church to be part of 'Churches Together' where it had not participated in the previous 'Council'. The approach, and especially an emphasis on working together in mission, also commended itself to the member churches of the Baptist Union of Great Britain, which in 1995 re-affirmed membership of 'Churches Together' by very large majorities.[7] Three of the four main Pentecostal denominations in the UK are also in membership of the various national bodies of 'Churches Together',[8] along with some smaller black-led Pentecostal and Holiness churches.[9] The recent creative move of the Church of England on making 'local covenants' with other churches for significant sharing in worship and

---

[5] 'The Word of God in the Life of the Church. A Report of International Conversations between the Catholic Church and the Baptist World Alliance 2006-2010', *American Baptist Quarterly* 31 (2012), pp. 28-122.

[6] British Council of Churches & Catholic Truth Society, *Not Strangers but Pilgrims: The Next Steps for Churches Together in Pilgrimage* (London: British Council of Churches, 1989). p. 12.

[7] The Baptist Assembly at Plymouth, 6 May 1995, reaffirmed membership of Churches Together in England by 90.21% of those present and voting, and membership of the Council of Churches for Britain and Ireland by 81.27%.

[8] Assemblies of God, Elim Pentecostal Church, and New Testament Church of God. The exception among traditional Pentecostal churches is the Apostolic Church.

[9] The Church of God (Cleveland) in America is the origin for the New Testament Assembly, although the latter derives more immediately from the New Testament Church of God in the Caribbean. The international headquarters of the Church of God of Prophecy is likewise in Cleveland, Tennessee, USA. The Redeemed Christian Church of God has its roots in Nigeria.

mission (under Canon B44) is another instance of lightness of touch in working together.

Not just in the UK but in many places, ecumenism begins with local clusters of churches engaged in theological education or mission or with chaplaincies to hospitals, prisons, education, and industry or with the sharing of buildings or with a local campaign against injustice or with a joint participation in inter-faith dialogue.

A second general trend I detect is towards talk of 'full communion' rather than 'one world Church'. The picture of visible unity with which people are working is a variety of churches, each with their own heritage, tradition, and emphases but each in full communion with the other. The goal of union as envisioned by the World Council of Churches (WCC) Assembly at Canberra in 1991 was 'when all the churches are able to *recognize* in one another the one, holy, catholic and apostolic church in its fullness'. Such a communion, the statement spells out, will be nurtured in a common sacramental life, will confess a common faith, will have a common life in which members and ministries are mutually recognized and reconciled, and will exercise a common mission in the world.[10]

This stress on communion or fellowship, *koinonia*, is rooted in a theological vision of God who lives in a fellowship of love as Father, Son, and Spirit. This has been expounded at length in the basic document of the Fifth World Conference on Faith and Order (1993), called 'Towards Koinonia in Faith, Life and Witness':

> The terms koinonia and communion have a wide reference. Koinonia is used to refer to the life of the Trinity or to that gift God offers in all its fullness to the whole of humanity and creation. They refer to the Church of Jesus Christ and to the way in which Christian communions understand their own life experienced at a local, national or worldwide level.[11]

---

[10] 'The Unity of the Church as Koinonia: Gift and Calling' ('The Canberra Statement'), in Michael Kinnamon (ed.), *Signs of the Spirit. Official Report. Seventh Assembly of the World Council of Churches* [Canberra, Australia, February 7–20, 1991] (Grand Rapids: Eerdmans/Geneva: WCC Publications, 1991), §2.1, p. 173; cf. §66, p. 250.

[11] 'Towards Koinonia in Faith, Life and Witness', in Thomas Best and Günther Gassman (eds.), *On the Way to Fuller Koinonia. Official Report of the Fifth World Conference on Faith and Order* (Faith and Order Paper 166; Geneva: WCC Publications, 1994), §45, p. 276.

This stress on *koinonia* in the triune God is to be found in both Baptist and Pentecostal theologians.[12] The abiding of the communion of the Church in this communion of God means that in spite of separation the various churches are already in communion. This is a new note that has been struck in ecumenical conversations in recent years, a sense that churches are not 'out of communion' – they *cannot* be if they exist in God's communion. But they can be said to share 'an existing though imperfect communion' or a 'degree of communion',[13] both phrases agreed between the World Council and the Roman Catholic Church. Recent conversations between the Baptist World Alliance and the Roman Catholic Church also conclude with the joint affirmation that 'we enjoy a "certain, though imperfect communion", though we continue to grieve over the divisions between us'.[14]

The document 'Towards Koinonia' admits that it is difficult to find the language to describe this 'growing conviction', this increasing experience of 'already sharing in one communion of God's own life ... a reality that already binds Christians together'.[15] Before some Baptists (and perhaps some Pentecostals) claim too hastily that others now accept their understanding of a purely *spiritual* unity of all Christians and churches or that visible unity is a state for which we hope only in the eschaton,[16] we should notice that the document 'Towards Koinonia' goes on to say that this experience

---

[12] Baptist examples are: Paul S. Fiddes, *Participating in God: A Pastoral Doctrine of the Trinity* (London: Darton, Longman and Todd, 2000), pp. 11-61; Stanley J. Grenz, *The Social God and the Relational Self: A Trinitarian Theology of the* Imago Dei (Louisville: Westminster John Knox, 2001), pp. 23-57, 304-36. For Pentecostal examples see Simon Chan, *Liturgical Theology: The Church as a Worshipping Community* (Downers Grove: IVP, 2006), pp. 23-43; Miroslav Volf (whose theological origins are in Pentecostalism though he is now an Episcopalian), *After Our Likeness: The Church as the Image of the Trinity* (Grand Rapids: Eerdmans, 1998), pp. 191-214.

[13] *Ut Unum Sint.* Encyclical Letter of the Holy Father John Paul II on Commitment to Ecumenism (London: Catholic Truth Society, 1995), p. 11. See *Unitatis Redintegratio* 3, in Austin Flannery (ed.), *Vatican Council II: The Conciliar and Post Conciliar Documents* (Dublin: Dominican Publications, 1975), pp. 455-56. Also, *The Church, Local and Universal.* A Study Commissioned and Received by the Joint Working Group between the Roman Catholic Church and the World Council of Churches (Faith and Order Paper 150; Geneva: WCC Publications, 1990), p. 10.

[14] 'Word of God in the Life of the Church', §212.

[15] 'Towards Koinonia', §45, p. 277.

[16] Volf, *After Our Likeness,* pp. 203, 213, 250.

should encourage us to move forward to *visible* unity in the midst of history for the sake of God's reconciling activity in the world.

A third general trend arises from this stress on full communion – that is the acceptance of diversity in the unity. As the triune God lives in unity and true diversity as three persons in one God, so the church in God's image can and should show *legitimate diversity*. The catchword here is 'reconciled diversity' not uniformity. This does raise the question, however, of what are legitimate and illegitimate diversities. 'Towards Koinonia' suggests that diversity is not acceptable where it denies the 'common confession of Jesus Christ as God and Saviour', where it justifies discrimination on the basis of race or gender, where it prevents reconciliation, where it hinders the common mission of the church, and where it endangers the life in *koinonia*.[17]

This is fairly wide-ranging, and while it clearly and properly rules out – for instance – a church based on apartheid, it might also rule out uncomfortable challenges to the *status quo* that are truly prophetic. Perhaps life in *koinonia* sometimes *needs* to be 'endangered'. The report of the Lambeth Conference of the Anglican Communion (1998), entitled 'Called to be One', makes the important point that diversity must include pain. Noting that churches exist in different cultural contexts with particular stories and marked by sin, the report says:

> If visible unity is about living in the world the communion of God's own life, then our portrait of visible unity must show that tension, even conflict, will always be part of life this side of the kingdom. 'Sharp things that divide us can paradoxically turn out to be gift ... the world with all its divisions is not used to such a possibility as this: that those on opposing sides should stay together ... bearing each other's burdens, even entering one another's pain'.[18]

These last words about one another's pain take us into the heart of the triune life of God, for there we find brokenness, desolation, and loss as communion is open to receive the impact of the cross.

---

[17] 'Towards Koinonia', §57, p. 280.

[18] *Called to be One,* Lambeth Conference 1998, Section IV (London: Morehouse Publishing), p. 24, citing a response to the Archbishop of Canterbury at the Lambeth Conference of 1988.

In this rich harmony, the wounds of Jesus are not absorbed but remain as a witness to the suffering of the world.

A particular contribution to an ecumenical ecclesiology of diversity is made here by the Pentecostal theologian Amos Yong. He argues that rooting the church in a usual free-church way in personal
confession of Christ can encourage a conformity of patterns of experience, as well as provoke the accusation of proselytism in an
ecumenical setting. But if the 'One Catholic Church' has its reality
through the shared gift of the Holy Spirit, there is bound to be diversity as well as unity because this gift will be received and shaped
in different contexts.[19]

So, to summarize where we have come so far, the sense of ecumenical call that is widespread at present is a calling to work from
the roots, to work towards full communion, and to live with diversity, painful though it is. I have been speaking of an ecumenical 'calling' because this echoes the statement of Ephesians 4 that we are
'*called* to be one', and so reminds us that all true movements for unity have their origin in the desire, initiative, and summons of God
(cf. the prayer of Jesus in John 17). The opening verses of Ephesians 4 have been often quoted in the dialogues of the modern
ecumenical movement,[20] in which the readers are urged to be:

> ... eager to maintain the unity of the spirit in the bond of peace.
> There is one body and one Spirit, just as you were *called* to the
> one hope that belongs to your *call*, one Lord, one faith, one bap-
> tism, one God and father of us all, who is above all and through
> all and in all.

This passage either states or hints at three theological ideas that
define the call to unity, and I want now to go on to use them as the
framework for the rest of this essay. First, there is the image of the
body; second, there is an evoking of the fellowship in which God
lives as 'one Spirit ... one Lord (Christ) ... one Father'; and third,
there is the language of covenant with the phrase 'bond of peace'.
One body, one fellowship, one covenant. Although these ideas
overlap and intertwine, I am going to take them each in turn.

---

[19] Amos Yong, *The Spirit Poured out on all Flesh: Pentecostalism and the Possibility of Global Theology* (Grand Rapids: Baker, 2005), chapter 3.

[20] For example, in the 'Called to be One' process of Churches Together in England; see *Called to be One* (London: CTE Publications, 1996).

2. The Call to One Body

A fundamental image of unity is the one on which Paul concentrates in 1 Corinthians 12, that of the Church as the body of Christ. The daring manner with which the early Christian community used this title, and the startling claim it makes, has perhaps been dulled by over familiarity. The early Christians were not just describing themselves by analogy as a 'body' of people – as we might speak today of soldiers as 'a fine body of men and women'. They were asserting that they were the body of *a particular person* – Jesus Christ, Jesus of Nazareth who was now the risen Lord of the universe.[21] They were venturing to say that people could touch and handle the risen Christ by touching the outstretched hands of the Church. As Christ was once to be seen on the streets of Nazareth and Jerusalem, so he is visible in the Christian congregation (1 Jn 1.1-4). He lives out his life through all his members. *Body is about visibility.*

Now, what I want to underline here is that the *primary* meaning of the 'body of Christ' is the whole, universal Church. Since Christ is the Lord of the universe, the exalted ruler of the cosmos, his body must be the universal company of all the redeemed. This link is brought out clearly in Eph. 1.22-23 (cf. Col. 1.24):

> And God has put all things under his feet and has made him the head over all things for the church, which is his body, the fullness of him who fills all in all.

So Paul states in 1 Cor. 12.13 that 'by one Spirit we were all baptized into one body – Jews or Greeks, slaves or free – and all were made to drink of one Spirit'. This 'all' cannot simply mean all in one local community, or Paul would not – for instance – include himself within it, writing as he was to Corinth. This perception ought to shape our understanding of the familiar picture that immediately follows it in verses 14-30, that of the many members making up the body: 'now you are the body of Christ, and individually members of it'. This body too cannot only be the single congregation.[22] Baptists

---

[21] So John A.T. Robinson, *The Body: A Study in Pauline Theology* (London: SCM, 1952), pp. 57-58.

[22] So *Relating and Resourcing: The Report of the Task Group on Associating*, approved at the Council of the Baptist Union of Great Britain, March 1998, §2.6, p. 4: 'The Body of Christ is not confined to local churches but finds expression in the relations between churches as well as within them'; cf. *The Nature of the Assembly and*

have, of course, insisted that the local company of believers can *also* be called the 'body of Christ'. Wherever two or three are gathered together, wherever the body of the communion bread is broken (1 Cor. 10.16-17), there is the body of Christ. However, the local congregation is always a '*manifestation* of the one Church of God on earth and in heaven'; [23] it derives from the one body. It not then a question of many small bodies making up one large body, by a kind of spiritual arithmetic; rather, the small bodies exist as an 'outcropping' of the whole body.[24] Separate churches already relate together because the body exists before us, and we are called to enter it.

Similarly, while Pentecostal ecclesiology has often centered on baptism in the Spirit, Simon Chan places equal stress on the image of the body of Christ; he sees Church in terms of the 'total Christ', and argues that since Christ came before the world did, so the Church is a divine humanity, created by the Spirit of God, 'before the creation of the world'.[25]

This sense of the one, trans-local body of Christ is prominent in early Baptist thinking. For instance, the (Particular Baptist) London Confession of 1644 asserts that '*although* the particular Congregations be distinct and severall Bodies … *yet* are they all to walk by one and the same Rule … as members of the one body in the common faith under Christ their onely head'.[26] That was in the context of congregations in one city, but in the more dispersed situation of the countryside, the 'Somerset Confession', drawn up in Bridgewater in 1656, also asserts that it is 'the duty of the members of Christ … *although* in several congregations and assemblies (being one in the head) if occasion be, to communicate each to other in things spiritual and things temporal'.[27] We note in both confessions

---

the Council of the Baptist Union of Great Britain (London: Baptist Union, 1994), pp. 6-7, 9-11.

[23] *The Baptist Doctrine of the Church* (1948), reprinted in Roger Hayden (ed.), *Baptist Union Documents 1948–1977* (London: Baptist Historical Society, 1980), p. 8.

[24] The metaphor is from the Congregationalist P.T. Forsyth, *The Church and the Sacraments* (London: Independent Press, 2nd edn, 1947), p. 66.

[25] Ephesians 1.4. See Simon Chan, *Liturgical Theology*, p. 23.

[26] *Confession of Faith* (London: Matthew Simmons, 1644), §47, in William L. Lumpkin, *Baptist Confessions* (Chicago: Judson Press, 1959), pp. 168-89 (emphasis added).

[27] *A Confession of Faith of Several Churches of Christ* (London: Henry Hills, 1656), §28, in Lumpkin, *Baptist Confessions*, p. 211.

that the separateness of the congregations is regarded as a matter of 'although'. The *London Confession* of 1644 even goes so far as to describe this situation as being a matter of simple practical necessity:

> though wee be distinct in respect of our particular bodies, for conveniency sake, being as many as can well meete together in one place, yet are all one in Communion, holding Jesus Christ to be our head and Lord, under whose government wee desire alone to walk ...[28]

It is not just that the terms 'body' and 'Christ as head' are used in these examples to *describe* wider assemblies than the local congregation. The point is being made that local churches are therefore under a *necessity* 'to hold communion among themselves for their peace, increase of love and mutual edification',[29] just as members in any congregation are called by Christ to gather together.

Now, belonging together in one body has implications for 'visible unity'. The one, universal body of Christ cannot be totally invisible, as this would undermine the whole point of the metaphor, which is about visibility and tangibility. Churches have the *duty* to relate together because they are summoned to allow Christ to become manifest through his body. If he is to become visible at every level of human society – local, regional, national and international – and if his word of challenge is to be heard in every human forum, then he will be humble enough to take on the rags and tatters of our human organizations. This is the meaning of incarnation: the divine Word is willing to come among us even in the poverty stricken form of an association of Baptist churches or an ecumenical council of Christian churches, with all their mixed motives and failures.

One sometimes hears it said among Baptists that there is indeed the local and the universal body of Christ, but only the local body is visible. The universal body is claimed to be completely *invisible*, a purely spiritual reality with no material embodiment. So (it is said) there is no need to make this visible through structures of association or churches together having an ecumenical unity which can be

---

[28] *Confession of Faith* (1644), Introduction, in Lumpkin, *Baptist Confessions*, p. 155 (spelling follows the original text).

[29] *Confession of Faith* (London, 1677), §26.14–15, in Lumpkin, *Baptist Confessions*, p. 289.

seen by the world.[30] Now, Baptists certainly reflected from their earliest days on the relation between the 'invisible Church' and 'visible saints'. They *did* think that there was an invisible Church here and now on earth as well as in heaven, but they did not use this concept as a justification for rejecting wider visible structures of the Church beyond the local congregation.[31] Early Baptists understood the 'invisible Church' to be the total company of all the redeemed, whether they were inside or outside the visible Church, and whether they lived in the past, present, or future. They certainly laid stress on the importance of the local church as a place where this universal Church became visible but did not imply that that there was no visibility anywhere else. The *Orthodox Creed* (General Baptist, 1679), for instance, equates 'the visible church of Christ on earth' with 'several distinct congregations', and is careful to place in apposition 'church' and 'congregations' (plural). It is clear that the body of Christ becomes visible, not only in *each* congregation, but in the gathering of congregations together.[32] As the eighteenth-century Baptist ecclesiologist Daniel Turner makes clear, there is a 'visible Catholic Church' as well as an 'invisible Catholic Church' and a visible local church.[33]

Pentecostals have made a similar affirmation in recent ecumenical conversations.[34] Further, Clark Pinnock (who may be counted as having been both a Baptist and a Pentecostal theologian) emphasizes that the church makes visible Christ's life of loving, suffering service, a manifestation extending beyond the local sphere. Through baptism in the Spirit, members of a church participate in the divine

---

[30] An influential voice here was Augustus Hopkins Strong, *Systematic Theology* (Philadelphia: Griffith & Rowland, 1909), pp. 887-91.

[31] See my argument in Paul S. Fiddes, 'Church and Salvation: A Comparison of Baptist and Orthodox Thinking', in Anthony R. Cross (ed.), *Ecumenism and History: Studies in Honour of John H.Y. Briggs* (Carlisle, Paternoster Press, 2002), pp. 134–38.

[32] *An Orthodox Creed* (London, 1679), §29, in Lumpkin, *Baptist Confessions*, p. 319.

[33] Daniel Turner *A Compendium of Social Religion* (London: John Ward, 2nd edn, 1778), pp. 2-4.

[34] See 'Perspectives on Koinonia. Report from the Third Quinquennium of the Dialogue between the Pontifical Council for Promoting Christian Unity and Some Classical Pentecostal Churches and Leaders', in Jeffrey Gros, Harding Meyer, and William G. Rusch (eds.), *Growth in Agreement II: Reports and Agreed Statements of Ecumenical Conversations on a World Level, 1982-1998* (Faith and Order Paper 187; Geneva: WCC, 2000), pp. 735-52, §35.

life of the triune God; through the Eucharist, the church is renewed
in this participation; and through the use of spiritual gifts, there is a
making visible of the same present and power of God as was manifest in Christ. As the church becomes an ever-widening community,
Pinnock urges, the world becomes more and more 'christomorphic'
at every level of human life.[35]

The ecumenical challenge facing both Baptists and Pentecostals
is thus to allow Christ to become visible through his body, giving
him a place to take form in his world. This is equally a challenge to
ecumenical mission. The New Testament image of the Church as
the body of Christ indicates that he uses all his members in order to
become manifest, to become graspable by people today. The members together make up the visible form of Christ. This is the point
of fellowship (*koinonia*) and the exercise of spiritual gifts as Paul describes it in 1 Corinthians 12. We are not assigned gifts for our self-
fulfillment. Schisms have happened in churches when people are
aggrieved because they feel that they are not being given proper
scope for their gifts, as they believe them to be; if they cannot exercise them where they are, they will go and form another church
where they can. But the point of the gifts (the *charismata*) is not to
find satisfaction for ourselves but to allow Christ to become visible,
and everything must be subordinated to that.

All this applies to the uniting of churches together. It will mean a
gathering together of *charismata*. As I suggested earlier, the picture
of the body in 1 Corinthians 12 applies on the level of churches living and working together: 'the eye cannot say to the hand, I have no
need of you'. Referring to the whole Communion of Saints, the
(Particular Baptist) Second London Confession of 1677 speaks of
'communion in each others' gifts and graces'.[36] A single local church
will be very unlikely to have all the gifts needed for mission in our
modern, complex society. Allowing Christ to become visible means
a sharing of gifts and also material resources. It is not charity when
a richer church gives assistance to a poorer one; it is a matter of
sharing life within one body, for 'if one member suffers, all suffer
together'. Here Pentecostal theologian Frank Macchia has greeted
as 'of interest to Pentecostals' the argument that the unity of diverse

---

[35] Clark H. Pinnock, *Flame of Love: A Theology of the Holy Spirit* (Downers
Grove: Inter-Varsity Press, 1996), pp. 113-21.
[36] Confession of Faith (1679), §27, in Lumpkin, *Baptist Confessions*, p. 289.

gifts within a local assembly has its analogy in 'a worldwide "federation" of churches, each with its own distinctive gift to offer Christianity'.[37]

Concern to fulfill the mission of God in Christ actually motivated the beginning of the modern ecumenical movement. This is usually dated to 1910 with the International Missionary Conference in Edinburgh, the first international meeting of church leaders from all denominations in modern times. As they considered mission strategy it became clear to them that there were wider issues of disunity on the agenda and especially disagreements about doctrine between the churches; from this discussion there issued the First World Conference on Faith and Order at Lausanne in 1927. These two streams of the ecumenical movement, the International Missionary Council and 'Faith and Order', were eventually brought together with the 'Life and Work' movement of the churches into the formation of the World Council of Churches in 1948. The letter of invitation sent to churches in 1938 to take part in the establishment of a World Council urged the churches to see this move towards unity 'against the background of the Church's primary task of World Evangelization'.[38] But the link between mission and unity had already been understood by the Baptist William Carey, one of the earliest and major influences on the missionary movement of modern times. In a letter of 1806 to the Secretary of his missionary society, Carey proposed 'a general association of all denominations of Christians, from the four quarters of the world', to meet every ten years or so. Proposing the Cape of Good Hope as a convenient, central venue, he called for the first meeting to be in 1810 or no later than 1812, commenting that 'we could understand each other better, and more entirely enter into one another's views by two or three hours conversation than by two or three years epistolary correspondence'.[39] Carey's vision, dismissed as a 'one of bro' Carey's

---

[37] Frank Macchia, 'The Tongues of Pentecost. A Pentecostal Perspective on the Promise and Challenge of the Pentecostal/Roman Catholic Dialogue', *Journal of Ecumenical Studies* 35 (1998), pp. 1-18 (16).

[38] *Documents of the World Council of Churches* (Amsterdam: WCC, 1948), p. 9.

[39] Letter from William Carey (Calcutta) to Andrew Fuller, 15 May 1806; original at St Mary's Church, Norwich, copy in the Angus Library, Regent's Park College, E13 (16).

pleasing dreams' at the time,[40] had to wait another hundred years before its realization at Edinburgh in 1910.

Making Christ visible together, in wide association, means the sharing of gifts and resources to make Christ known. While there are evident advantages in efficiency, this also means facing a deep challenge to established convictions and practices, calling for risk and trust in each other. The Swanwick Declaration, the founding document of Churches Together in Britain and Ireland, observes that any kind of resource sharing means 'taking holy risks' for the sake of common mission. One risk it suggests is allowing one church or agency to act on behalf of others, whether in evangelism or social service, without everyone feeling *they* have to be there.[41]

3. The Body of Christ and Conciliar Forms

Mission will be effective when we act in a way that makes Christ visible in his body; but to do this, we need to be able to make decisions together, to discern the purpose of Christ. Being the body of Christ means receiving the promise of knowing his mind when members are gathered and Christ becomes manifest among them. On and beyond the local level, this means the development of conciliar forms through which member churches can meet and consult. In its envisaging of what it would be like for churches to be in full communion, the Canberra Statement of the WCC (1991) stresses that if fullness of communion is to be sustained, it must 'be expressed on the local and universal levels through conciliar forms of life and action'.[42] That is, we are urged that communion is only possible if churches take responsible decisions together in some kind of council or assembly ('conciliar forms'). Baptists and Pentecostals are thus challenged to rethink their structures at a local, intermediate, and global level in the light of this call to conciliarity.

The later Faith and Order document, 'Towards Koinonia', makes clear that 'conciliar communion' is not just required for questions of strategy and resources between the churches; more fundamental is the need for churches to meet under the guidance of the

---

[40] Letter from Andrew Fuller to William Ward (December 2, 1806); Angus Library H/1/1.

[41] *Not Strangers But Pilgrims*, p. 13.

[42] For details of the Canberra Statement, see n. 9 above.

Holy Spirit to discuss the nature of the apostolic faith and to discern the ways that it should be discerned and proclaimed in the
context of our modern world. 'It is only when churches are in
communion with each other that they will be able in conciliar delib-
eration and decision-making to teach together the one faith in ways
that are acceptable to all.'[43] We might say that it is essential that
churches should hear the way that scripture is read and understood
in contexts quite different from their own; a church in the affluent
west is not in a position to know what scripture 'means' until it has
heard how it is interpreted, for instance, by a church in the poverty
of the shanty towns of South Africa or Brazil or by a church living
as a minority faith in the Middle East. However, 'Towards Koinonia' also points out that:

> Decisions taken in such conciliar communion will require recep-
> tion by the whole church. Such structures and forms of authority
> should be seen as gifts of God to keep churches faithful to the
> Apostolic faith and enable them to witness together in evangeli-
> cal freedom.[44]

Baptists have an opportunity to make a special contribution to
this matter of receptivity, as well as to consider how their ecclesial
forms might evolve in the face of the ecumenical challenge. This
lies, I suggest, in their view that authority is a matter of finding the
mind of Christ. It is precisely their convictions about the place of
the local church meeting and the freedom of the local church from
outside human constraint that should make Baptists very open to
listening to others. The church meeting is not about preserving in-
dependency or showing how self-sufficient a local church might be
but is about finding the mind of Christ. This is a proper quest for
the body of Christ gathered together, wherever it might be, at whatever level of society. In church meeting, members should thus take
very seriously the decisions and the advice of their own regional
associations and national (union or convention) councils and assemblies; this openness is easily, then, extendable to ecumenical
councils in which the church has a representative part. The church
meeting cannot be *imposed* upon by outside church authorities, but
this is because the final authority, according to Baptist understand-

---

[43] 'Towards Koinonia', §62, pp. 281-821.
[44] 'Towards Koinonia', §61, p. 281.

ing, is not the church meeting but the rule of Christ himself present in the meeting. And the same Christ is present to make himself visible in his body not only in the local congregation but in wider assemblies. In Baptist polity, the local congregation can thus relate to churches of other confessions in exactly the same way that it does to other Baptist churches. The Baptist Patristics scholar Henk Bakker has argued that conciliarity in the early church is a precedent for Baptist congregationalism, especially as evidenced in Cyprian's view of the 'voice of the people (*suffragium populi*)'.[45]

All churches are being urged by the WCC Faith and Order Commission to move towards common decision making. It is important for the churches together to understand the nature of the Apostolic Faith and the way it should be proclaimed in our modern world. Baptists should have no problem with this, as they are concerned not to defend a historic set of church dogmas but to find the mind of Christ. However, this very concern to find the mind of Christ will lead to a delicate balance between insights and decisions at conciliar level and the freedom to receive those decisions in the local fellowship. Baptists will insist that whatever decisions and resolutions are reached in wider councils, the local congregation keeps the freedom and the responsibility to test them, though it may not always insist on doing so. The relation between this local and conciliar authority is, for Baptists, not governed by regulation but is a matter of living in bonds of trust with others. The wider fellowship is the body of Christ, and can search for his mind with an outcome to which the local congregation must pay heed, but the *local* church is also the body of Christ gathered in one place. Here, I believe, is a particular Baptist contribution to the ecumenical movement, and it adds a great deal to what is often called the 'issue of reception'.

While I am not venturing to prescribe the way that this challenge might be heard by Pentecostal churches today, I observe that there too a tension or dialectic evidently exists between the freedom of the local congregation and the authority of centralized structures. This takes different emphases in various Pentecostal groups: Elim Pentecostalism is quite highly centralized, for instance, where As-

---

[45] Henk Bakker, 'Towards a Catholic Understanding of Baptist Congregationalism: Conciliar Power and Authority', *Journal of Reformed Theology* 5 (2011), pp. 180-83 (159-83).

semblies of God in the UK[46] places more emphasis on decisions made for themselves by local churches. In fact, there was a split in 1939 within the Elim Church when a key founder of the church, George Jeffreys left, citing the failure to devolve powers to local congregations.[47] Difference on this matter was probably the reason for the failure of a move to unite Elim and Assemblies of God in the 1920s. The situation is also complicated today by the phenomenon of the 'mega-church' which tends to acquire forms of a denomination in itself. But whatever structures different forms of Pentecostalism adopt, there is surely a challenge to think creatively about whether traditional principles might be re-imagined in an ecumenical context.

Whatever the status of decisions taken centrally, most Pentecostal churches take them at a regional and international level through 'national assemblies' and 'general assemblies' at which any local church member can choose to attend. Considerable confidence is placed in the 'moving' of the Spirit to form a consensus. Business will generally have been prepared and given to the Assembly for decision by leaders who will have been chosen by the ecclesial organization centrally on the basis of recognizing their spiritual gifts. The challenge is to ask whether this element of the charismatic – in both call to office and in decision-making – could remain within, and even transform, more conciliar structures as envisaged by the WCC, just as I have suggested that Baptist ideas of 'finding the mind of Christ' might be integrated and make their particular contribution. The experience of Pentecostals in handling the dialectic between charisma and institution could thus be fruitful for the rest of the Church of Christ.

4. The Call to One Fellowship

A second New Testament image for the church is that of a 'fellowship' – *koinonia* (κοινωνία)– and around this cluster other words like 'sharing', 'participation', 'communion', and the many phrases with

---

[46] Harold D. Hunter, in 'Reflections by a Pentecostalist on Aspects of BEM', *Journal of Ecumenical Studies* 29 (1992), p. 343, draws attention to the authority of the headquarters of Assemblies of God in Springfield, MO, USA.

[47] Kay, *Pentecostals in Britain*, p. 25. A more implicit reason was Jeffreys' adherence to British Israelitism.

'one another' in them. The ecumenical calling is a call to *koinonia*. This fellowship certainly has a *local* reality (in Acts 2.42 we read: 'and they devoted themselves to the ... fellowship, the breaking of bread and the prayers'.) But once again there is a larger and a wider fellowship to which Christians belong, which is not just an accumulation of warm feelings, as if it were made by adding all local fellowships together into a mega-fellowship.

Like the body of Christ, *koinonia* is an *existent reality before* us. In the first place, it already exists in God, in the mutual giving and receiving of love between the Father and the Son in the communion of the Spirit; Jesus is portrayed as praying in Jn 17.21 'that they may all be one, even as you Father are in me, and I in you, so that they may also be in us, so that the world may believe that you have sent me'. The doctrine of the Trinity, as the church developed it, was not a kind of holy mathematical puzzle in which belief was required to demonstrate how spiritual a believer was. God as Trinity is not a game with numbers, but a conceptualizing of an experience of fellowship. We find ourselves embraced in a network of relationships in God, and so we can only speak of God as communion. We share in the Father's sending of the Son on mission, the Son's obedience to the Father and glorification of the Father, and the sorrow and joy of the Spirit that unites them.

This fellowship that God experiences in God's self is what God intends for the whole of creation. God's purpose is to bring the whole universe into *koinonia*, into reconciled relationships and harmony (Rom. 8.21; Eph. 1.10; Col. 1.19-20). Meanwhile the Church bears witness to this fellowship, and shows it as a foretaste of the communion which is to come. Thus we enter a fellowship that is greater than ourselves, greater than the local scene, greater than the present age, greater than the finite world. This theme, which is common in ecumenical discourse, has been developed with a Pentecostal flavor by Veli-Matti Kärkkäinen, stressing Spirit baptism as immersion into the divine *koinonia*; while all life in the Spirit must then be linked to participation in local fellowships, we must go beyond the local to find the Spirit opening up *koinonia* in the wider world.[48] Similarly, Frank Macchia envisages Spirit baptism as not

---

[48] Veli-Matti Kärkkäinen, *Toward a Pneumatological Theology* (ed. Amos Yong; New York: University Press of America, 2002), pp. 105-108.

only for the forming of the people of God, but as a transformation of the whole of creation as the Spirit is 'poured out on all flesh', filling the universe.[49] In both these Pentecostal theologians, a new note seems to me to be struck in Pentecostal theology: Spirit baptism keeps the Church as the focus of God's working, and yet at the same time is an orientation towards the world, towards a kingdom of cosmic proportions whose goal is union with God.

Now, if the church is the foretaste of *koinonia*, an advance advertisement for the *koinonia* of the whole universe, brokenness of fellowship is a scandal to the world. It means hindrance to mission, because it prevents witness by life to the fellowship that God intends for his creation. It prevents the church working for peace and justice, for the renewal of human life, and for care of the natural world. Perhaps the key text of the ecumenical movement has been Jn 17.21, the prayer of Jesus for his disciples 'that they may all be one ... so that the world may *believe* you have sent me'.

Nevertheless, a Baptist and Pentecostal view of the visibility of the church universal will be a mixture of realism about broken *koinonia* and determination to overcome the scandal of division. Where Baptists and Pentecostals will take issue with the Orthodox and Catholic vision of the church universal is in the equating of *visibility* with *indivisibility*.[50] It is the tragedy of the church to have been broken through the contingencies and conflicts of history. It is visible indeed, but in pieces whose fragmentation is a scandal to the world and which enters the heart of God as a cause of grief and pain. It is an aspect of the divine humility, we may say, to allow the church to be divided, and it is a dimension of God's experience of the cross. The claim of any confession to be the one and only indivisible Catholic Church seems a too swift moving on from the Good Friday of history, which must always be held in tension with the brightness of Easter morning. Like the Orthodox Church in the East, the Roman Catholic Church in the West deduces from the unity of God's *koinonia* that the one undivided church *must already exist*, in reality and visibility. This conviction leads to a certain understanding of the relation of churches to each other. Several recent

---

[49] Frank Macchia, *Baptized in the Spirit: A Global Pentecostal Theology* (Grand Rapids: Zondervan, 2006), pp. 100-106.

[50] See 'Perspectives on Koinonia', §34; 'Word of God in the Life of the Church', §25.

Catholic documents have followed Vatican II in affirming that 'the One Church of Christ ... subsists in the Catholic Church, governed by the Successor of Peter and by the Bishops in communion with him'.[51] The non-Catholic Christian communities in the West, stemming from the Reformation, are thus 'not Churches in the proper sense', but may be called 'ecclesial communities'. This fine distinction results partly from a view of apostolic succession and episcopacy, but even more fundamentally from a certain doctrine of the divine *koinonia*. If the *unity* of God is the predominant basis for ecclesiology, then we must ask where the one Church is *already* visible as a unitary structure. Having established that to our satisfaction, we will then see in others only 'aspects' or 'elements' of that way of being the church, where the church in its fullness exists only in what is undivided. But if we hold the unity of God in tension with the suffering and brokenness of God, as one whose *koinonia* is disturbed by lack of love in the world, then we may be able to see the one Church of Christ in each other despite our imperfect communion together.

Another instance of living with brokenness is the practice of baptism. Being willing to live in a fragmentary state of the church means that we will be ready to compare *whole stories* of initiation not just the single moments of baptism. Those of us who are Baptists, rather than asking whether infant baptism is equivalent to believers' baptism, will listen to people's story of their beginning in the Christian life, perhaps stretching over many years, as a process that includes a number of key moments. In these journeys, baptism of one kind or another will have been central, but other elements will also belong to the journey – among them the prevenient grace of God in the human heart, Christian nurture, various moments of filling with the Holy Spirit (sometimes accompanied by laying on of hands), personal confession of faith, receiving spiritual gifts for service in the world, and sharing for the first time in the Lord's Supper. If we can recognize a common initiation despite these aspects appearing in a different order or at different ages, then we may indeed be able

---

[51] Vatican II, 'Lumen Gentium 8', in A. Flannery (ed.), *Documents of Vatican II* (New York: Pillar Books, 1975), p. 357; cf. *Unitatis redintegratio* 4, in Flannery (ed.), *Documents*, p. 457; *Ut Unum Sint*, §§10, 86; *Dominus Jesus*, Congregation for the Doctrine of the Faith, August 6, 2000, §16: text at <http:// www.vatican.va/rom an_curia/congregations>.

to say that we are called to 'one Lord, one faith, one baptism'. In various ecumenical conversations, Baptist participants have been aiming to move the conversation from 'common baptism' to that of 'common initiation' or a common process of beginning in Christ.[52] This way forward was already indicated by *Baptism, Eucharist and Ministry* in recommending the recognition of different 'patterns' of initiation as 'equivalent alternatives for entry into the Church'.[53] Despite this, many ecumenical documents simply assert that all churches share a common baptism, and Baptists – along with many Pentecostals[54] – appear to be the 'awkward squad' by not joining in a common baptismal certificate. But pinning all ecumenical hopes on baptism like this does not seem to have led, among those who affirm common baptism, to a mutual acceptance in other areas such as ministry and the Eucharist.

Placing single moments side by side (infant baptism, believers' baptism) will accentuate differences, but comparing whole journeys of faith and salvation may enable mutual recognition to happen; as people listen to each other's stories, they may be able to say, 'It is the same journey!'[55] I venture to say that we might be able to take the same approach to the question of 'baptism in the Spirit', a matter sometimes in dispute between Pentecostals and Baptists, as well as between Baptists themselves. Some Baptists place a Spirit baptism before water baptism, the latter being only a sign of what has already happened in regeneration by the Spirit. Others take a more sacramental view of baptism and insist on holding Spirit and water baptism in one event. For many Pentecostals, baptism in spirit is understood as a 'second blessing' after conversion and water baptism as a further gift of God for the increase of holiness. But if we

---

[52] See *Conversations Around the World. The Report of the International Conversations between the Anglican Communion and the Baptist World Alliance* (London: Anglican Communion Office, 2005), §§42-4; *Dialogue between the Community of Protestant Churches in Europe (CPCE) and the European Baptist Federation (EBF) on the Doctrine and Practice of Baptism* (Leuenberg Documents 9; Frankfurt: Verlag Lembeck, 2005), pp. 19-22; *Pushing at the Boundaries of Unity. Anglicans and Baptists in Conversation* (London: Church House Publishing 2005), pp. 31-57; *The Word of God in the Life of the Church*, §§103-104.

[53] *Baptism, Eucharist and Ministry* (Faith and Order Paper 111; Geneva: WCC, 1982), p. 5.

[54] See *Perspectives on Koinonia*, §55.

[55] The language of journey for initiation appears in the *Catechism of the Catholic Church*, 12229. This is available at <http://www.vatican.va/archive/ENG0015>.

understand salvation to be a process, wherever we locate water and Spirit baptism we may still be able to recognize a common journey into Christ and his Church.

5. The Call to One Covenant

We have been thinking about the ecumenical call as a summons to one body and one fellowship. It is also, I proposed earlier, the call to one covenant. In Baptist understanding, a covenant has horizontal and vertical dimensions: when members enter the local church, they promise to be faithful to each other and to God who makes the covenant in Christ and calls disciples into covenant. As expressed by the early Baptist John Smyth, 'A visible communion of Saints is of two, three or more Saints joined together by covenant with God and themselves'.[56] So covenant is not a mere human decision to ally strategically with others to achieve certain ends, or even to worship in a way that suits one's own choice. Covenant is based on the calling of God through Christ, and from their beginnings, Baptists have understood that the eternal 'covenant of grace' between God and humanity, initiated by God, is actualized in a particular time and place when believers covenant together in a local church.[57] Traditionally, Baptist covenant-making took the form of a pledge to 'walk together and watch over each other'. 'Watching over' is, of course, the early English translation of the Greek word *episkope* (ἐπισκοπή), meaning 'oversight'. It is basic to the Baptist perspective on ministry that pastoral oversight is based in covenant relations, within a single congregation and between churches.

Ecumenical documents urge us all to recognize three dimensions of *episkope* – personal, collegial and communal – within and

---

[56] John Smyth, *Principles and Inferences concerning the Visible Church (1607)*, in W.T. Whitley (ed.), *The Works of John Smyth* (2 vols.; Cambridge: Cambridge University Press, 1915), I, p. 252.

[57] For the making of the proto-Baptist (Separatist) covenant at Gainsborough in 1606-1607, see William Bradford, *History of Plymouth Plantation, 1620-1647* (ed. W.C. Ford; 2 vols.; Boston: Massachusetts Historical Society, 1912), I, pp. 20–22. For 'consenting to walk together', see *Confession of Faith* (London: 1677), §26.5-6, in Lumpkin, *Baptist Confessions*, p. 286. For a thorough review of the Baptist idea of covenant, see Paul S. Fiddes, '"Walking Together": The Place of Covenant Theology in Baptist Life Yesterday and Today', in Fiddes, *Tracks and Traces*, pp. 21-47.

among the churches. That is, oversight should be exercised by the whole community (communal), by individuals with special commissions (personal) and by those persons working together (collegial).[58] Baptists have in fact always had these dimensions of watching over the people of God. They understand that the basic personal ministry of 'oversight' is given to the minister or pastor in the local church, whom many early Baptists called either 'elder' or 'bishop' without distinction.[59] While the local church has the freedom and responsibility to appoint its own local ministry, or 'deacons', the Baptist practice has been for the minister or pastor to be recognized and ordained by a wider fellowship of churches acting together. However, oversight in the community flows to and fro between the personal and the communal, since the responsibility of 'watching over' the church belongs both to *all* the members gathered in church meeting and to the pastor. The 'London Confession' of 1644 makes clear that while all members enter into covenant to 'watch over' each other spiritually, they also recognize that Christ has called some to an office in which they have a special responsibility for oversight:

And as Christ for the keeping of this Church in holy and orderly Communion, placeth some special men [*sic*] over the Church, who by their office are to govern, oversee, visit, watch; so likewise for the better keeping thereof in all places, by all the members, he hath given authority, and laid duty upon all, to watch over one another.[60]

Although holding that the local minister is a bishop, or an 'overseer', most Baptists do recognize *episkope* at an inter-church level. Oversight is exercised communally by a regional association of churches which have covenanted together and which in assembly seeks the mind of Christ for the life and mission of the member churches, while having no power to *impose* decisions on the local church meeting. Similarly, churches or representatives of associations meet in an assembly at national level ('Union' or 'Convention'). Oversight flows freely between the communal and the per-

---

[58] See *Baptism, Eucharist and Ministry*, p. 26.

[59] See e.g. *Confession of Faith* (1677), §26.9, in Lumpkin, *Baptist Confessions*, p. 287.

[60] *Confession of Faith* (1644), §44, in Lumpkin, *Baptist Confessions*, p. 168.

sonal here too, as personal oversight is exercised by various kinds of senior ministers who are linked either with the association or with the national Union and who work together in collegiality for such purposes as assisting the settlement of ministers in congregations. This does not necessarily imply a threefold ministry – for the most part the regional or national minister is not 'consecrated' beyond his or her initial ordination as a minister of word and sacrament.[61]

While there is much in all this that Baptists share with other Christian communions, there is often a difference in the way that *episkope* is connected to apostolicity. There is, to be sure, a general agreement growing on the ecumenical scene that apostolic succession is not in the first place about handing on a particular ministry through the laying on of hands in an unbroken chain from the earliest Apostles to today. It is not a strict sequence of one bishop ordaining another from Peter to the present. Rather, it is about the succession in faith and life of the *Church* as a whole, as each Christian community continues to participate in the mission of Jesus and is faithful to 'the words and acts of Jesus transmitted by the Apostles'.[62] Apostolic succession is thus about the continuing story of the covenant community. This is the kind of emphasis that was made in the document *Baptism, Eucharist and Ministry* and which the Anglican church made in its agreement with the Lutheran churches of the Baltic countries at Porvoo.

Baptists will generally be in sympathy with this understanding of what it means to be apostolic. They have a strong sense of continuity in faithfulness of the covenant community. This is expressed in a typical Baptist way in the church book, which records all the deliberations and decisions of the church meetings over the years; in this way the current generation acknowledges that it is part of the story of God's faithful people in that place in the past, who have themselves aimed to stand in the succession of the earliest Church. However, the growing ecumenical consensus adds that while the

---

[61] Historically, there was an exception among certain General Baptists in the latter part of the seventeenth century, for whom the trans-local bishop or messenger was a distinct office: see the *Orthodox Creed* (1679), §31, in Lumpkin, *Baptist Confessions*, pp. 319–20.

[62] E.g. *Together in Mission and Ministry: The Porvoo Common Statement. The British and Irish Anglican Churches and the Nordic and Baltic Lutheran Churches* (London: Church House Publishing, 1993), §41, p. 24; cf. *Baptism, Eucharist and Ministry*, pp. 28–29.

ordination of bishops is not the essence of apostolic succession, the bishop is a *sign* of the apostolicity of the community.[63] To have those who watch over God's people ordained continuously in one place is a testimony to the unbroken nature of the covenant.

Here is a challenge to both Baptists and Pentecostals. It does not seem that there will be any hope of visible unity in the church of Christ without some agreement on this personal sign of being apostolic. Those churches who have bishops understand them at the least as being a God-given sign and focus of standing in the tradition of the faith. They are a key part of the plot of the story. My account of Baptist understanding of *episkope* suggests that it would not in fact be a great leap from the existing situation into a more formal understanding of a threefold ministry, and 'senior ministers' with an inter-church or trans-local role are in fact *named* bishops in several Baptist unions and conventions in the world.[64] Regional ministers are also named 'bishops' in several classic forms of Pentecostalism such as the Church of God. Commenting on *Baptism, Eucharist and Ministry*, Pentecostal theologian Harold D. Hunter judges that 'major Holiness Classical Pentecostal denominations in the USA have essentially episcopal infrastructures' and that 'when guided by the admission that "the New Testament does not describe a single pattern of ministry"[65] ... Pentecostals should be able to interact responsibly with the concept of a threefold ministry'.[66]

This Pentecostal view need not be in contradiction with the view on episcopacy offered by the Pentecostal participants in dialogue with the Roman Catholic Church when they state that 'On the whole, Pentecostals propose that presbyteral and/or congregational ecclesial models express better [than episcopacy] the mutuality or reciprocity demanded by koinonia'.[67] In this section of *Perspectives on Koinonia*, Pentecostal theologians are reacting against a certain view of episcopacy, that in which the whole structure depends on the primacy of one see, the papacy, as having 'universal power over the whole church'. Neither Baptists nor Pentecostals can accept this

---

[63] *Together in Mission and Ministry*, §§46–51, pp. 26–28.

[64] For example, Republic of Georgia, Moldova, Russia, and several African conventions.

[65] *Baptism, Eucharist and Ministry*, p. 24.

[66] Hunter, 'Reflections', p. 343.

[67] *Perspectives on Koinonia*, §87.

version of the link between bishops and apostolicity. However, t. challenge for both traditions is to re-think the issue of *episkope* in a creative way. For Baptists, this is likely to be guided by faithfulness to the concept of a covenant community, drawn together under the rule of Christ. For Pentecostals, institutions must always be shaped by the energy of charismatic gift, implying – as *Perspectives on Koinonia* expresses it – that 'ordination is a public acknowledgement of a God-given charism which a person has received prior to the act of ordination'.[68]

My hope is that all churches will be open to re-thinking, re-visualizing in an imaginative way, what this 'sign' of apostolicity might look like. If those churches which have episcopal structures think that they must always continue as they are now, then they themselves are not open to the new forms that covenant can take. As body, fellowship, and covenant community, the ecumenical calling of the church must be a summons to move on, to tread the pilgrim path into the future in 'ways known and yet to be made known'.[69] God help the church if she gets stuck when she should be walking steadily on, her face turned to the coming kingdom.

---

[68] *Perspectives on Koinonia*, §85.

[69] This was the wording of the covenant made in Gainsborough, 1606-1607: see n. 124 above.

3

A GLOBAL SHIFT OF WORLD CHRISTIANITY AND PENTECOSTALISM

WONSUK MA[*]   *He is a Korean Pentecostal*

This contribution will present a very broad picture of the landscape of global Christianity today, and it will set an extremely important context for our life, our mission engagement, and our churches. In the first part, I will cover the 2,000 years of church history followed by several observations. In the final section, I will pick up with the implications for global Pentecostal and Charismatic Christianity.

1. Millennial Shifts

The first millennial shift is the shift towards global Christianity. Todd Johnson makes this case clearly in his book, *Atlas of Global Christianity*, which was published as part of the Edinburgh Centenary publications. Global Christianity has made a drastic shift in the past one thousand years. We are currently in the beginning of the third millennium.

1.1 First Millennium

In the first millennium, Christianity started in what is known today as the Middle East, in the city of Jerusalem to be more precise. Christianity flourished in Asia Minor and Northern Africa in particular. In spite of its continuous expansion toward the West, the center of gravity of global Christianity was still below what is Turkey

[*] Wonsuk Ma (PhD, Fuller Theological Seminary) is Executive Director and David Yonggi Cho Research Tutor of Oxford Centre for Mission Studies, Oxford, United Kingdom.

today. Because of the expansion of global Christianity in Northern Africa, this vast area was not only a Christian seedbed, but also a theological cradle. For example, the monastic movement came from Egypt, and early Christian theologies were shaped by forefathers from Northern Africa. It is a fascinating story to see how, for example, this monastic movement traveled all the way to the Celtic region – Ireland and today's Great Britain, which eventually Christianized the country.

Thus, in the first millennium, global Christianity was a religion of the South. Among several others, Syriac Christians were major Christian players in the first millennium Christianity, and they made important missionary moves, not only to India, but also to China and other parts of the world, especially Northern Africa, including the Sudan and Ethiopia.

The rise of Islam in the seventh century certainly impacted global Christianity. Nonetheless, if you follow the story of Syriac or Nestorian Christianity, that part of Christianity was never sanctioned by the state. It was always under persecution, partly because of their doctrinal controversy as Nestorians, but also because they were constantly under Persian Islamic rulers in later centuries.

This is an important clue that we need to pick up later. But, what makes a church missional? What is it going to take for us to recognize and develop mission? Are we going to seize the historic moment and strive for the unprecedented opportunity at hand?

1.2 In the Second …

The rise of Islam practically eradicated Christianity slowly but steadily in some of its heartlands, from Northern Africa and Asia Minor. The theory of Andrew Walls is very disturbing.[1] He argues that Christianity made a serial move while Islam made a progressive move. By serial move, he is arguing that there is a life-cycle: birth, growth, flourishing, expanding; but at some point, it will lose its own vitality and eventually disappear. At the height of its life, that part of Christianity will give birth to a new territory with new forms of Christian spirituality and worship almost like human life. This is a very disturbing concept!

---

[1] Andrew F. Walls, 'Christianity across Twenty Centuries', in Todd M. Johnson and Kenneth R. Ross (eds.), *Atlas of Global Christianity* (Edinburgh: Edinburgh University Press, 2009), pp. 48-49.

In contrast, Islam takes over a territory; the territory will remain as an Islamic region and then they will continue to expand and expand. So, it is a progressive work. Now, I do not like it, but it is definitely a valid historical observation. My personal question is: 'Do we have to live with this or is there a way that we can break this pattern?' I think this is a 2000-year-old question that is worth asking. It is interesting to note that when Orthodox Christianity in Northern Africa and Asia Minor was completely eradicated by Islam, it founded new territories – Eastern, Central Europe, and the vast region of Russia. So in terms of territory, the new Orthodox region was so much larger than the older ones. Of course, how we wish that the move had been more progressive rather than serial, so that it was Northern Africa, Asia Minor, plus Eastern Europe, Central Europe, and the former Soviet territories all under the banner of Christianity. However, I am not here to correct history!

In the second millennium, Christianity was practically a northern and later a western religion with a center of gravity above what is Turkey today. During this era, Christianity began to make both a westward and a northward movement, making global Christianity a northern religion. The rise of Islam (especially in the places of Orthodox Christianity in Northern Africa and Asia Minor) and also Orthodox expansion in new territories enhanced this move. The rise of European powers and their colonial campaign, the discovery of the Americas, and the expansion of Christianity further helped this move. The characteristics of Christianity in this period are still fresh in our memory. There are several important global mission players, beginning with Jesuits as a Catholic missionary order and nations such as Britain and now the United States of America.

1.3 Now …

According to Todd Johnson, during the second millennium, global Christianity as a northern religion came to an end in 1981. Not many people remember this year as a very critical watershed point, but as far as global Christianity is concerned, 1981, if this observation is correct, is the year that Christianity, for the second time, became the southern religion. Therefore, in our own generation, the center of gravity for the global Christian has moved toward the South. The secularization of the West, especially in Western Europe, and the significant growth of Christianity in Asia, Africa, and South America, has added to this move. The question is: 'Who will be the main player in mission?' We will have to wait and see, but I would like to see Korea as a major player but as one of many.

2. Observations

What do we observe from here?

2.1 Global Changes in Christianity

First of all, you and I are in an exciting and historic generation. If we can suspect some of the causes of this global shift, definitely the missionary movement must have contributed to it. So, there has been a radical change in the spread of global Christianity during the last 100 years. When the world church celebrated a historic mission corporation in Edinburgh (in 1910), about 80 percent or more of the world's Christians were found in the global North. Today, about 63 percent of global Christians are found in the southern continents.

When it comes to mission, it follows the pattern of global Christianity, but in a decade or two. When the Edinburgh conference was held about a hundred years ago, almost all the Christian missionaries came from what is called the West. Today more than 50% of Protestant missionary forces are coming from the South. This change has affected North American missionary movements as well. Today, North American missionaries are no longer the same group of people who served as missionaries fifty years ago: 'Americans' now come in different colors, such as Latinos, Asians, and Africans as well as the traditional whites. Politically speaking, it was the height of the colonial era a century ago. About 80 percent of the world's territory was occupied by the West. But today, we are talking about the post-colonial era, and changes are everywhere, including in economics and mission paradigms.

2.2 No Growth at All

Our excitement at this global change, however, stops here. This vast, global, seismic, historic move of global Christianity has not brought any change in the proportion of Christianity against the world's population. This harsh reality is before us, in spite of concerted efforts to bring partnership and cooperation within world evangelization over the last 100 years – far more than all the efforts combined in the rest of the Church's history. More journals, more

programs, more mission organizations, and far more resources have
been invested into the evangelization of the world in the last 100
years than ever before. In fact, Todd Johnson argues that 100 years
ago Christianity was about 34.2 percent of the world's population.
Today, it is slightly under 33 percent. We lost! Therefore, the shift,
the unprecedented global shifts, are all in-house.

   Although it is quite true that the maintenance of the current level
of global Christianity is not a small feat and owes greatly to the missionary movement and the rise and expansion of Pentecostal Christianity, why have we still not made definite progress? Of course, we
can argue that every generation is a new mission field. But in the
Centenary Celebration of the Edinburgh Conference in 2010, there
was a satiric hush that we are lucky to still have 1/3 of the world as
Christian. At the back of my mind, we were asking: 'What will it be
like when we come back 100 years from now? Will we still have
one-third of the world's population as part of this great religion of
truth that we proclaim?' This sad mood was greatly troubling to me
as a Pentecostal and also as a Korean. While world Christianity has
struggled to maintain this status quo, the only group that made a
significant growth was Islam.

2.3 Can It Grow?

I am sure you have some burning questions, just as I do. First, are
we destined just to protect what we have, or is there any possibility
and real potential that we can grow beyond the one-third wall?
Does world Christianity, with the heavy shift to the South, have a
better chance to grow beyond the one-third mark of the world's
population for the first time in its 2,000 years of history and stay
there? This is not just a mental game: it is a fact that we need to
face. Even with the growth and spread of Pentecostal Christianity
and the wonderful missionary feats, it is still in-house. Now, if we
believe that there is a possibility for growth beyond that line, what
reason do we see for this possibility, especially in the global South?
Of course, the rest of the world is not going to say, 'O great! South,
it is your turn.' We all know that in every place, we will have to give
everything we have.

   Thus, we need to ask some 'what if' questions. One of these hy-
pothetical questions would be: 'What if Western Europe did not
decline in the last fifty years; what if they were able to hold the line?'
I am sure that we would have been better off than 33 percent today.

Then, of course, the real question is for the future and to ourselves: 'If in the last 100 years, it was Pentecostal Christianity that has been contributing significantly to the maintenance, at least, of global Christianity to this level, what would be its role in the next 100 years or fifty years or thirty years?' This is a very serious question because it is a 2,000-year-old question!

I am sure that certainly you would like to join with me in believing that we are a generation of a new possibility, that a 2,000-year-old Christianity has never been seen yet.

2.4 Mission as Usual or as We Know?

If we are to be a radical generation, then what kind of Christian mission are we going to look for? Can the new shift open up to a new missionary paradigm? The missionary paradigm that we have known, seen, and practiced in the last 300 years, starting from Church Mission Society of the Church of England and London Missionary Society and on and on and, of course, North America – let me ask you these questions: 'Can this missionary paradigm be workable, for example, for the missionaries of the eight million strong and missionary-sending Ethiopian Kale Heywet Church? Would it be possible for some of the churches in Africa (Zambia, for instance) to carry the missionary baton to fulfill this real possibility in the next generation?' This leads us to analyze critically key elements of the established or 'received' missionary paradigm.

2.5 Call for New Missionary Paradigm

Let us be very practical here. How much money would it take to maintain one family on the mission field for a four-year term? Can this be applied to churches in Ethiopia? Unfortunately, Korea has tried to emulate this, and I think Korea is realizing that it is not our 'clothes'. The people do not deny the validity of the established or received system, but it is one thing to ask if this will fit the newer churches. Another much deeper question, beyond practicality, is: 'Is this missionary understanding and paradigm very close to what we read in the book of Acts and the Gospels?'

We all know that the western missionary system was a product of its age and social context. I am not denying its validity; it was perfectly all right for that time, for that circumstance, for that situation, for particular gifts and resources. In fact, the steady and impressive expansion of world Christianity in the southern continents in the past owes much to this missionary commitment and method. But this, and any system for that matter, cannot universalize as it is. Therefore, we need to ask ourselves what a new missiology will look like if a new southern context is taken into account. And, as one member of the church in the global South, I would even ask a much deeper question: 'How would the practices of the Early Church guide us to reshape mission understanding and mission practices?' I believe that is the question that is relevant to the West as well. What is the average time for a newly appointed missionary to fully raise their budget? Can the current growth sustain the kind of number of missionaries we envision in the next thirty years? Deeper than this practical inquiry will be: 'What is a missionary paradigm that will reflect faithfully our Pentecostal spirituality and theological values?'

2.6 A Pentecostal Question

Sometimes the gap between our claimed theological convictions and actual practices can tell us where we need to do some work. For example, how Pentecostal missiology is clergy–laity division blind. That means the composition of our missionaries should be well represented by an overwhelming number of lay professionals along with a smaller number of clergy missionaries. This is so if we are to be faithful in our theological values and if we really believe that our mission practice is based on the conviction that everyone is called to proclaim God's Kingdom. This will have an implication for every aspect of mission operation including recruitment, training, deployment, and support. And this is necessary if we want to see the global church finally cross the one-third line and stay there or even continually make headway.

2.7 Adding Asia

Now, let me speak as an Asian Pentecostal. We can almost say that the twentieth century was the century of Africa. It is amazing how 100 years ago, when top mission minds and leadership gathered in Edinburgh, they never talked about Latin America, partly because of the political issues with the Roman Catholic Church. They paid very little attention to Africa because they knew it was a Lost Continent. A lot of attention, almost full focus, was on China, India, and Japan. In fact, in the early 1910s, people like John Mott almost believed in a Christianized China just as much as the whole conference believed that the whole evangelization of the world in their generation was possible. They believed that they had all the resources. More than 80 percent of the world's territory was theirs or under their (or Christian) domination. They not only had religious hegemony, but also political power, military influence, and a superior culture. Therefore, the move of Christianity was from developed to developing or underdeveloped nations. They knew that if nothing worked, they still had guns. They knew that in one way or another, world evangelization in their generation was not just a prayer but a good possibility and was imminent. What an irony it was in 1949 when China fell to a Communist regime. That shook the Christian mindset. Of course, also consider what we saw in that generation – two World Wars, mostly fought by Christian nations among one another and the killing of millions of lives. That is the Asian part, now the Pentecostal angle.

The world Christian leaders in Edinburgh did not notice the Azusa Street Revival, an obscure group meeting somewhere in downtown Los Angeles in a smelly barn, where weird people babbled. Of course, they were not even decent enough to be considered for the Edinburgh missionary conference. No! How the Holy Spirit surprised the world and us! We are no better than anyone else; the best gift that we had was marginality. We do not belong to the mainstream; we are different. So, suddenly, the twentieth century was also the century of the mission of the Spirit.

Look at eighteenth-century Africa from the perspective of the historic churches, especially Roman Catholic and the/Anglican Church, which had full access to much of the sub-Saharan continent. In the twentieth century, especially in its second half, the African independent churches rose and transformed the landscape of Christianity in that continent. It is only one part of the Pentecostal story that surprised all of us, the delegates of Edinburgh 2010.

Christians comprise about one-third of the total population. In the last 2,000 years of Church history, Christianity has never exceeded one-third of the world's population. Today, Pentecostal Christians are about one-third of the Christian population. We know that this is the strongest and fastest growing segment of global Christianity evolving into endless new forms and varieties of expression. This dynamic and also unpredictable 'evolution' will greatly challenge us because we want to keep the work of the Spirit. But, who are we to tell the Holy Spirit how to operate if we are truly to be people of the Spirit?

Among the three southern continents, Asia is the least evangelized, about 12%. Among them, 50% are Pentecostal and Charismatic in their orientation. Many of them would not use this nomenclature; but their worship, spirituality, orientation, and religious worldview is clearly Pentecostal and Charismatic. This is compared with 33% of Christians in Africa who are Pentecostal and Charismatic and 28% in Latin America.[2]

3. Wrapping with Possibilities

All the three southern continents have similar numbers of Pentecostal and Charismatic Christians. Conversely, look at Asia. It holds more than 60 percent of the world's population, but the evangelization rate is less than the world average (33.3%) of which 50% are Pentecostals and Charismatics. Do you see which is the biggest and yet last frontier? And who holds the key to the quest for the evangelization of this vast continent and ultimately to the 'one-third' question of world evangelization? It is plainly clear: you and I, Pentecostals and Charismatics, embody this possibility. Thus, you and I represent the generation of the first possibility – sustained growth of Christianity beyond the one-third line. It can stay there or it can grow even further. I live with this possibility, and I pray that you do too. This has huge missional implications for challenges, yes, but great opportunities as well that will require very radical and creative thinking as we rely on the creativity of the Holy Spirit. Mission in the Spirit!

---

[2] Johnson and Ross (eds.), *Atlas of Global Christianity*, pp. 102-103.

SECTION II

THE GLOBAL SOUTH

4

PENTECOSTALISM AS SUFFERING: HOUSE CHURCHES IN CHINA (1949-2012)

CONNIE AU[*]

Background of Chinese House Churches

In the nineteenth and the early twentieth centuries, China was regarded as the 'darling of mission' as far as western missionaries were concerned. Soon after the Chinese empire was forced to open treaty ports and offer settlements to western countries, thousands of missionaries of all denominations were sent to China. No matter how much missionaries had sacrificed for the Chinese millions and their contribution to modernization and to humanitarian improvement in China, Christianity was stigmatized as a subtle force of western imperialism. The Boxer Uprising in 1900 and the Anti-Christian Movement in the 1920s demonstrated utter hatred against missionaries through verbal and physical violence assisted by governmental back-up. The latter campaign was even fueled by the communist power in China, assisted by the Union of Soviet Socialist Republics (USSR).

Some Chinese Christians had resented being controlled by western missions and became independent. They founded indigenous

* Connie Au (PhD, University of Birmingham) is a part-time lecturer in western church history and an associate researcher of the Divinity School of the Chinese University of Hong Kong. She is the Project Officer (Ecumenical Formation) of the Hong Kong Christian Council, coordinating two ecumenical courses for students and adults. She is also a member of Echos, the Youth Commission of the World Council of Churches. Her doctoral thesis was published as *Grassroots Unity in the Charismatic Renewal* (Eugene, OR: Wipf & Stock, 2011).

churches based on the 'three-self' principles (self-support, self-propagation, and self-governance) first introduced by Henry Venn of the Church Missionary Society and Rufus Anderson of the American Board of Commissioners for Foreign Mission in the nineteenth century. These churches expanded quickly as the gospel was preached in the Chinese language and developed in the local culture. Signs and wonders accompanied the preaching, which concretely answered the physical and spiritual needs of the people.

Meanwhile, the communist party grew stronger through military support from the USSR and other ideological influences. It was determined to take over the sovereignty from the Nationalist Party, but this plan was interrupted by the Second World War. To fight against the Japanese, their common enemy, the Nationalists and Communists joined forces. But once WWII ended, they brought the country into the turmoil of civil war. Eventually, the Nationalists headed by Jiang Jieshi retreated to Taiwan and the Communists led by Mao Zedong came to power. The People's Republic of China was founded on October 1, 1949; but beforehand, many businessmen and Christians had already fled to Hong Kong and other countries as they had predicted that oppressive political campaigns against capitalism and Christianity would soon happen. It did not take long for their prediction to come true.

To regulate Protestant and Catholic Christianity effectively, the communists established the National Committee of Three-Self Patriotic Movement of the Protestant Churches (National TSPM) in 1954 and the Catholic Patriotic Association in 1957. Those Protestants and Catholics who could not align themselves with the official churches went underground. Although most of the house churches were developed from indigenous churches whose practices were in line with Pentecostalism, some do not follow this trend. No matter whether the house churches are Pentecostal, non-Pentecostal or Catholic, they are all illegal and face the risk of persecution for their faith.

The Birth of the Unfriendly Twins: Three-Self and House Churches

The atheism of the communists did not give birth to the Three-Self Patriotic Movement immediately after 1949; rather it was formed through a gradual process. Being inspired by the premier, Zhou En-lai, Wu Yaozhong, who had not been a significant Christian leader, drafted a manifesto called 'The Pathways for Chinese Churches to Contribute to the Establishment of the New China' in 1950, also called the 'Three-Self Declaration'.[1] The communists used the missionary terminology to develop their own political agenda and impose it on churches. Instead of showing love and loyalty to God, churches should bear this attitude to the party. The Declaration instructed churches, stating, 'Under the leadership of the government, the church must reject imperialism, feudalism, and bureaucratic capitalism so that they can diligently participate in the building of an independent, democratic, peaceful, united, and affluent new China'.[2] It demanded of churches

> to clearly identify the evil of imperialism in China, to know about the fact that Christianity was used by imperialism, to drive out the influence of imperialism within Christianity, and to be alert of any conspiracies of imperialism, especially American imperialism, using religion as a way to develop dissident power.[3]

The Declaration was first signed by more than forty church leaders but many others disagreed with it and kept silent under political pressure. It was signed by 320,000 people between August 1950 and December 1951. On September 23, 1950, the government's official newspaper, *People's Daily* (*Renmin Ribao*), announced that through signing the Declaration, 'all religious believers obtain a new direction. It is only by following this direction that the religious sector can develop its own normal religious business.'[4]

The antagonism against the 'American imperialism' was fueled by the outbreak of the Korean War in 1950. The policy of 'resisting the United States and aiding Korea' was applied not only to the War itself, but to churches. In April 1951, the State Administration of

---

[1] Chinese Romanization: *Zhong Guo Ji Du Jiao Zai Xin Zhong Guo Jian She Zhong Lu Li De Tu Jing.*

[2] Quoted in Deng Zhaoming, *The Vicissitudes of the Three-Self Patriotic Movement in the 1950s and Its Predicament Today* (Hong Kong: Christian Study Centre on Chinese Religion and Culture, 1997), p. 11.

[3] *A History of Wenzhou Churches (Wen Zhou Di Qu Jiao Hui Shi)*, p. 101. Since this book was published for internal use of churches in Wenzhou with confidentiality, the author, publisher, year, and city of publication are not provided in the book.

[4] *A History of Wenzhou Churches*, pp. 102-103.

Religious Affairs held a meeting to discuss Christian organizations receiving American subsidies. It was attended by church leaders of all regions, including Ni Tuosheng (Watchman Nee, 1903-1972), founder of the Little Flock, and Jing Dianying (1890-1957), founder of the Jesus Family. The meeting declared, 'Under the leadership of the people's central government, imperialism which has invaded Chinese people's culture for more than a century must be eventually, thoroughly, eternally, and completely terminated'. To achieve this goal, the meeting formed the Preparatory Committee of the Resisting America and Aiding Korea Three-Self Reform Movement of Chinese Christianity.[5] It decided that churches that had received American sponsorships should register and achieve self-support without delay.

To wipe out all 'counter-revolutionary' and 'imperialist' churches thoroughly, the Committee launched an Appealing Movement in the whole country. Wu justified this action with Matthew 23, which was about Jesus criticizing the Pharisees and scribes.[6] Missionaries like F.W. Price of the Church of Christ of China[7] and E.H. Lockwood of the Young Men's Christian Association (YMCA) were publicly accused of working as spies for the United States in the name of mission. Chinese church leaders like Chen Wenyuan of the Chinese Methodist Church, general secretary Liang Xiaocuo of the Chinese Young Men's Christian Association, and the renowned independent preacher, Gu Renen, were condemned as making connection with American missions. They were rebuked as 'American imperialists' and the 'running dogs of American imperialism'.[8] By the end of 1951, there were 108 public accusatory assemblies in the

---

[5] Quoted in Zhaoming, *The Vicissitudes*, p. 12. Chinese Romanization: *Zhong Guo Ji Du Jiao Kang Mei Yun Qiao San Zi Ge Xin Yun Dong Cou Bi Hui Wei Yun Hui.*

[6] Zhaoming, *The Vicissitudes*, p. 13.

[7] F.W. Price was ordained as a missionary of the Presbyterian Church of the United States in 1923. He was the principal of the Nanking Theological Seminary until 1952. He was closely related to Jiang Jieshi and his wife and worked at the Church of Christ in China from 1948 to 1950. Since the communists took over, Price and his wife were under persecution for three years and expelled in 1952. Frank (Francis) Wilson Price Collection at the George C. Marshall Research Foundation, <http://marshallfoundation.org/library/documents/Price_Frank_Wilson.pdf.> (accessed May 16, 2012)

[8] Liu Jianping, 'China's Christianity Appealing Movements during the Korean War', *Twenty-First Century Bimonthly* 121 (October 2012), pp. 123-33 (124), <http://www.cuhk.edu.hk/ics/21c/issue/articles/121_0911011.pdf>.

whole country.[9] To enforce communist education within churches, church leaders were required to attend the 'Three-Self' learning classes so that they would understand the political situation and be self-critical about their political position.

Since foreign support was cut off and church leaders were arrested, many churches and Christians organizations, including schools and hospitals, were either controlled or shut down by the government. Those Christian schools that were allowed to remain were managed by communist members appointed by the government and had to teach dialectical materialism, historical materialism, and the new democracy. By 1953, Christian education was diminished, including theological training. Many Bible colleges were forced to merge together, and Christian publishers were monitored by the government. All their publications were censored and those considered to be pro-American and anti-Soviet Union were destroyed. The Three-Self Steering Committee also reinterpreted the Bible according to communist ideology. Missionaries were forced to leave the country, and by the end of the 1950s, fewer than five missionaries remained in China.[10]

In 1954, the Chinese Christian Three-Self Patriotic Movement Committee was formed.[11] Since denominational churches were deprived of foreign support, they were forced to incorporate into the Three-Self system. Churches that had been independent from missionary support before 1949 and had implemented the missionary version of 'three-self' refused to be part of the system. They condemned the Three-Self churches as 'Babylon' and 'the whore' since their ministers were appointed by the atheistic government.[12] Among the religious dissidents, Wang Mingdao (1900-1991) was the most prominent person rebuking the system. He and his wife were arrested after his final sermon, entitled as 'The Son of Man Is Betrayed into the Hands of Sinners', on August 7, 1955. He was sentenced to a fifteen-year imprisonment but later was given life im-

---

[9] *A History of Wenzhou Churches*, pp. 103-104.

[10] *A History of Wenzhou Churches*, pp. 106-107

[11] Chinese Romanization: *Zhong Guo Ji Di Jian San Zi Oi Guo Yun Dong Wei Yun Hui*.

[12] Lian Xi, *Redeemed by Fire: The Rise of Popular Christianity in Modern China* (New Haven: Yale University Press, 2010), pp. 206, 212

prisonment and was released at the age of eighty. His co-worker in Guangzhou, Lin Xiangao, was also arrested.[13]

Indigenous Pentecostal and charismatic churches were under more severe political attack. Some churches that tried to incorporate themselves into the Three-Self system institutionally and to follow the communist ideology doctrinally soon disappeared. Miraculous practices including healing, exorcism, dancing, and singing spiritual songs were condemned as 'depressive', 'leading people to spiritual gloom, producing a pessimistic, world-denying, and escapist sentiment, being unhealthy to the contemporary society'. Their teachings on the end time and imminent second coming of Jesus were criticized as 'hyper-political, hyper-national, hyper-world, and unrealistic'.[14] Although they did not receive any foreign support, they relied on donations from Christian landlords and capitalists, which for the communists meant that they approved of feudalism, bureaucratic capitalism, and imperialism.

The leader of the True Jesus Church, Isaac Wei, son of the founder, Paul Wei, was arrested and disappeared in 1957. The 'Spiritual Gifts Society' was seriously attacked.[15] Watchman Nee was arrested in 1952 based on the charge of organizing a 'counter-revolutionary cooperation' and was sentenced to imprisonment for fifteen years in 1956. As he was severely ill in prison, he was released in April 1972 but passed away in less than two months.[16] The Jesus Family was 'reformed' by a working team sent by the Preparatory Committee of the Resisting America and Aiding Korea Three-Self Reform Movement for four months. In 1952, their leader, Jing Dianying, was accused of collaboration with the Japanese during the occupation in the Second World War and of working with the British and Americans to oppose communism.[17] These indigenous Pentecostal churches did not reappear in the country after 1976. They were oppressed not only by communist atheists but also by adherents of the TSPM. The incidents of betrayal in that period sowed

---

[13] Zhaoming, *The Vicissitudes*, pp. 46-47.

[14] Zhaoming, *The Vicissitudes*, pp. 36-37

[15] Zhaoming, *The Vicissitudes*, pp. 36-37.

[16] Zhaoming, *The Vicissitudes*, pp. 38-41; *A History of Wenzhou Churches*, pp. 108-109.

[17] Deng Zhaoming, 'Indigenous Chinese Pentecostal Denominations', in Allan Anderson and Edmond Tang (eds.), *Asian and Pentecostal: The Charismatic Face of Christianity in Asia* (Oxford: Regnum International, 2005), p. 460

the seeds of mistrust between the Three-Self and the house church-es, and even today, they have not been completely removed.[18]

From the 1950s to the 1970s, the communists launched a series of political movements, and Christians were one of the main targets of political attack. In the Anti-Right Movement in 1957,[19] they were identified as the 'right-wing' and had to be re-educated. In the Great Leap Forward Movement in 1958, they were condemned as the 'ex-ploiting class' who helped the capitalists and were forced to do la-bor work. Under the leadership of the TSPM, many church build-ings were converted into factories as a way to support the govern-ment's scheme of increasing production. Churches in the same re-gion were merged into a few churches to save expenses and to achieve 'unity'.[20] All denominations were eliminated and churches used the same form of liturgy in their services. Regarding this 'ecu-menical achievement' in 1958, the official Christian periodical *Tian Feng* said:

> The Western churches had called for 'collaboration' and 'unity' for forty years but achieved nothing. We surpassed them within a short time (three days only). What we Chinese Christians have been hoping for in the last forty years has been realized in this generation ... This is indeed 'one day as twenty years!'[21]

In Henan province, officials announced '15 Nos' against Chris-tians in 1959: 1. No preaching outside the church building; 2. No prayers for healing; 3. No exploitation; 4. No discrimination and harassment against women; 5. No illegal meetings; 6. No hindrance of production; 7. No wandering; 8. No membership of teenagers and children under 18 years old; 9. No protection for landlords; 10. No attack against socialism and collective economy; 11. No rumors and pessimistic counter-revolutionary propaganda; 12. No setup of churches and house meetings; 13. No private ordination; 14. No

---

[18] Zhaoming, 'Indigenous Chinese Pentecostal Denominations', pp. 442-43.

[19] The movement identified five types of people who were a threat to the so-ciety, including landlords, rich farmers, counter-revolutionists, bad people, and the right-wing. They were called the 'black five'.

[20] For example, the number of churches in Shanghai decreased from 140 to 8; Guangzhou, from 52 to 1; Beijing, from 66 to 4. The number of people in at-tendance for Sunday services decreased drastically. See *A History of Wenzhou Churches*, p. 114.

[21] Quoted in Zhaoming, *The Vicissitudes*, p. 97.

fusion of Christian doctrines and the Party's policy; 15. No overseas connection.[22] The severity of persecution against Christians accelerated during the Cultural Revolution from 1966 to 1976. Torture and public humiliation were justified because Christianity represented imperialism, superstition, and theism, which were condemned as the enemies of the Revolution. Christians were commanded to confess their 'crime' in public, but some of them took the opportunities to preach about the gospel, healing, and heaven. Many Christians secretly worshipped in houses, and cases of baptism in the Spirit and healing frequently happened. Some of the persecutors converted to Christianity because of the gospel message and personal experience of healing. They changed from a persecutor to protector for Christians when they were worshipping in houses.[23]

In those ten years, the legal Three-Self churches stopped public worship and activities; house churches were the only form of Protestant Christianity that remained active and growing. In 1976, Wang Hongwen, one of the members of the Gang of Four and the expected successor of Mao Zedong, sent a decree to all provinces and counties to kill all Christians. But soon afterwards, he was arrested with the other three Gang members, Jiang Qing (Mao's wife), Zhang Cunqiao, and Yiao Wenyun.[24] The government was subsequently controlled by reformists led by Deng Xiaoping who allowed public worship and returned church buildings and land to congregations. Church leaders and Christians were released, including Wang Mingdao. The TSPM resumed its work under the leadership of Ding Guangxun (or K.H. Ting, 1915-2012), a former Anglican bishop and president of Nanjing Theological Seminary since 1952. He founded the China Christian Council (CCC) to deal with 'pastoral work' such as printing the Bible and hymn books and training ministers.[25] Nowadays, TSPM and CCC, called the 'two associa-

---

[22] Zhang Yinan, *Sixty Years of Chinese House Churches* (*Zhong Guo Jia Ting Jiao Hui Liu Shi Nian*) (Hong Kong: Revival Chinese Ministries International, 2010), p. 4. The author was followed and investigated by the police for nine years as he was collecting materials and interviewing house church leaders for this book. He eventually was sentenced to imprisonment for two years in 2003.

[23] Xi, *Redeemed by Fire*, pp. 208-209.

[24] *A History of Wenzhou Churches*, p. 137.

[25] Xi, *Redeemed by Fire*, p. 210.

tions' (*liang hui*) in short, are monitored by the State Administration of Religious Affairs and Ministry of Civil Affairs.[26]

Although the government has been more open to religions since the 1980s, house churches remain illegal and their suffering has not ended. They refuse to register as a Three-Self church because their faith, based on their understandings of the Bible, cannot compromise with the Three-Self rules. For instance, the government prohibits cross-provincial evangelistic activities, but house churches believe that preaching the gospel to the end of the world is a biblical teaching which they have to follow. They resist the law which prohibits Christians from preaching to children and teenagers under eighteen and connecting with foreign Christian organizations. They feel offended by the regulations which only allow those who have a preaching license to preach and grant the authority to the State Administration of Religious Affairs to appoint ministers for a particular church.[27] They believe that these rules violate the missionary nature of the church and hinder Christians from fulfilling the Great Commission.

Most of the house churches in China share the common vision of mission and principles as the followers of Christ, but the level of persecution that they bear as the cost of their vision varies from region to region. It depends on the attitudes of the local government towards house churches. Economic and geographical factors can also affect their attitude. The following explains two extreme cases: Henan and Wenzhou. They are one of the poorest and richest areas in China respectively and reflect the contrasting harsh and gentle treatment meted out to house churches.

---

[26] 'Articles of the National Committee of Three-Self Patriotic Movement of the Protestant Churches', <http://www.ccctspm.org/quanguolianghui/zhang cheng_sanzi.html> (accessed May 16, 2012). The Catholic churches in China are managed by the Chinese Catholic Patriotic Association and the Bishops' Conference of Catholic Church in China, which is called 'one association, one conference' (yi hui yi tuan). They are also monitored by the State Administration of Religious Affairs and Ministry of Civil Affairs. See 'Articles of the Chinese Catholic Church in China' and 'Articles of the Bishops' Conference of Catholic Church in China', <http://www.chinacatholic.cn/index.php/yhyt/zczd/400-tianzhujiao-zhujiaotuan-zhangcheng> and <http://www.chinacatholic.cn/index.php/yhyt/zczd/399-zhongguo-tianzhujiao-aiguohui-zhangcheng> (accessed May 16, 2012.)

[27] <http://www.chinaaid.net/2006/07/7.html> (accessed April 27, 2012).

Henan: Suburban House Churches

Henan is an inland province in the east of China. According to the census launched by the National Bureau of Statistics of China in 2010, Henan has the third largest population. Of the Chinese population, 7.02% is from Henan, 94,023,567 in total.[28] It is one of the poorest provinces in China. Most of the people are farmers and sell their blood for extra income. Due to the unhygienic equipment for blood transmission, many people have been infected by the HIV virus. Henan is therefore notorious for its 'AIDS villages'. Churches provide support to the AIDS patients and take care of hundreds of orphans who have been affected by the fatal virus.[29] Since farmers cannot afford to pay for medication, the last problem that they want to have is disease. If one member gets ill, the whole family will collapse. In this difficult circumstance, healing is good news, and people become Christians because of the miracles that happen to them or to their family members.[30] This social hardship indirectly contributes to the prominence of the Christian population in the province and the whole country.

Henan has been the cradle of Christianity in China. Hudson Taylor of the China Inland Mission started his mission in this province in 1883.[31] He established churches with local Chinese, including Lao Yian, Ma Cuansheng, Sung Fun, Bo Cunshen, and their wives. Baptists, Lutherans, Presbyterians, Wesleyans, Anglicans, Seventh Day Adventists, and Assemblies of God also launched missions in the province until 1949.[32] In the last 63 years of the communist regime, Henan is also the home of three major networks of house churches: China Gospel Fellowship (also called Tanghe Fellowship) led by Shen Yiping; Fang Cheng Fellowship led by Zhang Rongliang; and the Born-again (also called Word of Life Movement) led by Xü

---

[28] The largest population is in Guangdong, 104,303,132 (7.79%) and the second largest is in Shandong 95,793,065 (7.15%). <http://www.stats.gov.cn/was40/gjtjj_detail.jsp?searchword=%C8%CB%BF%DA%C6%D5%B2%E9%B7%D6%B5%D8%C7%F8&channelid=6697&record=2> (accessed April 30, 2012).

[29] Zheng Cun Qiao, *Why Is Henan a Christian Province but Full of Vicious Sects?* (Hong Kong: Alliance Bible Seminary, 2006), pp. 20-21.

[30] Qiao, *Why Is Henan a Christian Province*, p. 14.

[31] Yinan, *Sixty Years of Chinese House Churches*, p. 1.

[32] Yinan, *Sixty Years of Chinese House Churches*, p. 1.

Yongze. Another large network is located in Anhui province called Fu Yang Church led by Chang Xianqi.

Zhang Rongliang is regarded as one of the most prominent leaders of house churches in China. He was secretly baptized in 1969 and became a brigadier of a rail-building team of a hundred workers. As he was categorized as a 'poor farmer' by the government,[33] he was promoted to be a chief leader of workers and vice-secretary. In 1970, he made a vow to become a communist member and believed that the eternal life taught by Christianity was consistent with socialism. Unfortunately, his Christian identity was found when he was caught in an evening prayer meeting. He was sent to religious classes to be brainwashed by police and security guards and forced to abandon his faith. During this trial, he was encouraged by some elderly Christians, presbyters, and deacons of churches of the former China Inland Mission which had joined the TSPM, but they also betrayed him. They reported to the police about his house meetings and contacting other persecuted Christian leaders. He was detained in 1974 and sentenced for seven years of imprisonment in 1976 due to his so-called 'counter-revolutionary crime'.[34] After the Cultural Revolution, he was vindicated by the reformists and was released in 1980, but he was not excited about it since he considered prisons and labor camps as his Bible colleges. As he answered a British pastor's question about his theological training in 1985, he said, 'Prisons are the Bible colleges for house church pastors. Security guards are our teachers. Whips and truncheons are teaching tools. We experience God's presence in prisons more than in a comfortable classroom of a Bible school.'[35]

---

[33] During the Land Reformation in the 1950s, the communist government categorized people in villages into five classes. First, there were landlords who owned land and employed workers to work for them. This class was condemned as the enemy of the whole country. Second, rich farmers, who had land and employed workers to work for them, but they also worked on the farm. Third, middle-class farmers, who had land for self-supply and only employed temporary workers. There were three types of middle-class farmers: rich middle-class, upper middle-class, and lower middle-class. Fourth, poor farmers, who did not have much land and worked for others for a living. Fifth, employed farmers, who did not have any land and totally relied on employment for a living. They were the major supporters of communism. <http://zh.wikipedia.org/zh-tw/%E8%B4%A B%E5%86%9C> (accessed May 14, 2012).

[34] Yinan, *Sixty Years of Chinese House Churches*, pp. 33-37.

[35] Yinan, *Sixty Years of Chinese House Churches*, p. 46.

After being released, he immediately rejoined some churches in Henan and was amazed by the revival when he saw many young people involved. The revival was also spread by some former members of indigenous Pentecostal churches. An elderly woman, Zhang Oirong, had participated in Jesus Family before 1949. She talked about being filled with the Holy Spirit and miracles and encouraged young people to preach the gospel bravely.[36] Some zealous youth ministers, both men and women, were dedicated to evangelism and were called 'Fire ecstatics'. They adhered to 'preaching with mouths, preaching with blood, preaching with pens, preaching unceasingly to Jerusalem as there was nothing that they desired in the world'. Gao Guofu was the most prominent youth preacher in the early 1980s and was sentenced to serve in Xihua Labour Camp as a result of his evangelistic work.[37] Unsurprisingly, the number of house church members grew rapidly. According to the statistics in 1985, there were 18,361 members in 46 Three-Self churches and over 100,000 in house churches in Fangcheng.[38] Nevertheless, Zhang still felt that he and his church had not fulfilled the command of the Great Commission, so he organized the 'Gospel Month' in 1994. He encouraged his members to fast and commit themselves to preach the gospel in a particular village. The church provided tracts, videos, Bibles, and books for them to introduce the gospel to villagers, but they also believed in the use of spiritual gifts, which is stated in the creed endorsed by leaders of the house church networks in Henan.[39] Some of them preached in public, which was illegal, and were persecuted by the local authorities. The persecutors got sick or died immediately and the evangelists prayed for their forgiveness and recovery. The miracles that people experienced and witnessed convinced them of the living God, and they were converted.[40] As the community was growing, Fangcheng Fellowship has become the mother church of thousands of churches in the whole country, claiming more than ten million members.

---

[36] Yinan, *Sixty Years of Chinese House Churches*, p. 41.

[37] Yinan, *Sixty Years of Chinese House Churches*, p. 45.

[38] Yinan, *Sixty Years of Chinese House Churches*, p. 42.

[39] 'The Creed of Christian House Churches in Henan', in Yinan, *Sixty Years of Chinese House Churches*, p. 140.

[40] Yinan, *Sixty Years of Chinese House Churches*, pp. 53-54.

Although the practice of spiritual gifts had been common in Fangcheng Fellowship, it did not emphasize Spirit baptism until Dennis Balcombe preached about it in the 1980s. He was born in El Centro, Southern California in 1945, but he believes that he was born for China. He felt this calling at sixteen and went to Hong Kong in 1969.[41] He founded the Revival Church in the colony, and a mission to China has been the main vision of the church. He entered China for the first time in 1978 when the country was open for foreigners to visit again after almost thirty years.[42] Local leaders requested that he preach for ten hours a day for about two weeks. Eight hundred leaders representing about 100,000 house church Christians gathered inside and outside a small room to hear the message of the baptism in the Holy Spirit. Some of them were laughing, crying, and speaking in tongues, but some senior Christians had never seen such reactions in the Spirit, having been told by missionaries about the cessation of spiritual gifts, and they were skeptical about what was happening.[43] They were also concerned about the suffering that members had borne for the church and would not want them to be misguided by cults and wrong teaching.[44] But their doubts could not extinguish the hunger for revival; the leaders of Fangcheng invited Balcombe to preach all over the country about Spirit baptism. Many Christians were empowered by the experience and prepared to preach the gospel.

To avoid being seen by the police, Balcombe sometimes pretended to be a dead corpse lying in a cart to be taken to burial, or he laid in a coffin and the local Christians took him into the village to preach.[45] However, as his work became more influential, the police began to inspect his activities in Henan. In 1990, Zhang was imprisoned for one year and two months because of inviting foreigners to preach. After his release, he sent a young woman, Lü Xiaomin, to preach in churches. She was caught by the police, but was eager to have a taste of prison like other experienced preachers. As she was in the prisoners' room, she began to sing in the Spirit, 'In

---

[41] Dennis Balcombe, *One Journey, One Nation: Autobiography of Dennis Balcombe, Missionary to China* (Chambersburg: eGenCo. LLC, 2011), p. 1.

[42] Balcombe, *One Journey, One Nation*, p. 156.

[43] Balcombe, *One Journey, One Nation*, p. 161.

[44] Yinan, *Sixty Years of Chinese House Churches*, p. 48.

[45] <http://www.youtube.com/watch?feature=player_embedded&v=ssRwcpi FRYk> (accessed May 15, 2012).

difficult time, we are tested; in difficult time, we grow'. She was locked up for nine days and was guided by the Spirit to compose eight songs. She has written more than a thousand songs which were collected into *Song of Canaan* and are sung all over China.[46] In 1994, Balcombe visited Fangchen with seven other foreigners at the Chinese New Year. They were discovered by the police and were detained for six days. Their arrest became international news and within a few days was reported by the Voice of America. President Bill Clinton was concerned about the case and the American ambassador in China negotiated with the Chinese Ministries of Foreign Affairs. Zhang and his co-workers were released after two weeks as the police realized that the incident had caught international attention. Balcombe was strongly criticized by the vice-chairperson of the National TSPM, Han Wenzao, in his article published in *Tian Feng* in 1994.[47] The government also annulled his visa for seven years from 1995, but his church in Hong Kong continued to send thousands of Bibles to Chinese Christians and organized mission trips to the mainland.[48] He founded the Revival Chinese Ministries International to serve house churches in 1997. Its branches in Australia and Germany work for the same goal.[49]

Zhang is not only concerned about evangelism and being filled with the Spirit but also unity with other house church networks as he sees that unity is the foundation of revival.[50] In 1996, he invited leaders of the four major networks to discuss this matter. They continued to meet once a year and invited ministers from other provinces and Taiwan to speak at their meetings. In 1998, they gathered together in the north of China to draft *A Declaration of Faith of Chinese House Churches*, stating their understandings of the Bible, the Trinity, Christology, soteriology, pneumatology, ecclesiology, and eschatology. They were hoping that by announcing their common faith to the government and churches inside and outside of the country, people would not consider them as cults. It was signed by Chen Yiping (Tanghe Church, Henan), Zhang Rongliang (Fang-

---

[46] Yinan, *Sixty Years of Chinese House Churches*, p. 51.

[47] Yinan, *Sixty Years of Chinese House Churches*, pp. 53-54.

[48] Balcombe, *One Journey, One Nation*, p. 161.

[49] <http://rcmi.wordpress.com/about-rcmi/what-we-do/> (accessed May 11, 2012).

[50] 'The Creed of Christian House Churches in Henan', Yinan, *Sixty Years of Chinese House Churches*, p. 141.

cheng Fellowship, Henan), Chang Xianqi (Fuyang Church), and Wang Junlü (representative of other house churches) on November 26, 1998.[51] In the following year, 36 leaders gathered again, but this large group was quickly found by the police. Their cash of 100,000 Chinese Yuan and their mobile phones were confiscated.[52]

Zhang was charged with interruption of social order and sent to labor camp for three years. After being released, he was invited to speak about the house churches and mission overseas, but the security office refused to issue him a passport, so he applied for a travel document with another name. He successfully traveled to Chicago for a Chinese Christian conference, went on a pilgrimage to Jerusalem, attended ecumenical meetings in Hong Kong, and visited Australia, Singapore, and Egypt.[53] However, he was arrested in 2004 for counterfeiting travel documents and was sentenced for seven and a half years of imprisonment. The parliament of the European Union demanded his immediate release in 2006, but this only happened on August 31, 2011. During his imprisonment, he suffered from diabetes and was sent to Xinmi County People's Hospital from September 9, 2005 to January 23, 2006. His hands and feet were locked up on the sick bed.[54]

House churches in Henan represent the growth of Christianity among the poor, who have been exploited by local officers politically, economically, and medically. Through the preaching of a mighty God, hope of eternity, and the concrete experience of miracles, Christianity has been a source of self-empowerment to the oppressed. Because of their humble social and economic context, Christians in Henan have painfully borne any persecution and oppression imposed by the security office and religious bureau without questioning the legitimacy of these unreasonable actions. However, what happens in Henan does not represent the circumstances in all other provinces and regions. Especially in a wealthy city like Wenzhou, Christians of the house churches have more bargaining

---

[51] Yinan, *Sixty Years of Chinese House Churches*, pp. 136-39.

[52] Yinan, *Sixty Years of Chinese House Churches*, pp. 55-56.

[53] Yinan, *Sixty Years of Chinese House Churches*, p. 31.

[54] News report of China Aid Association, July 2006, <http://www.China aid.net/2006/07/7.html>; News report of China Aid Association, 14 September 2011, <http://www.chinaaid.net/2011/09/7.html> (accessed April 27, 2012).

power developed from their economic superiority to fight for rights from local officials.

Wenzhou: Urban House Churches

Wenzhou is on the east coast of China, adjacent to the East Sea. Its geographical location provides economical privileges to the city. Its harbor is one of the twenty major harbors in China. There are more than 150 rivers running across the city, providing abundant fishing and agricultural produce. It has three major railway systems, three motorways, and an airport.[55] Its outstanding natural water resources and infrastructure provide citizens with easy access to knowledge, religions, and culture of the outside world. They can also actively engage in business and trading, especially when the former president, Deng Xiaoping, implemented the 'open door' policy and strategy of 'letting a few get rich first' in the 1980s. Wenzhou business people responded to this policy before any other parts of the country. They invested in small businesses such as clothes and eyeglasses. Its shoes, being famous for good quality, have won the city the title, 'Shoe Capital'. The commercial success has been recognized by the central government by calling it 'Wenzhou model'.

Wenzhou is not only an eminent business center, but also a Christian center.[56] David Aikman recorded that about ten percent of the population is Christian, not only business people, but also government officials.[57] This expansion of Christianity earns Wenzhou the title 'China's Jerusalem', where religious freedom seems to be securely guaranteed through the trusting relationship between the entrepreneurs and government officials instead of through the law. House churches in Wenzhou are registered not as 'Three-Self' churches but as 'places of religious worship'.[58] These house churches are not only above ground but are also eye-catching mega churches. Their gigantic buildings marked by a red cross on top accommodate over a thousand people. Churches openly hold Christ-

---

[55] *A History of Wenzhou Churches*, pp. 20-21.

[56] Cao Nanlai, *Constructing China's Jerusalem: Christians, Power, and Place in Contemporary Wenzhou* (Stanford: Stanford University Press, 2010), p. 7.

[57] David Aikman, *Jesus in Beijing: How Christianity Is Transforming China and Changing the Global Balance of Power* (Grand Rapids, MI: Monarch Books, 2003), p. 204.

[58] Aikman, *Jesus in Beijing*, p. 203.

mas celebration events and arrange performances by children, teen-agers, and adults, followed by huge banquets.[59] These events attract migrant workers, bosses, students, government officials, Christians, and non-Christians alike. Flocking to the same church on one occasion caused traffic congestion and the Public Security Bureau intervened.[60] As most of the affluent business people are Christians who are known as 'boss Christians', their increasing financial power enhances their political bargaining power.[61]

In 2002, the State Administration of Religious Affairs (SARA) prohibited any Sunday school to be held for children under eighteen, but some pastors complained about the ban to Ding Guanxun, who was the chairperson of the National TSPM and the China Christian Council. Ding accepted their complaint and wrote a letter to the Chinese People's Political Consultative Conference (CPPCC). Although the CPPCC did not reply to Ding's letter, Wenzhou pastors, with the assistance of business Christians, negotiated with the government in Beijing and the All-China Federation of Industry and Commerce. The SARA eventually withdrew the ban.[62] In the context of China where religious freedom is not protected by law, materialistic wealth does not necessarily lead to spiritual poverty and secularization as it does in the West; rather, it enables upward social mobility for elites. They enjoy more privileges in the society; even though belonging to an 'illegal' house church, they are less likely to be prosecuted. To a large extent, Christianity in Wenzhou is shaped by 'boss Christians', not only because of their financial support and diplomatic influence, but also their spiritual engagements. They regard their business as a way of serving God, which is similar to Max Weber's observation of Calvinist Protestants who perceived working hard as a way to fulfill God's calling. Some of them also preach in services and sponsor evangelistic resources.[63] They endeavor to achieve a 'holistic economic-spiritual-moral way of life'. They consider themselves as integrated into western modernity because capitalism and Christianity are parts of western civilization.[64]

---

59 A video of a Christmas celebration in 2008 is available online, <http://www. tudou.com/programs/view/NTLERLo5DZs/> (accessed May 5, 2012).

60 Nanlai, *Constructing China's Jerusalem*, p. 2.

61 Nanlai, *Constructing China's Jerusalem*, p. 7.

62 Aikman, *Jesus in Beijing*, p. 206.

63 Nanlai, *Constructing China's Jerusalem*, pp. 169-70.

64 Nanlai, *Constructing China's Jerusalem*, p. 166.

'Boss Christians' arise in Wenzhou not just because of the geo-graphical, economic, and political advantages, but also due to the Christian foundation developed by the forerunners who persevered through all the political trials. It is incredible that 'China's Jerusa-lem' was once designated by the communists to be an 'experimental site for an atheist zone' in 1959.[65] During the Cultural Revolution, Christians and leaders in Wenzhou were as severely persecuted as those in other provinces, but they managed to form a general coun-cil in the turmoil. In 1967, five Christians gathered together in a loft to pray every Friday night in the mountain area of Ruian County. They were burdened by the persecution against the church and were devoted to pray for millions of lost souls and the revival of the church. In less than a month, the prayer group expanded so quickly that the loft was too small for them. Many villagers were healed through their prayers and the number of Christians in the village increased. About 300 Christians of other villages also joined it. There were about 271 groups for about 50,000 Christians in Ruian. The same happened in other counties, including Pingyang, Leqing, Yongjia, Dongtou, and the city center.

As the number of Christians was growing rapidly, leaders desig-nated several meeting regions, and regional leaders formed a council in their own county in 1970.[66] As the political persecution worsened and civil war took place in Wenzhou, council leaders formed a gen-eral council to lend strength to each other. They met twice in 1971 and chose three people to be chairpersons. Thirty of them would represent their counties to attend a meeting every three years, and several hundred people would attend the annual meeting. Since the majority of the general council was youth, they decided to hold sev-eral meetings for young people every year. Before the establishment of the general council, churches in Wenzhou had identified them-selves according to western denominationalism, so they had not had much contact with each other. If the TSPM is the official mecha-nism to erase denominationalism by force, then general councils of this kind represent the effort of house churches to bring about uni-ty.

---

[65] Nanlai, *Constructing China's Jerusalem*, p. 2.
[66] *A History of Wenzhou Churches*, pp. 120-22.

Members of the council agreed to baptize with full immersion and use one bread and one cup to celebrate the communion. Healing, exorcism, raising the dead to life, and signs and wonders continued to happen. At a prayer meeting in the city, many people were filled by the Holy Spirit and firemen came to put out the 'fire'.[67] Churches in Wenzhou experienced an unprecedented revival from 1971 to 1980. It was the 'brightest' and 'golden' period, but persecution was also severe. One of the chairpersons of the general council, Miao Zhitung, was mercilessly tortured and other members were sent to labor camps. Several hundred Christians worshipped loudly on Sunday regardless of the threat of local officers as they were prepared to bear any suffering. Despite all humiliation, torture, imprisonment, and political propaganda, local officials never succeeded in eliminating house churches during the Cultural Revolution.[68]

Although reformists had been in power since 1978, persecution against house churches in Wenzhou continued but in a different form. As the TSPM functioned again, house churches were forced to register as Three-Self churches; otherwise, they were identified as illegal religious groups. From 1997 to 2000, when former president Jiang Zemin was amazed at the crosses and Buddhist mirrors hanging on many religious buildings during his visit to Wenzhou, the local State Administration of Religious Affairs launched a 'destroy-the-mirrors-and-remove-the crosses' movement. Many non-Three-Self church buildings and Buddhist temples were destroyed, imploded, or confiscated.[69] These church buildings were built by local Christians with their own saving and effort, but some leaders of the TSPM supported the action.[70] The prosperous scenario of house churches has just happened in the last ten years. As their survival depends on the relationship between the boss Christians and local

[67] *A History of Wenzhou Churches*, pp. 126-28.
[68] *A History of Wenzhou Churches*, pp. 132-34.
[69] Aikman, *Jesus in Beijing*, p. 204.
[70] *A History of Wenzhou Churches*, p. 184. In Yongjiang County, a group of Christian raised money to build a church as the brother's house was too small for the group. They did not only spend their saving, but also built it up themselves. One of them was an old man over seventy years old and his back was injured when building the church. When he saw the building being demolished, he was grieving tearfully. The leader of the Three-Self reported to the police about his grief and they twisted his arms immediately. He fainted on the ground out of sharp pain.

officials rather than the law, they remain in a vulnerable position and their activities and leaders still have to be kept secret.

An Ambivalent Reality

It is undeniable that more recently, persecution against house churches has been less serious than from 1950 to 1980, but the idealistic goal of respecting individuals' religious freedom in China is still a long way off. The positive sign is that the 'open door' policy allows Chinese and foreigners to travel in and outside China. If Chinese Christians can pay the tuition fees and travel expense with their own savings or sponsorships, they can enroll in courses overseas.

Some go to the Philippines, to other Southeast Asian countries, or to the United States if they can study in English. Most of them come to Hong Kong, where they can learn in Chinese. David Wang, a pastor from Hong Kong and president emeritus of the Asia Outreach International[71] and the general director of Hosanna Foundation, has been ministering to house churches since the 1960s. He has organized Master and Doctor of Ministry programs with Jack Hayford's King's University for leaders of house churches in recent years. The degrees are recognized by the Ministry of Education in China and in the United States. He identifies the goal of Hosanna to 'pastor the pastors to pastor; train the trainers to train; lead the leaders to lead' to meet the rapidly modernizing and changing China.[72] These courses attract some affluent house church members from Wenzhou and other cities to attend. Lectures are conducted by Chinese and English teachers from Hong Kong, Southeast Asia, and the King's University in either Hong Kong or the mainland.

The majority of Chinese Christians rely on foreign missionaries to come and teach courses for them, especially as the house churches cannot study in official theological seminaries; but most of the time, they consolidate their theological understandings through self-study of the Bible or sermons. However, because of visa issues

---

[71] Asian Outreach was founded by Paul Kauffman, a missionary from the Pentecostal Assemblies of Canada, and David Wang from Hong Kong in 1966.

[72] 'China Connect' (leaflet of Hosanna Foundation, January-February 2011), pp. 1-2.

and financial limitations, voluntary foreign missionaries can only offer some irregular and unsystematic programs. They also have to take the risk of being arrested. If they have planned to come for a long period, they have to enter China to do investment or teach English and thereby reach out to the locals. Increasingly, as Three-Self churches find more cases of healing and exorcism but have not learned about the Holy Spirit and spiritual gifts in the official theological seminaries, they invite Pentecostal and charismatic leaders from overseas to provide theological guidance in this regard. Although Dennis Balcombe has been active in supporting house churches for more than three decades, he has also been invited by Three-Self pastors to teach about the Holy Spirit and revival. He has seen that some of these pastors are 'evangelical and Spirit filled leaders', and they have freedom to preach all sorts of message.[73]

Some Three-Self churches which were founded by Classical Pentecostal denominations before 1949 still practice speaking in tongues, healing, and exorcism and hold prayer meetings featured by spontaneous worship but not in Sunday services. The Yuanfeng Church and Pingnan Church in Zhongshan in Guangdong province were established by the Hong Kong Pentecostal Mission in 1917 and 1922 respectively. After the Cultural Revolution, members of these two churches gathered in the nearby Taiping Church for services as their own church buildings had been severely damaged. Their mother church in Hong Kong sponsored the rebuilding of both churches in the 1990s, and the general superintendent preached there occasionally. Older members still firmly believe in the work of the Holy Spirit and the importance of sanctification.[74] Some former Assemblies of God (AG) pastors, who now work in Three-Self churches, still identify themselves as AG pastors and have regular unofficial meetings. The AG's headquarters in Springfield, Missouri, is also involved in theological training and humanitarian support in China through the Northern Asia Network.[75] For more than a century, missionary and theological organizations and

---

[73] Dennis Balcombe, 'New Wine in New Wineskins – Fires of Holy Ghost Revival Burning in China's Official and Registered Churches', <http://rcmi.word press.com/2012/02/17/new-wine-in-new-wineskins-fires-of-holy-ghost-revival-b urning-in-chinas-official-and-registered-churches/> (accessed May 8, 2012).

[74] Interview with members of the Yuanfeng Church, Zhongshan, Guangdong Province, on November 27, 2011.

[75] <www.nothernasianetwork.org> (accessed May 17, 2012).

churches of any denomination in Hong Kong have frequently sent pastors or people with expertise to hold intensive courses on worship, biblical studies, leadership, and counseling training in China. Pentecostal churches like the Yoido Full Gospel Church in Seoul and its branch, Full Gospel Church in Hong Kong, have been ministering to Chinese of Korean ethnicity in the mainland.

Although the government has become more tolerant of foreign missions and house churches, it is still suspicious of them. Since foreign missions and house churches remain illegal, if the government is controlled by conservative communists, severe persecution can be reinforced. House churches still function under this shadow, even though they may have good relationships with local authorities. The China Aid Association, a non-governmental organization in Texas, working for human right issues and house churches in China, has reported that China's government has decided to eradicate Protestant house churches since September 2011. The action is to be completed through three phases in ten years. First, local authorities are required to investigate house churches and file reports from January to June 2011. Second, they will urge them to register as a Three-Self church in two to three years. Finally, those churches which refuse to do so will be cracked down on. Besides, authorities will replace the term 'house churches' with 'house gatherings' on websites or other media as the latter refers to the legal meeting related to the National TSPM. They are also responsible for dispersing large house churches into small groups.

Protestant ministers will be registered or their churches will be forced to close down. Ministers also have to attend 'Training Sessions for Ministerial Certification' held by the National TSPM and CCC, introducing regulations on religious affairs and patriotism. Some of the house churches have been registered. One of the most controversial cases is the repression against the Shouwang Church in Beijing, which caught international attention. This church has neither been able to register nor rent a place for worship successfully as landlords have been under pressure from the security forces, so it can only worship in public areas, which is illegal.[76] From April to December 2011, security authorities caught more than a thou-

---

[76] Sarah Page, 'China Plans to Eradicate House Churches', *Compass Direct News* (April 25, 2012). <http://www.chinaaid.org/2012/04/compass-direct-news-china-plans-to.html> (accessed April 30, 2012)

sand members in 38 weeks; more than a hundred of them were put under house arrest, and some were abused physically and verbally. The church has attracted university students, lecturers, and professionals.[77] One of the members, who is a lecturer at a university, sent a pleading letter to the president, the premier, and the Standing Committee of the Political Bureau of the Communist Party's Central Committee. By explaining the charity works that the church has done, such as sending a donation to the victims of the earthquake in Sichuan in 2008 and its positive influence on the degrading moral standard in society, he exhorted leaders of the government to give up its hostile policies against house churches.[78] However, his request did not really bring much change to the situation. From January to April 2012, China Aid recorded members of house churches and foreign workers being arrested in Beijing, Heilungjiang, Henan, and Hubei.

In some cases, church offerings were confiscated, church buildings damaged, and leaders beaten. Moreover, since some of the famous human right lawyers are members or leaders of house churches who are crippling the policy of social 'harmony' from the government's perspective, it justifies the necessity of eliminating house churches. They have been imprisoned, kidnapped, or beaten.[79] A woman who was beaten up by police forces and has become disabled due to her resistance against the local authority's forceful clearance of private residential housing in Beijing was sentenced to imprisonment for two years and eight months in April 2012, despite the protest of the European Union. Her husband who had been faithfully supporting her campaign and looking after her was also imprisoned.[80] A renowned Christian author had been under house arrest and abused along with his family for criticizing the government in his writing. For the sake of his freedom of speech, he ap-

---

[77] China Aid Association, *2011 Annual Report: Chinese Government Persecution of Christians and Churches in Mainland China, January-December 2011.* <https://docs. google.com/file/d/0B_YUgSyiG6aIZTlmNjNmMmItYzZkNy00OTUyLWIyZjg tNDA0MWM5NjdmZTk3/edit?pli=1> (accessed May 9, 2012), p. 4.

[78] Due to the sensitivity of this document, the name of the writer and the source cannot be provided.

[79] China Aid Association, *2011 Annual Report*, p. 5.

[80] <http://www.bbc.co.uk/zhongwen/trad/chinese_news/2012/04/120410 _china_lawyer_sentencing.shtml> (accessed May 11, 2012).

plied for asylum in the United States and left China in January 2012.[81]

Freedom is indeed a luxury in China. True and honest academic discussion requires a space of freedom to be implemented, but this is even more luxurious. Scholars have affirmed the contextual flexibility of Pentecostalism, that there cannot be a single definition for Pentecostalism to be imposed on all groups. If we consider the element of human rights and freedom, its definition can vary from context to context. In the West where freedom is fully embraced as the core value of human dignity and the foundation of law and in some Latin American and African countries which respect religious freedom, Pentecostalism is naturally defined by the manifestations of the power of the Spirit through Spirit-baptism and charisms. In the context of house churches in China, Pentecostalism is not just about these manifestations, but more importantly, about suffering for the faith and the praxis of these manifestations and other fundamental doctrines.

If Pentecostalism has been portrayed as a movement bringing biblical healing, exorcism, and raising of the dead into the contemporary world, then Christians of Chinese house churches consider it as sharing the biblical suffering of Christ and the apostles in modern times. If gifts demonstrate the power of the Spirit, then suffering is certainly a gift as it requires the power of the Spirit to endure. The stories recorded in Lukan texts of apostles fleeing from persecutors, being imprisoned, beaten, and killed are not scriptures to be analyzed with hermeneutical techniques but are living texts to be experienced and analyzed with personal experience. Some scriptures giving guiding principles during persecution are not regarded as historical statements but are read literally and practiced sincerely by house church Christians, such as Mt. 10.23, 'But when they persecute you in this city, flee ye into another'. Wherever they flee, they preach the gospel as the apostles did. They consider persecution as the acts of evil forces rather than human intention, so they organize fasting prayer meetings and prayer walks to fight against spiritual power. They also pray for the officials and learn to forgive and bless them as the Bible teaches.[82]

---

[81] Due to political sensitivity, the names of these human right lawyers are not mentioned in the article.

[82] Yinan, *Sixty Years of Chinese House*, p. 193.

Although they desire theological training provided by foreign efforts, theological knowledge is in fact secondary. What they have already obtained is *theologia prima*, which is unique and personal, developed through their own physical, emotional, and spiritual suffering. Biblical passages in the book of Revelation are not to be eschatologically decoded by theologians, but they are the sources of hope and strength during persecution, which was also John's purpose of writing when Christians were anxiously waiting to be caught and taken to the Coliseum under Nero's regime. The charism of martyrdom is accompanied by the faith in the imminent second coming of Jesus and the hope for the new life in heaven. Pentecost is not primarily regarded by the house church Christians as the birth of the church and the beginning of Christian mission accompanied by the work of the Spirit but the prologue for martyrdom throughout church history, as conveyed in one of the songs that house church Christians sang during the Cultural Revolution, *Martyr for the Lord*.[83]

1. Since the Pentecost when the Church was born, followers of the Lord are willing to sacrifice their lives.

Thousands of people died for the gospel. They are rewarded with the crown of life.

2. The disciples who truly love the Lord follow the Lord to walk on the suffering road.

John was imprisoned on the Island of Patmos; Stephen was stoned to death;

3. Matthew was pierced in Persia; Mark's legs were torn by horses and he died;

Doctor Luke was cruelly hung; Peter, Philip, and Simon were crucified;

4. Bartholomew's skin was peeled off by pagans; Thomas was pulled apart by five horses;

James was beheaded by Herod; James the Younger's head was sawn apart from the body;

---

[83] Yinan, *Sixty Years of Chinese House*, pp. 5-6. The quotation is translated by the author from Chinese into English.

5. The Lord's brother, James, was stoned; Jude was bound on a pillar and killed by arrows;

Matthias was stoned and beheaded in Jerusalem; Paul was beheaded by Nero;

6. I am willing to bear the cross, to follow the Lord and apostles to walk on a sacrificial road;

To save thousands of precious souls, I am willing to lay everything down and die for the Lord.

Chorus: Martyr for the Lord, martyr for the Lord, I am willing to be a martyr for the Lord's glory.

This Pentecostal theology and hermeneutic are based on a reconciled acknowledgment that persecution is the cost of revival, just as God is saving people from the devil through his Son's crucifixion. Through persecution, Chinese believers identify themselves with Jesus Christ and so deserve to be called 'Christian', which is glorious on earth and heaven. After being released from imprisonment, they testify to their members about God's protection and miracles in the prison, which strengthen their faith and prepare their hearts for suffering.[84] As Lian Xi suggests, martyrdom is their 'spiritual asset' for self-identification and apprenticing others to be a Christian.[85]

Epilogue

If Pentecostalism means suffering in Chinese Christianity, then it is not just about persecution but also about division caused by political intervention. The hopeful sign is that more and more Three-Self churches have been open to the work of the Holy Spirit, which brings about common experiences in the Spirit and ushers deeper fellowship and theological dialogue between the Three-Self and house churches. Another trend is that as the younger generation has been taking up the pastoral positions of house churches and while not feeling so strongly about the betrayal and persecution of the TSPM that their older generation experienced, they are more open

---

[84] Yinan, *Sixty Years of Chinese House*, p. 44.
[85] Xi, *Redeemed by Fire*, p. 214.

towards the Three-Self churches. Certainly, the ecumenical venture between the Three-Self and house churches takes a great risk of being discovered by national security officials. Some Three-Self pastors were arrested because of inviting house church ministers to preach in their churches. It is my hope that these unfriendly twins, the Three-Self and house churches, would lay down the past betrayal and pursue reconciliation like Esau and Jacob.

5

Introduction to the Church of the Arabs

Yohanna Katanacho[*]

I studied ten years in the United States at some of the best institutions. Even though I took several classes in theology and church history, I was never taught about Arab Christians and their contributions to the global church.[1] The failure to address the presence and contributions of Arab Christians is intensified in light of false assumptions related to equating the term Arab with the label Muslim as well as characterizing the Arab–Israeli conflict as a religious conflict between the Judeo–Christian faith and Islam.[2] Some people view Arabs only through the lens of Arabic stereotypes shown in mass media. Following some Arab Americans, Qumsieh coins this distortion in a noticeable sarcasm calling it 'the Three B Syndrome'.

---

[*] Yohanna Katanacho (PhD, Trinity International University) is a Palestinian Evangelical who serves as the Academic Dean for Bethlehem Bible College. He has authored several books in English and Arabic including *The Land of Christ: A Palestinian Cry* (Bethlehem: Bethlehem Bible College, 2012), and *The King of Peace and His Young Followers* (Nazareth: Arab Israeli Bible Society, 2012). He is also one of the authors of the Palestinian Kairos Document.

[1] The label 'Christian Arabs' points out that there are Christians among Arabs. It is an ethnic label that dismisses the myth that all Arabs are Muslims. Conversely, the label 'Arab Christians' is a religious label. Further details are found in Tarek Mitri, 'Who are the Christians of the Arab World?', *International Review of Mission* 89 (2000), pp. 12-13.

[2] It is unfortunate that people use the misleading label 'Judeo-Christian' faith. Christianity and Judaism have many disagreements. Admittedly, Christianity accepts the Old Testament but the latter is not equivalent to Judaism.

He points out that Arabs are mainly stereotyped as bombers, billionaires, and belly dancers.[3]

I hope to dismiss these myths by providing a chronological sketch of Arabs who followed Yahweh from the times of the Old Testament until today. The data is enormous, which makes the peril of reductionism unavoidable, and the label 'Arab' might mean different things at different times in different discourses. Nevertheless, there is still merit in seeing the big picture and in using the label Arab, which entails common linguistic, cultural, and historical grounds. At the cost of oversimplification, I will divide my presentation into four periods: Arabs in the Old Testament, Arabs from Christ to Muhammad, Arabs from Muhammad to Germanos, and Arabs from Germanos to the Arab Spring. My main focus will be on Arab followers of Yahweh, i.e. Arabs in the Old Testament, Arab Christians in the New Testament, and throughout history.

Arabs in the Old Testament Period

The label Arab appears in extra biblical texts in the ninth century BCE.[4] In 867 BCE, an Assyrian king, King Shalmaneser III, defeated an Arab leader called Jundub and his 1000 camels at the battle of Qarqar.[5] Rosmarin affirms that Arabs have appeared in several ancient Assyrian writings in the eighth and seventh centuries BCE.[6] In addition, Arabs can be found in the Bible, confirming their antiquity. The label Arab appears several times in the Old Testament itself (1 Kgs 10.15; 2 Chron. 9.14; 17.11; 21.16; 22.1; 26.7; Neh. 2.19; 4.7; 6.1; Isa. 13.20; 21.13 (twice); Jer. 3.2; 25.24 (twice); Ezek. 27.21).[7] It

---

[3] Mazin Qumsieh, '100 Years of Anti-Arab and Anti-Muslim Stereotyping'. See <http://www.ibiblio.org/prism/jan98/anti_arab.html> (accessed March 26, 2012).

[4] For further details see Israel Eph'al, *The Ancient Arabs: Nomads on the Borders of the Fertile Crescent 9th–5th Centuries B.C.* (Leiden: Brill, 1982), pp. 1-3. See also Jan Retso, *Arabs in Antiquity: Their History from the Assyrians to the Umayyads* (London: Routledge Curzon, 2002), p. 105.

[5] The Arabic term Jundub or Jundubu means grasshopper.

[6] Trude Weiss Rosmarin, 'Aribi und Arabien in den Babylonisch-Assyrischen Quellen,' *Journal of the Society of Oriental Research* 16 (1932), pp. 1-37.

[7] Yohanna Katanacho, 'Al Mstlh 'rb fi al 'hd al qdym' [The Label Arab in the Old Testament], *Middle East Association for Theological Education Journal* 5 (2010), pp. 1-11.

also appears in Deuterocanonical books such as: 1 Mac. 5.39; 11.15, 17, 39; 12.31; 2 Mac. 5.8; 12.10, 11. Admittedly, its denotations and connotations might have been different at different times; however, we cannot deny that Arabs existed before Islam and even before Christianity. The Anchor Bible Dictionary asserts this understanding, giving different labels that denote certain Arab groups in ancient times.[8] Eph'al also provides a well-documented study testifying to the same argument.[9] In a recent study, Maalouf stresses the antiquity of Arabs, pointing out several Arab persons in the Bible.[10]

Montgomery further affirms that studying the existence of Arabs is not confined to the label 'Arab'.[11] Several Arab figures and tribes appear in ancient writings (1 Mac. 5.4, 25; 9.35-36; 9.66-67; 11.17, 39; 12.31; 2 Mac. 5.8). In addition, Kitchen insists that Queen Sheba who interacted with King Solomon is an Arab (1 Kgs 10.1-13).[12] Other Old Testament scholars point out the testimony of the appendix in the Septuagint concerning Job's wife. It says,

> This man is described in the Syriac [Aramaic] book as living in the land of Ausis on the borders of Idumea and Arabia: and his name before was Jobab; and having taken an Arabian wife he begot a son whose name was Ennon. And he himself was the son of his father Zare, one of the sons of Esau, and of his mother Bosorrha, so that he was the fifth from Abraam.[13]

The locale of his dwelling and of his friends – Eliphaz king of the Teimanites, Baldad king of the Shuhaites, and Sophar king of the Minaeans – as well as his Arab wife, strengthened the belief that Job himself was an Arab. Others argue that the last two chapters in

---

[8] Robert Smith, 'Arabia', in D.N. Freedman and G.A. Herion (eds.), *Anchor Bible Dictionary* (New York: Doubleday, 1992), I, pp. 324-27.

[9] Eph'al, *The Ancient Arabs*, pp. 60-63.

[10] Tony Maalouf, *Arabs in the Shadow of Israel* (Grand Rapids: Kregel, 2003), pp. 17-42.

[11] James Montgomery, *Arabia and the Bible* (Philadelphia: University of Pennsylvania, 1934), pp. 37-53.

[12] Kenneth Kitchen, 'Sheba and Arabia', in Lowell Handy (ed.), *The Age of Solomon: Scholarship at the Turn of the Millennium* (Leiden: Brill, 1997), pp. 126-53.

[13] Sir Lancelot C.L. Brenton, *The Septuagint Verson: Greek and English* (Grand Rapids: Zondervan, 1970), p. 698.

the book of Proverbs are written by Arabs.[14] In short, we have to accept that even though more work needs to be done in order to clarify the identity or contributions of Arabs in the Old Testament, it is clear that Arabs existed before the New Testament era and were used by God to spread His Kingdom.

Arab Christians from Christ to Muhammad

The term 'Arab' or one of its cognates occurs three times in the New Testament (Act 2.11; Gal. 1.17; 4.25). We also know that 2 Cor. 11.32 (cf. Act 9.24-25) mentions Aretas IV, a Nabatean Arab who ruled from 9 BCE to 40 CE.[15] He is the father-in-law of Herod Antipas who left his Arab wife, desiring the wife of his brother Philip. This led Aretas to rage war against Herod Antipas and later defeat him. Put differently, John the Baptist, a Jewish prophet, lost his head defending the rights of an Arab woman. This good interaction between Arabs and Jews is further confirmed by the legendary correspondence between King Abgar and Christ. In his well-known Church History, Eusebius presents King Abgar's letter to Christ. Abgar writes:

> I have heard of Thee, and of Thy healing; that Thou dost not use medicines or roots, but by Thy word openest (the eyes) of the blind, makest the lame to walk, cleansest the lepers, makest the deaf to hear; how by Thy word (also) Thou healest (sick) spirits and those who are tormented with lunatic demons, and how, again, Thou raisest the dead to life … Wherefore I write to Thee, and pray that thou wilt come to me … and heal all the ill that I suffer, according to the faith I have in Thee … I possess but one small city, but it is beautiful, and large enough for us two to live in peace.[16]

---

[14] Tony Maalouf, 'Ishmael in Biblical History' (PhD, Dallas Theological Seminary, 1998), pp. 143-53.

[15] David Graf, 'Aretas', in *Anchor Bible* Dictionary, I, pp. 373-76. There are other Arab Kings also named Aretas.

[16] Further details can be found in Abgar V, <http://en.wikipedia.org/wiki/Abgar_V> (accessed March 26, 2012). See also *Historia Ecclesiastica* I, xiii; Eusebius, *Church History*, Book I, <http://www.newadvent.org/fathers/250101.htm> (accessed March 26. 2012).

Inspired by this tradition, Shahid argues that 'Arabs were one of the first groups in the Orient, and indeed in the world, to adopt Christianity'.[17] He has written several books presenting Arab Christians before Islam.[18] Based on his writings, we can divide the period between Christ and Muhammad into Arabs in the Roman period (63 bce–305 CE) and Arabs in the Byzantine period (4th–7th Centuries). Shahid points out that Arabs lived in Palestine, Jordan, Syria, Lebanon, Mesopotamia, Egypt, and other places.[19] Sadly, however, many overlooked their influence and contributions because historians did not use the label 'Arab'. Instead, they employed different terms such as Herodians, Nabataeans, Idumaeans, Itureans, Osroeni, Palmyrenes, Saracens, and Scenitae.

Indeed, many Arabs supported Christianity and became Christians themselves. They continued the tradition that started on Pentecost when Arabic was employed to lift up the Lord Jesus Christ (Acts 2.11). The following list of leaders should demonstrate the veracity of my argument. Eusebius informs us of the exchange of letters between Christ and King Abgar VIII.[20] Another Arab Christian King (also called Abgar) ruled Edessa around 200 CE. He was the first ruler in history to adopt Christianity. He proclaimed Christianity the official religion of his state.[21] In his state, the Syriac Peshitta was translated from the Greek and Hebrew. Later, Edessa became the mother of the Syrian Christian Church and the rival of the Greek Antioch.[22] In the third century, Philip the Arab (204-249 CE) was the first Christian Roman Emperor.[23] On one occasion,

---

[17] Irfan Shahid, *Rome and the Arabs: A Prolegomenon to the Study of Byzantium and the Arabs* (Washington DC: Dumbarton Oaks, 1984), p. 154.

[18] Irfan Shahid, *Rome and the Arabs; Byzantium and the Arabs in the Fourth Century* (Washington, DC: Dumbarton Oaks, 2006); *Byzantium and the Arabs in the Fifth Century* (Washington, DC: Dumbarton Oaks, 2006); *Byzantium and the Arabs in the Sixth Century* (Washington, DC: Dumbarton Oaks, 2009).

[19] Shahid, *Rome and the Arabs*, pp. 4-5. It might be interesting to note that Herod was an Idumean on his father's side and an Arab on his mother's side.

[20] Some argue that Abgar I (4 BCE–50 CE) was the first Christian among the Abgarids. Shahid says, 'Eusebius relates the apocryphal story of the exchange of letters between Christ and Abgar (4 BCE to CE 50) and the mission of Thaddaeus, one of the Seventy, who succeeds in healing Abgar and converting him together with many of the Edessenes'. See Shahid, *Rome and the Arabs*, p. 102.

[21] Shahid, *Rome and the Arabs*, p. 155.

[22] Shahid, *Rome and the Arabs*, p. 156.

[23] Shahid, *Rome and the Arabs*, pp. 65-93.

Bishop Babylos required that the Arab Emperor confess his sins before joining the Easter service. The Emperor was humble enough to repent. We also encounter in the third century Cosman and Damian. They were the Arab twins who offered free medical care and were known for performing medical miracles by the power of God. In the fourth century, the Arab Queen Mavia defended orthodox Christianity, fighting the Roman Emperor Valens who accepted the Arian heresy. Her bishop, Moses, the bishop of the Arabs was known as a miracle-worker and a fighter against Arianism. Further, in the same century many Arab Bedouins in Palestine believed in Jesus through the ministry of St Hilarion (291-371 CE).[24]

It might surprise some of us to know that Arab Christians participated in formulating the ecumenical creeds. At the Council of Nicea (325 CE), we find Pamphilus and Theotimus the Tanukhids, Petrus of Ayla, and Marinus of Palmyra. At the Council of Constantinople (381 CE), we find five bishops who represented the province of Arabia. At the Council of Chalcedon (451 CE), we find seventeen Arab Christian leaders; among them is Youhanna from Edessa, Youhanna from Palestine, and Youhanna bishop of the Bedouins.[25] Their presence reflects the spread of Christianity among Arabs before Islam. Shahid confirms this point by explaining the Christian roots of three major Arab Christian tribes: the Lakhmids in the fourth century, the Salihids in the fifth century, and the Ghassanids in the sixth century.[26]

Arab Christians from Muhammad to Germanos (7th–16th century)

Muhammad the prophet of Islam (570-632 CE) brought a new era to Arabs. He founded the religion of Islam and was followed by the Ummayyad and then the Abbasside Caliphates. During this period Arab Christians 'began to compose theological works in Syriac and

---

[24] Nicola Zeida, *Al Masihit wa Alarab* [Christianity and Arabs] (Damascus: Cadmus, 2000), p. 121.

[25] Zeida, *Al Masihit wa Alarab*, p. 150.

[26] Shahid, *Byzantium and the Arabs in the Fourth Century*, p. xvi.

Arabic to counter the religious challenges of Islam'.[27] Interestingly, John of Damascus (655-749 CE) might be considered the 'first classical systematic theologian'.[28] John of Damascus, also known as Youhanna b. Mansour b. Sargun (يوحنا بن منصور بن سرجون), is one of the major Arab theologians who responded to Islam in its early stages. He considered Islam as a Christian heresy arguing that some Arab clergymen translated apocryphal Bibles into Arabic and their works stand behind the distorted similarities between the Quran and the New Testament. John of Damascus not only engages Islam but also discusses free will and predestination, icons, and other theological concerns. Theodore Abu Qurrah (ثيودور أبي قرة) is one of the primary vehicles for the transmission of Youhanna b. Sargun's thoughts into the Melkite church. Other well-known Arab theologians include 'Ammar Al-Basri (عمار البصري), Habib Ibn Hidmah Abu Ra'itah Al-takriti (حبيب ابو رائطة التكريتي), Severus ibn al-Muqaffa' (ساويروس ابن المقفع).[29] In short, Arab Christians produced many theological works. *Summa Theologiae Arabica* is one example of such works.[30] To illustrate the depth of its arguments, I will give one example that relates to the incarnation of our Lord.

The pertinent document states that the incarnation of our Lord has at least four sides.[31] First, God wants to honor us through the

---

[27] Sidney Griffith, *The Beginnings of Christian Theology in Arabic: Muslim-Christian Encounters in the Early Islamic Period* (Burlington: Ashgate, 2002), p. vii. See also Spencer Trimingham, *Christianity among Arabs in Pre-Islamic Times* (London: Longman, 1979).

[28] Daniel Sahas, *John of Damascus on Islam: The Heresy of the Ishmaelites* (Leiden: Brill, 1972), p. 52. In the work of John of Damascus known as the *Fountain of Knowledge*, he presents philosophical concerns. Then he talks about the orthodox faith and its relevance to knowledge of truth. Last, the pertinent work mentions the different heresies. Islam is considered one of the heresies.

[29] See the outstanding work of Mark Beaumont, *Christology in Dialogue with Muslims* (London: Regnum, 2005). See also Mark Swanson, "'Folly to the Hunafa'': The Crucifixion in Early Christian-Muslim Controversy', in Emmanouela Grypeous, Mark Swanson, and David Thomas (eds.), *The Encounter of Eastern Christianity with Early Islam* (Leiden: Brill, 2006), pp. 237-56; Kenneth Gragg, *The Arab Christian* (Louisville: John Knox Press, 1991).

[30] For further details see Sidney Griffith, *Arabic Christianity in the Monasteries of Ninth-Century Palestine* (Burlington: Ashgate, 1992), IX; pp. 123-41.

[31] The following explanation is based on my interpretation of the Arabic texts of chapters six, seven, and eight of *Summa Theologiae Arabica* as found in Joshua Blau, *A Handbook of Early Middle Arabic* (Jerusalem: Hebrew University, 2002), pp. 73-82.

incarnation of Jesus Christ. He dealt with us like a great king who chose a daughter for his son in order to transform her family into his household and to make them inheritors. Through the incarnation of God, humanity is honored. Second, incarnation is the means of revealing the Trinity and the one divinity. God dealt with us like a man who is able to speak and listen but because he is communicating with a deaf person, he uses signs. In other words, anthropomorphisms are an expression of his mercy and kindness. Similarly, the incarnation expresses God's mercy and plan to speak at a level in which we can understand. Third, the incarnation is an expression of liberty and its means. God wants to liberate us from the curse of failing to obey the law. This liberty is like a man who committed himself to work long hours. He worked part of the hours and was not able to continue. His master came and worked on his behalf and then paid him the full wages. This is exactly what Jesus Christ has done for us. Fourth, the incarnation is the means to nourish in our hearts the assurance of life after death and the victorious resurrection. In the resurrection of the incarnated Christ is the proof of our resurrection. Furthermore, the story of our victory is like the story of a man who has sheep. His sheep were attacked by a wolf. The man slaughtered one of the sheep and wore its wool.[32] Then he was in the midst of the sheep. When the wolf came the disguised man attacked it. The wolf thought that the sheep were becoming so strong. So he decided to escape. In other words, Jesus became a sheep and conquered the wolf by his incarnation. The devil defeated the human race in paradise but lost the battle before the incarnated Christ.

In addition to theological works, historians point out that many Arab Christians lost their lives as they were defending their faith. David Vila points out that many Arab Christians were martyred.[33] He discusses the powerful stories of Rawh Al-Shareef Al–Qurayshi (روح الشريف القريشي), Michael of Mar Saba (ميخائيل من مار سابا), and Abd al Masih an Najrani al Ghassani (عبد المسيح النجراني الغساني). Vila rightly points out that many Arab Christians worked on creating an

---

[32] Admittedly, this part of the story presents theological problems but the main point of the story is still valid.

[33] David Vila, 'Christian Martyrs in the First Abbasid Century and the Development of an Apologetic against Islam' (PhD, Saint Louis University, 1999).

apologetic of affinity instead of an apologetic of distinction. He explains that Byzantine Christians looked down at the Arabic culuture and at Islam. Conversely, Arab Christians rejected Islam but highlighted the common cultural and linguistic grounds with Arab Muslims. They were further faithful in sharing Christ respectfully and courageously. The story of Abd Al Masih should make this clear.

Abd al Masih was a Christian from Najran.[34] He became an invader with the Islamic army. He joined them in their prayers and fought against their enemies. One day, he entered a church and heard a priest reading from Scriptures, 'whoever loves a mother or a father or a brother or anything more than me is not worthy of me' (cf. Mt. 10.37 and Lk. 14.26). Abd al Massih was convicted and started crying. The priest helped him to repent and Abd al Massih sold his weapons and gave the money to the church. Later, he became a monk in Jerusalem and also in Sinai. When he went to Ramlah, the capital of Palestine in the ninth century, in order to pay some taxes, he declared to many Muslims that he had left Islam and become a Christian. Later, he was caught and brought before the governor of Ramlah who told him to recant from his faith for he was a man of great honor. Like some followers of Christ who come from a Muslim background, Abd Al Massih was under the threat of death. He answered the governor saying that life from Christ is better than life from him. The governor put him in jail for three days then asked him to accept Islam. But Abd Al Massih refused and consequently he was beheaded. Arab followers of Christ continue in the footsteps of this faithful martyr. They built good relationships with many moderate Muslims and do not recant before some violent extremists.

Later, the crusaders tried to liberate the Holy Land and its Christians from Islam. They waged several major wars from 1096 to 1215 CE.[35] Interestingly, during this period many local Arab Christians suffered. Their Christian expressions and Arab identity were unde-

---

[34] The story of Abd Al Masih is found in Sidney Griffith, *Arabic Christianity in the Monasteries of Ninth-Century Palestine* (Burlington: Ashgate, 1992), pp. 331–74. I focused on the Arabic text that is available on pp. 361–70.

[35] Further details are found in Samih Ghnadry, *Al Mahd Al-Arabi* [The Arabic Cradle] (Nazareth: Ghnadry, 2009), pp. 363-419.

sirable to the crusaders who in the name of God were killing their Muslim neighbors as well as many Arab Christians. Gladly, the exclusive violent worldview of the crusaders faded and was replaced by a peaceful and sacrificial approach. The Catholic Church in Palestine has been very active during the 18th–21st centuries. Its followers have been pioneers in advocating education, relief, peace, inter-religious dialogue, inter-denominational interaction, and justice.[36] It is fitting now to look at the fourth period, i.e. from Germanos to the Arab Spring.

Arab Christians from Germanos to the Arab Spring

While Martin Luther and Calvin were changing the Western World, Germanos was Hellenizing the Middle Eastern church. Germanos was a Greek who went to Egypt and became fluent in Arabic. Then he served the Orthodox Church in Palestine and Syria. He was able to collect tax monies and increase his power. He was further able to deceive the Arab Patriarch Attallah and guarantee his support. The old Arab Patriarch resigned and named Germanos as his successor in 1534.[37] During 45 years in which he was the Patriarch, Germanos succeeded in Hellenizing the church by replacing every deceased Arabic bishop with a Greek one. Since that time the Arab Orthodox in the Middle East struggled with ethnocracy and Hellenization.

Hourani writes about this period, dividing it into the Ottoman age (sixteenth-eighteenth century), the age of the European empires (1800–1939), and the age of nation-states.[38] During the Ottoman age, the *Millet* system dominated; it is a system for confessional communities. Put differently, Christian communities have their legal courts for personal matters, and they collect the taxes for the Turks.

---

[36] For further details, see Michael Prior and William Taylor (eds.), *Christians in the Holy Land* (London: World of Islam, 1994). It is, however, worth mentioning that the relationship between the Catholic Church and Evangelicals in Israel/Palestine is marked with exclusion and animosity. Both sides need to take courageous steps towards honoring each other.

[37] Randa Muryba, 'The Struggle between Greek Clergymen and the Orthodox Community in Palestine during the First Half of the Twentieth Century' (MA, Beir Zeit University, 1999), p. 14.

[38] Albert Hourani, *A History of the Arab Peoples* (Cambridge: Harvard, 1991), pp. 207-458.

The *Millet* system facilitated the growth of an identity centered on religion and consequently the emergence of the protectorate *Millet* system. Many European Christians acted as protectors of local Middle Eastern Christians. This expedited the growth of Catholic and Protestant missionary work. At the same time it paved the way for the Arab renaissance as well as the dominance of European imperial powers.

Eventually, the Ottoman Empire collapsed, and European imperial powers occupied the Middle East. European empires dominated from 1800 to the beginning of the twentieth century. During this period, the state of Israel was established. Many western Christians supported Zionism in the name of the Bible, and one of the results was hurting Arab followers of Christ, especially in Palestine. In short, due to wars associated with the establishment of Israel and its preservation by military force, Palestinian Christians became oppressed refugees.[39] They, along with other Arab Christians, thought that nationalism was the answer to their problems.

Arab Nationalism developed and several Arab states were declared. During the period of nationalism, Christians were co-citizens, and many of them were prominent leaders of nationalist movements. However, nationalism failed to develop in the right way and was hindered by several dictators who abused their powers. People started looking for alternatives such as communism or radical Islam. Radical Islam dominated over several minds, and people started breaking the barrier of fear and challenging the dictators who ruled the Arab world.

In short, the Arab Spring emerged. It was sparked by the self-immolation of Mohammed Bouazizi in Tunisia. On December 17, 2010, Bouazizi protested against the harassment of municipal officials. He set himself on fire and consequently died. His death sparked the Tunisian evolution and its domino effect that led to many other revolutions in Egypt, Yemen, Libya, Syria, and other places. One of the consequences of the Arab Spring is the growing influence of radical Islamic voices and the growing persecution of

---

[39] For further see Alex Awad, *Palestinian Memoires: The Story of a Palestinian Mother and Her People* (Bethlehem: Bethlehem Bible College, 2008); Yohanna Katanacho, *The Land of Christ: A Palestinian Cry* (Bethlehem: Bethlehem Bible College, 2012).

Christians. Several Christians from Iraq became refugees. Churches in Egypt were attacked. Some Christians were transformed from citizens to refugees; others lost their security and are extremely concerned. At the same time, some decided to hope in God and empower the prophetic role of the church.[40] The Evangelical church in Cairo is a good illustration. They not only participated in nonviolent demonstrations singing hymns, but they also opened their church as a temporary hospital for the injured demonstrators. In short, the church can choose to adopt the victim mentality and live in fear or be clothed with love and courage in order to be prophetic light and salt. They can be a voice of love in the midst of hatred and a voice of peace in the midst of trouble.

Concluding Remarks

Against common western perceptions, we have shown in this paper that Arabs followed Yahweh in the Old Testament. Furthermore, Arab Christianity preceded Islam, and Arab Christians were some of the earliest Christians who were faithful in loving God with all their minds and hearts. They participated in shaping the theology of the global church and defended orthodoxy, sacrificing their lives to win the smile of Christ. This rich history is a great encouragement for all Arab followers of Christ. It provides a framework in which our Arabic culture and history are related to the triune God.

It is also interesting to notice that Arab Christians were pioneers in theological thinking and sharing Christ at the cost of martyrdom. Their rich history is part of the tradition of the church of the Arabs as well as the global church. It has the potential of empowering the church of the Arabs and enriching the global church. Allow me to unpack this idea through the following points.

First, we cannot be responsible theologians or missiologists without a proper understanding of contextual rootedness. Unfortunately, many missionaries overlooked the history of Arab followers of Yahweh. Consequently, Arab followers of Christ who adopted

---

[40] The Palestinian Kairos document is a vivid example in which we see a prominent prophetic Arab Christian voice. For further details, see Katanacho, *The Land of Christ*, pp. 143-71.

the missionaries' perspective lost their identity and vision. Because they overlooked studying how the grace of God was working in their ancestors, they did not present Christian Arab heroes and heroines who can be models of faith and faithfulness. Instead, they adopted a western perception of the Gospel that enlarged the gap between the church of the Arabs and their Arab neighbors. Furthermore, the new emerging Evangelical Arab churches looked down upon other Christian traditions that had produced many Arab martyrs and theologians. In other words, highlighting the contextual rootedness of the church of the Arabs has the potential to contribute to the unity of Arab followers of Yahweh.

Second, overlooking the contextual rootedness led most missionaries to present a Gospel that lacked contextual relevance. It would be wiser to learn from the history of the Arab church and their response to Islam, violence, heresy, and church divisions. Many western missionaries came to present the gospel as a message or, more specifically, information, but the church of the Arabs has been presenting for centuries a community of Christians as a gospel. They presented an apologetic of affinity looking at Muslims not only through a doctrinal lens but also as fellow human beings who are their neighbors and fellow citizens. They wanted not only to bring about personal peace but also social peace so that both Muslims and Christians can live with honor in the same country.

Third, the church of the Arabs has many good models of interaction with the God of Israel. Queen Sheba would be one example of a fruitful interreligious dialogue that led to honoring the God of Israel. She would be a good way of presenting a contextual gospel.[41] Like many Muslims who read Sura 1.6 asking God for guidance, Queen Sheba is an Arab truth seeker. She heard about the Israelite King Solomon: his wisdom, faith, power, and great reputation. Solomon affirmed the uniqueness and superiority of his God. As a result, Queen Sheba decided to probe the news by taking a trip to Je-

---

[41] For another example of a contextual presentation of the Gospel, see my discussion on Hagar and Sarah in Yohanna Katanacho, 'Hagar: A Victim of Injustice', in Stephen Smith and Wendy Whitworth (eds.), *No Going Back: Letters to Pope Benedict XVI on the Holocaust, Jewish-Christian Relations & Israel* (London: Quill, 2009), pp. 96-100.

rusalem and visiting King Solomon, talking to him in person. She travelled at least 1400 miles from Yemen to Jerusalem. Although the trip might have been dangerous, she insisted on testing Solomon and on making sure that the information she received was correct and not one-sided. She was indeed a truth seeker who invested every effort to verify the news, hearing from the original sources and asking difficult questions. Queen Sheba was further a truth celebrator. Her openness to be fair and courageous transformed any confusion, doubt, or fear from the Other into an exciting adventure. When she discovered truth elements in the faith, culture, and life of Solomon, she accepted them. This is not only a form of Old Testament evangelism in which Queen Sheba was perhaps converted, but it is also a genuine openness to value truth with joy regardless of its source, for all truth is God's truth. In her celebration, she said: 'Praise be to the Lord your God, who has delighted in you and placed you on the throne of Israel. Because of the Lord's eternal love for Israel, he has made you king, to maintain justice and righteousness' (1 Kgs 10.9, NIV). Indeed, a truth celebrator is committed to celebrate love, justice, and righteousness wherever they are found.

Last, studying the history of the church of the Arabs should help to change the perception of many westerners. It will challenge them to view Arabic culture in a different light. It will help them to distinguish between Arabism and Islam. It will empower them to love all the Arabs in light of the fact that the church of the Arabs is full of love towards their Arab Muslim neighbors and is full of commitment to pursue justice nonviolently.

6

PENTECOSTALISM IN LATIN AMERICA: ITS CURRENT CHALLENGES

ELIZABETH SALAZAR-SANZANA[*]

In Latin America the multifaceted Christian reality has become pentecostalized, and this has happened in several ways. Since the mid-twentieth century we experienced a steady growth in Pentecostal denominations, meaning in some countries they have been established as the largest percentage of the Protestant Christian population.[1] Added to that is the rise of the charismatic renewal in the Roman Catholic Church and the increased presence of theological and liturgical Pentecostal elements in historic churches. All of this shows what has been happening in recent decades: a constant, plural, and dispersed 'pentecostalization' or 'spiritualization' of the Christian church in Latin America.

This movement introduces the new term/concept, 'pentecostalness' (Spanish '*pentecostalidad*'), as a universal experience, which expresses the event of Pentecost as the ordering principle of the lives of those who identify with the Pentecostal revival but not necessarily churches that call themselves Pentecostal.[2] These churches mani-

[*] Elizabeth Salazar-Sanzana (PhD, Methodist University of Sao Paulo, Brazil) is a Chilean theologian, historian, and religious scientist. She is Theological Advisor for the Evangelical Pentecostal Church in Chile. She has been part of various international theological commissions, working in theological reflection of the Global Christian Forum process in Latin America consultation also in the Latin American Council of Churches (CLAI), the World Council of Churches, Edinburgh 2010, CLADE V, and other ecumenical bodies.
[1] David Soll, *¿Se vuelve América Latina protestante? Las políticas del crecimiento evangélico* (Quito: AbyaYala, 1990).
[2] 'Se entiende por "pentecostalidad" como el principio y práctica religiosa tipo, informada por el acontecimiento de pentecostés. Se trata de una experiencia

fest the presence of the charism of the Spirit, who lives with different intensities in all religious expressions without exceptions.

Among this 'pentecostalness' we must consider those referred to now as 'neo-Pentecostal', which are widely present in our continent. With this rapidly changing movement, we can feel overwhelmed by its remoteness from what is the basis of the reformed Christian Church: grace and justification by faith. We know that pentecostalness is the essence of the faith of those who have received Christ and is older and broader than Pentecostalism. Nevertheless, they share the same basis of universal experience with the Risen Christ, which is not so evident in neo-Pentecostalism. In Pentecostalism, the euphoria and enthusiasm in worship and pastoral community life have a profound theology of justification by faith. Pentecostalism embodies this pentecostalness, this way of living the joy of salvation that transcends denominational categories.

That is, in Pentecostalism and 'pentecostalness', spirituality remains an ordaining principle of the practices, with a sense of life, of social identity; which is not so in the neo-Pentecostalism we are seeing in our society today.

These neo-Pentecostalisms have features of agencies based on sacred 'supply-consumption', and some are powerful churches/companies, promoting, with mass acceptance, a theology of material prosperity by divine intervention. It is propagated by the media and social networks, encouraged by privileged groups in major Latin American cities.

The neo-Pentecostal movement and their organizations are acquiring a business model, following the rules of marketing, getting installed in metropolitan centers, and managing large resources. They aspire to become mega-churches, reaching the maximum audience, and although they create spaces of proximity, they fail as a faith community and eventually lose their effectiveness. However, we must point out that their liturgy, their methods of recruitment, their permissiveness, attractive literature, and theology of material prosperity, have impregnated several American Christian groups, which are not strictly adherents of this movement. They adopt cer-

---

universal que eleva a la categoría de principio, las prácticas pentecostales que intentan ser concreciones históricas de esa experiencia primordial … es la fuerza del espíritu'. Bernardo Campos, *De la Reforma Protestante a la pentecostalidad de la Iglesia* (Quito: CLAI, 1997), p. 90, 92.

tain features because they consider them appropriate for the 'success' of their mission, especially its growth.

The obvious social changes that we have experienced as a society can be seen in the Christian church. These changes reflect the crisis of contemporary society, which is often considered the result of secularization. Undeniably, neo-Pentecostalism's approach effectively conforms to the requirements of the postmodern citizens of today, and even with members of the Christian churches, who are attracted by the versatility of its message. These churches do not go to the extreme of losing their identity as Pentecostals, though they do confuse that identity. Even the independent groups, with their celebrative strength and means of evangelization, face similar difficulties. Some academic work regarding this subject cautions that Pentecostals and pentecostalized groups gradually adopt this nefarious mercantilist style.

Pentecostal churches, when faced with the striking offerings of the religious marketplace, are seen as fragile. This is one of the problems that we face today throughout Latin America.[3] This situation has been a frequent concern in Pentecostal Congresses and Conferences as it is a reality that we cannot escape. It is also very evident in our theological institutions as we find students who have passed through various Christian communities and are willing to 'consume' the latest things that this religious market offers. The most dramatic part of this situation is that they understand this 'ecclesiological promiscuity' as healthy and even 'ecumenical', which is completely removed from what ecumenism and Pentecostalism really mean in Latin America.

Another antecedent, from sociological studies, reveals that a large proportion of Christians do not feel attached to their churches, and the friendly and affectionate community that once captivated them is just a distant memory. The sense of belonging, which is a constituent element of Pentecostal communities, is lost in this scenario. Numerical growth is favored over pastoral care, discipleship, and commitment. They apply morals over mercy and goodness, and dogmatism over tolerance and love. Immediacy and results are be-

---

[3] Paulo Barrera, *Tradicao, trasmissao e emocao religiosa. Sociologia do protestantismo contemporaneo na América Latina* (Sao Paulo, Olho dagua, 2001), pp. 275-77.

ing sought before the grace of the Cross and the commitment that means accepting Jesus Christ as Savior.

We are immersed in this postmodern crisis. The identity of the Christian churches in general has been strongly affected by it, and we have not handled these fluctuations well. We cannot ignore or demonize the postmodern global world in which we are called to testify, much less reach simplistic solutions when faced with such complex situations. We therefore believe that we must consider carefully 'pentecostalization' or 'pentecostalness' with bolder eyes and perceive this situation, where Pentecostalism and the pentecostalness of Protestant churches is being confused with the mercantilist neo-Pentecostalism.

In Pentecostalism, our spirituality is based on personal experience that creates community, an experience that transforms everything, that puts everything face to face in an encounter with God. The experience of personal faith is still what we want as a church to transform the lives of others and of the society. However, this situation has also undergone a series of transformations, and the way human beings see life is reflected in their multi-faith experiences. Living a *light life*,[4] implemented by the media, leads to also viewing religion in a *light* way: lack of commitment, relativity, and diversity. Today people are looking for immediate results from their faith experience; and if none are found, they inquire quickly into another area of faith. The transience of religion is one result of this postmodern social change, for the church as a faith community, where life is part of that emotional experience of the Spirit, does not respond to this phenomenon with immediate and magical necessity.

Sociological explanations have been varied in this field and have been warning of the phenomenon and its danger. However, the fact is that the main forms of Christianity, which today are exposed to this danger by their massiveness are Pentecostal congregations and large pentecostalized protestant groups. That is, the Latin American religious scene today is strongly pentecostalized and is being increasingly transformed into a neo-Pentecostalization out of a clear desire to renew mission. Pentecostalism, and obviously this pentecostalization, were not, nor ever will be a religious product to con-

---

[4] Enrique Rojas, *El hombre Light: una vida sin valores* (Barcelona: Temas De Hoy, 2000), p. 80.

sume. We as Pentecostals should believe in the Holy Spirit and not fall into the loss of grace just to be fashionable. This challenges the ecclesial and theological task of all Christianity, including Pentecostal churches and institutions themselves. As Pentecostals we know what we are by God's mercy and what we are not and what we do not want to be.

This uncomfortable situation shows us how vulnerable we are as the people of God, and we must take care (without fear) of this fragility and the possible loss of the Gospel. In this situation, various theological challenges have radically changed the face of the society which we affect in responding to the call of God's mission. I shall consider first the Latin American continent as a region and then prioritize what I consider the key challenges we face.

1. A Brief Look at Latin American

One of the factors currently affecting Latin America is unconsciousness, that is, the abstraction of the people themselves from their contextual reality. The society is founded on an economic model that drives the concentration of income to a minority and causes poverty in education, health, social security, and housing for the vast majority of the inhabitants of this continent. Fundamental rights are currently neglected by government projects since, despite the creation and implementation of state programs aimed at justice, the global economic system restricts the implementation of fair and just public policies.

Moreover, corruption in our countries, together with the inequalities of gender, race, ethnicity, and class are social injustices in which our faith communities seek to develop. Inequalities in housing, education, and health are the cries now heard in the streets of our major cities. Violence concocted by this situation makes any city that seeks to create systems of security vulnerable to crime. This causes a vicious cycle, unfair and difficult to overcome, as people seek spaces that guarantee safety, which in fact generate more violence.

This reality is exacerbated by international economic interests, resulting in the devastation of forests, the pollution of beaches, and the constant abuse of mining and agricultural soils. This places our Latin American countries into an economic situation that does not achieve the levels of self-sufficiency. At the same time, the great social debt to the indigenous peoples, land distribution issues, and the use of natural resources does not provide the justice that should sustain a multicultural coexistence so necessary in our Latin America. Despite international agreements signed by the Latin American States, caring for the environment is not considered a public policy priority when legislating or inspecting, and we live day by day with the deterioration of our continent.

Complete the sad situation in Latin America with the illegal production and trafficking of drugs, which causes more cumbersome daily conflicts. It is a problem that has been impossible to resolve by peaceful means; it attracts the youth who see in this trade an easy way to get money. Another problem is the 'traffic in women' and the slavery of the migrant population, among other scourges that threaten the most vulnerable in society.

These social problems are exacerbated when there are natural disasters such as droughts, floods, earthquakes, and tsunamis, which have been very common in our countries. Also we must acknowledge the genuine accidents that threaten workers because of a lack of proper care in the exploitation of minerals and forests.

2. The Current Challenges

Doing theology in Latin America today is to live with the constant challenge of the social situation affecting our continent. It is a spiritual challenge to the Christian churches as well as for theological institutions. As Pentecostal Christians we have the flexibility, spontaneity, and joy needed to endure or survive in the midst of daily adversity. There is confidence in the transformation promised by our good God. The grace of God that is creative guarantees us this, and in God's Spirit this grace can transform the world with the gospel of the Kingdom of God.

Pentecostalism in Latin America draws on various sources but mainly from experienced revivals within each country, living a different dynamic in their own doctrinal development. From this perspective, every Pentecostal theological current has a different way of meeting this challenge posed by the twenty-first century.

2.1. Impact on Society

We can mention, as a theological challenge to Pentecostal communities, the rereading of the Bible in the context of the demands of today's society, taking into consideration the reality of justification by faith, not subject to gaining merits or social/ecclesiastic positioning. In this we face the greatest challenge of not falling into a mercantilist response as promoted by neo-Pentecostalism. In other words, the Pentecostal church is called to be an instrument of social transformation, breaking free of its historic 'apolitical' speech to establish responsibility for the impact of the Gospel in society.

Pentecostal theology, with which we want to identify ourselves, appears extremely critical of certain alienating spiritualities, which come not only from the official Catholic Church but also from some Fundamentalist evangelical churches. They are able to justify (if only by omission) the official sectors that exert social oppression with a greater impact on the poorest sectors of society. We want a Pentecostal theological context capable of fostering a kind of spirituality that is committed to social justice.

A major contribution of Pentecostalism to society is personal dignity and community. The struggles in favor of social justice from a different platform from what we know as social struggle are recognized as significant in the continent. The contributions to society from the transformation of human beings and their world view is what we must now promote to influence society.

An important example of what we are suggesting is the incisive Pentecostal participation in social movements in Chiapas, Guatemala, Ecuador, and other Latin American countries. They are Evangelical Pentecostal communities who are playing an important role in the struggle for peasant and indigenous rights and the implementation of a new social order. The theological conception is a community of life, which leads each person to be and to feel part of the call to witness the risen Christ. A constant challenge is to ensure that pentecostalization leads to a consciousness of a spiritual transformation of society. It is not institutionalization from a dogmatic point of view that achieves this but the vitality of a community that has a clear vocation and can testify about their experiences of life which are opposed to injustice and oppression, not becoming part of it in any way. They are salt and light in the world and an oasis in the desert.

2.2. Challenge in Theological Formation

For First World Pentecostal churches, theological doctrinal preparation is essential. However, what is central to Latin American Pentecostalism is experience, including prioritizing the experience of faith over theological preparation of any kind. Pentecostalism is primarily an empirical religion, given expression by rationalizing the doctrine from faith.

Religious conversion experience shapes Pentecostal group membership. There has been work done on this in relation to the third generation of Pentecostals in Chile, and all come to the same conclusion: being born into a Pentecostal family 'is not enough to go through life as a Christian believer, nor does it guarantee their religious suitability'. Receiving a faith or being part of a religious group is not enough. Instead, 'a personal conversion experience is a prerequisite for receiving the Holy Spirit, His enthusiasm and fervor … stirring the spirit of the individual'.[5]

Pentecostal preaching constantly challenges everyday experiences, new or old, showing the relationship of people with God. Remembering the primarily religious experience of conversion helps us make sense of our other experiences in our spiritual walk. It makes Pentecost life itself. Without this, there is no starting point or meeting place for theological training. Pentecostalism itself, with its cross-cultural diversity, is a paradigm shift in classical theological thought, and that is why it has to recover its own way of thinking.

However, the massive influx of Pentecostal theological students who do not consider the theological stance of national groups has led to a loss of identity of these groups. Topics such as infant baptism, biblical literalism (biblical infallibility and inerrancy), glossolalia as a single test of Spirit baptism, Eucharist (open), the critique of hymnody, among other topical issues, lead some to reject studies in theology. This situation is compounded by the suspicion that 'theological' means 'instrumental rationalistic', a suspicion already present in the Pentecostal world. The contrast between spirituality and intellectuality has been constantly among the issues faced by the academy.[6]

---

[5] Carmen Galilea, *El predicador Pentecostal* (Santiago, CISOC, 1991), p. 12.

[6] Russell Spittler, 'Los pentecostales y carismáticos son fundamentalistas', in *Movimiento Pentecostal y Comunidad de Base en Latinoamérica* (Hamburgo, EMW, 2000).

Pentecostalism, as already noted, is not homogeneous; its diversity is generally positively accepted today. However, regardless of this current diversity, it is essential to ensure that the pastors and church leaders and Pentecostal movements have access to theological studies in order to strengthen their principles and mission and not to lose their identity. Studies are not meant to strengthen pentecostalness within churches but to strengthen the way we look and feel empowered as a church. The vitality of Pentecostalism is in breaking down stereotypes, confident in the strength of the Spirit. Today we respond to the postmodern, globalized world.[7]

It is also necessary at the same time that the theological institutions assume their coexistence within the diversity of Pentecostal churches and work through the most urgent and specific training needs. The urgency of formation can be observed in the leaders who occupy public spaces in Latin American society. Because of new laws in several countries that have established religious freedom and equality, Pentecostalism, being the majority evangelical religious expression, is driven to take on much larger roles with significant social impact. For example, training school teachers in religion classes, hospital chaplains, prison chaplains, military chaplains, university chaplains, chaplains in state institutions, among others.

This challenge of theological formation requires that we read the reality of Latin American Pentecostal churches according to the context and culture of each country. Our Pentecostal congregations in major metropolitan cities are diverse. Some concentrate on the second and third generation Pentecostals, with specific challenges and dilemmas, while others bring together migrants, indigenous, black people, who represent the forgotten ones in an impoverished society.

It is amid this plurality that we recognize Pentecostal communities living life in abundance, where they are still comfortable, where

---

[7] A Theology of the Pentecostal, or better, of 'Pentecostalness', has to be much more than a confessional, continental, regional, subjective theology. It has to be universal, inclusive, comprehensive (with a perspective of wholeness), not necessarily in the theme chosen, but rather in the spirit in which we deal with the theme, in our case, the complex realities of both continents in a Pentecostal perspective.

Translated by the WCC Spanish Language Service. B. Campos, 'Pentecostalism: A Latin American View' at <http://www.pctii.org/wcc/campos96. html> Recommendations Number 8.

there is love and they find a new way of giving meaning to their lives. Because of the preparation of their leaders, these communities knew how to respond to today's society. Between order and affection they creatively gathered previous generations and those that are added daily to the community with a clear counter-proposal, with a style of being and doing that needs to be recognized and affirmed. It is in this space where theological education must reach Pentecostal communities: to display and promote their way of living the faith, to socialize their faith experience, and make a recognized theological reflection part of their practice, to show that there is no need to lose their identity by becoming fashionable in order to be an effective instrument of God.

This accompanying context, from the experience already gained in this respect in small steps and under the degree of vulnerability to which Pentecostal communities are exposed, reaffirms their identity and allows them to guide their youth and leaders better.

Today we need to think in terms of theological training programs that address this contextual, dynamic, and economic situation, allowing us to meet these specific Pentecostal and *pentecostalizados* group needs. It is therefore essential to highlight the efforts of theological institutions that locally offer online courses and congregational courses in local dialects. However, they are still in deficit in Latin America since the Pentecostals do not have specialists that respect Pentecostal hermeneutics, theology of the way, theology and everyday experience, liturgy, and pastoral work.

The Pentecostal theological work currently circulating is in many cases not from specific contexts and so imposes stereotypes that damage the wealth of local Pentecostalism with its specificities and experiences. This causes rejection and distrust, especially among the Pentecostal tradition.[8]

2.3. Equity and Gender Justice

A major challenge not only to Pentecostalism but to Protestantism in general is the subject of gender. The gender issue allows us to see a contradiction between the principles of community which is lived among the converted and the practice of hierarchical inequality.

---

[8] José M. Bonino, *Rostros del Protestantismo Latinoamericano* (Buenos Aires: Nueva Creación, 1995).

One of the main ambiguities in this regard is reflected in the tension between community life and vision of the church dome.

The sense of belonging on the part of women is at the group level, community living; however, the inequality in social relations is still patent in Pentecostalism. This contradictory 'inclusion/exclusion' as a constituent part of the Pentecostal churches was very evident in some areas but has now receded. In the history of the Pentecostal movement, we recognize that women make their expression of faith in a way that breaks the social order of discrimination. We meet women who assumed leadership in revivals, amazing for their time, but today, women do not occupy the same space of equality in Pentecostal communities, despite the fact that they constitute more than 60% of its membership. What happened? The masculinization of the domes in Pentecostal churches continues being the face of the community.

The Pentecostal movement has constantly emphasized the theme of life in the Spirit. Simple faith discovers the dimension of affection, of sensitivity, of human warmth, of something that brings joy and divine hope. It is a component directly related to the conversion experience that testifies to the gift of God, which transforms the creature, freeing it from its violence, competitiveness, individualism, and selfishness and helps create up a new social order. It is the Spirit of life, the Creator Spirit, the Spirit of life in abundance, which is present in the lives of all people without distinction.

It is the before and after of the conversion experience that assures believers of a safe place to rest and creates a new way of relating. It is this experience of all transforming faith that we defend and that challenges us to seek just and inclusive communities. The Pentecostal experience is an experience that makes no exception of persons, which places no restriction on what is considered a useful life, unlike other human experiences, especially in this market of productivity. It is an inclusive and exclusive experience for every being in all its manifestations. We must seek to reverse the situation to which the women are exposed in Pentecostalism, to feel the current challenge of gender justice. That is, Pentecostal communities are not meant to be spaces where these patterns and values of a unjust and oppressive society will be repeated, because there have been other elements through which women, youth, and children are empowered to be subjects of their own lives.

Brief conclusions

Faced with this reflection, the great missionary challenge we have today as Pentecostals is to understand that God does God's work, and uses us as God's instruments, in places that are not always ideal; insofar as they are built upon economic, patriarchal, racist, and gender power, they may not be ideal for the constitution of the kingdom in the midst of time.

Today we are in this place of reflection, and we must dedicate ourselves to this process of reflection more frequently (1 Jn 4.1), a serious, personal, intimate, community reflection through our busy postmodern lives before it is too late. We must take forgotten Christian elements and make a call to consecration: back to family worship, a life of prayer, fasting, the affectivity of domestic and community activities, and include in this theological reflection the consideration of a rhythm different from what this globalized world forces us into, of explosive growth and immediate results.

We are being pushed to accept what we are not: religious mercantilist enterprises. We have to advance in the mission and meet the challenges of these times. We must go back to being a people thirsty for the message and for humility and devotion, to pick up again our dusty sandals and not yearn or aspire for palaces where the Lord does not dwell.

Being not afraid to promote and foster the ecumenical dialogue, we live in communion with Christ (Eph. 1.10; 4.1-6), learning to hear the voices of other Christians and other theological interpretations of Scripture without losing who we are, our identity, keeping away from danger and from current threats that keep us from the Gospel of grace in the wisdom of the Spirit.

7

APPROACHING CARIBBEAN THEOLOGY FROM A PENTECOSTAL PERSPECTIVE

AGUSTINA LUVIS-NÚÑEZ*

> *Al viento del Espíritu que se llevó,*
> *en Pentecostés, los prejuicios,*
> *los intereses y el miedo de los apóstoles*
> *y abrió de par en par las puertas del cenáculo,*
> *para que la comunidad de los seguidores de Jesús*
> *fuera siempre abierta al mundo*
> *y libre en su palabra*
> *y coherente en su testimonio*
> *e invencible en su esperanza.*
> *Al viento de su Espíritu*
> *que se lleva siempre los nuevos miedos de la Iglesia*
>
> – Pedro Casaldáliga[1]

I was born in Loíza, the heart of Puerto Rico's African heritage. I am an Afro-Latina Pentecostal woman. Loíza is on the northeast coast of the island, just beside the main city, San Juan. Loíza's history can be traced to the first Spaniard colonizers who found an in-

---

* Agustina Luvis-Nuñez (PhD, Lutheran School of Theology at Chicago) teaches at the Evangelical Seminary in Puerto Rico and is the Coordinator of the DMin Program. She is an ordained minister of the Defenders of Faith Church in PR, which is a native Pentecostal church, and founder and first coordinator of the Women and Gender Justice Pastoral of Churches (CLAI).

[1] Pedro Casaldáliga, *Fuego y Ceniza Al Viento* (Brasil: Mato Grosso, 1983), p. 1. English translation: 'To the Spirit's wind which took away,/in Pentecost, prejudices,/the Apostles' interests and fears,/and wide opened the dining room doors,/ so that Jesus' community of followers/were always open to the world/and free in their word/and coherent in their witnessing/and unbeatable in their hope./To the Spirit's wind/which always takes away the new fears of the church'.

digenous population (Taínos) living at the mouth of the river. However, it was not until 1719 that it was officially proclaimed to be a town. The city was named after Yuisa or Luisa, one of the women caciques of the island when the Spanish conquerors arrived.

Loíza was a very rich place, where many colonizers decided to settle. While there was abundant gold in the region, the native population survived as ethnic group in spite of the Spaniards hunger for that precious metal. During the first decades of the sixteenth century, the colonizers shifted the agricultural system from subsistence to sugar cane plantations. This farming stage required more forced labor than the native Indians could supply, and therefore the African slaves, kidnapped from their homeland, entered the scene.[2]

Sugar cane farming was a very productive business for plantation owners. During the second half of the nineteenth century Loíza was one of the most important producers on the island. However, the settlement started to lose relevance as other towns began to emerge under the impact of a general economic prosperity. But Loíza's way of life remained unchanged, whether in terms of population, or economically. There were only two stone buildings: the church, built in 1719, and the king's house. Many free blacks lived in the surroundings. The white landholders lived with their slaves on large ranches near the town. Some Irish families settled in Loíza, owned almost all the farms, and controlled the sugar cane production.[3]

Today, most of Loíza's population is of African descent.[4] It is not by chance that it is the blackest and also the poorest town in Puerto Rico. This socioeconomic reality does not impede *Loiceños* from celebrating an annual carnival called *Las Fiestas de Santiago*

---

[2] See Gonzalo Fernández de Oviedo, *Historia General y Natural de las Indias* (ed. José A. De los Ríos Madrid: Editorial, 1851), p. 466.

[3] Ricardo Alegría, *Las Fiestas de Santiago Apóstol en Loíza Aldea* (San Juan, PR: Colección de Estudios Puertorriqueños, 1954), p. 3.

[4] The population of the municipality was 32,537 at the 2000 census. As of the census of 2000, there were 32,537 people, 10,927 households, and 6,140 families residing in the municipality. The racial makeup of the town was 20.1% White, 67.2% Black, 0.7% Native American, 0.2% Asian, 0.1% Pacific Islander, 6.0% from other races, and 5.6% from two or more races. The median income for a household in the town was $8,962, and the median income for a family was $9,911. Males had a median income of $14,076 versus $12,903 for females. The per capita income for the town was $4,707. 67% of the population and 64.7% of families were below the poverty line. Out of the total population, 62.3% of those under the age of 18 and 59.5% of those 65 and older were living below the poverty line. (Demographics/Ethnic US 2000 Census Bureau).

Apóstol en Loíza. The antiquity of the celebration is such that the details of its origin are lost in the past. Some neighbors affirm that the feast has been celebrated since 'the times God walked in the world'. This carnival plays a central role in the popular culture of Loíza's people. To appreciate this, we must attend to their feast. *Loiceños* express their world vision, dreams, and resistance.

Steeped in centuries-old traditions and with a black-and-proud-of-it attitude, this carnival pretty much embodies Puerto Rico's African streak. People from other towns and from outside of Puerto Rico, including other Caribbean neighbors, visitors from many countries join with the *Loiceños* to the beat of the drum.

Loíza's people dedicate the July 25 of every year to the *Loiceños ausentes* (absent *loiceños*), those who have immigrated to other towns on the island or abroad. They come back every year to participate in the feast with their people and to share with them a special meal. It is a reunion to celebrate common roots, to foment the sense of community, and to share last year's stories far from their town. It is a way to overcome the syndrome that Puerto Rican writer René Marqués describes in the famous story *La Carreta*,[5] where a poor Puerto Rican family migrates from the country to the city and then to the USA never to return. For many *Loiceños*, it is very important to renew their friendship and to ask God to help them in a world where discrimination, marginalization, and racism are so pervasive. The Roman Catholic Church is uneasy with the carnival elements, with the spontaneity, loud music, and the masks that designate feasts that are out of its control. It is important to note that even among progressive movements such as Latin American liberation theology, there is some resistance towards accepting and understanding popular religion. Leonardo Boff, in the book that caused his censorship by the Vatican, *Church: Charisma and Power*, expresses that Base Church Communities as communities of faith 'will be left to themselves' and wishes them to be put in touch with the 'grand apostolic tradition ... and to reaffirm the unity of the church'.[6] In order to embrace the poor, the church must elevate the role that people play in the church. Boff is calling for a new church built upon the reformation of the old one. But this genuine, deep concern

---

[5] René Marqués, *La Carreta* (Puerto Rico: Editorial Cultural, 1963).

[6] Leonardo Boff, *Church: Charisma and Power: Liberation Theology and the Institutional Church* (New York: Crossroad, 1986), p. 47.

for the people causes him to insist that people must surrender to the grand tradition. Does this mean that in order to be part of the church the poor must give up their popular religion that sometimes is considered 'profane' by the 'sacred' church?

Regardless, Loíza's people celebrate as always in their own way and in their own order. Puerto Rican sociologist Angel Quintero affirms that there is a marked tendency in the history of Puerto Rico's popular feasts to appropriate some religious spaces within our own autochthonous context and in this way to evidence their no-strangeness.[7] The feast is the moment to affirm the tradition, to be more *Loiceños*, and to enjoy it. There is no distinction between the sacred and the profane; it is one unified life.

This socio-cultural, political, and religious background shaped my vision of what the church must be. Since I was a little girl, my parents, concerned with my sister's and my identities, reinforced in us our black roots. This meant that even though we grew up in a Pentecostal church context, they took advantage of any opportunity to immerse us in the Loíza's ethos. Every year, we religiously participated in the Loíza Feasts. We did not understand what every single ritual or song or dance meant. However, every year my sister and I anxiously expected the arrival of the summer season to participate in the carnival. My parents did not study the origins of Pentecostalism and knew nothing about Pentecostalism's black roots as identified by Walter Hollenweger.[8] However, they saw no contradiction to affirm both traditions in our lives.

From this lively experience comes a metaphor to describe what it means to be church: the church is a Loíza popular feast. The affirmation of my cultural, social, political, and religious identity as a Latina Pentecostal woman is the affirmation of my African heritage as an Afro Caribbean woman as well. Puerto Rico is a Caribbean country. What does that mean theologically?

---

[7] Ángel Quintero, 'De la Fiesta al festival: Los movimientos sociales para el disfrute de la vida en Puerto Rico', *David and Goliath* 54 (February 1989), pp. 47-54.

[8] Walter Hollenweger, considered one of the first researchers of global Pentecostalism, affirms that one of the five Pentecostal historical roots, the black root, comes from the Afro-American slave religion inherited from African traditional religion. See Walter Hollenweger, *Pentecostalism: Origins and Developments Worldwide* (Peabody, MA: Hendrickson Publishers, 1997), pp. 18-139.

The Caribbean is much more than sun and fun, or sun and rum, sand, beaches, and palm trees. It is a mosaic of languages, races, ideologies, cultural heritages, economic organizations, and religious backgrounds. It is a heterogeneous place that points to a pluralistic society predominantly shaped by its African heritage. The territories that form the Caribbean emerged from different and competing colonial powers: Spain, France, Holland, England, and Denmark. Its population represents a group of forced migrants that had to adopt new identities. Like the Phoenix bird, Caribbean people emerge, in the middle of a society that speaks Spanish, English, French, Dutch, and Papiamento or French Creole languages to reflect critically on their lives through the lens of their faith. This variety is evident also in its religious plurality where non-Christians, Jews, Hindus, Muslims, Bahais, Voodoo practitioners, Santeros, and Rastafarians (considered a Caribbean Theology of Liberation) live with a plurality of Christian believers named Roman Catholics, Protestants, Orthodox, and Pentecostals.

The Caribbean was marked by the violent hunger for wealth, power, and dominion that featured the European colonial enterprise of the fifteenth century. The colonial impact provoked the disappearance of the indigenous people and the exploitation of African slaves kidnapped from their homeland. The history of the Caribbean is one of colonialism, racism, militarism, exploitation, genocide, imperialism, deculturization, and neocolonialism. Economically, the region has experience persistent, structured, and endemic poverty.

More relevant than anything else is the fact that the Church, being part of this process of dehumanization, sanctioned all these enterprises. The invasion of the Caribbean arrived together with the theological argument that God had given to the European powers these territories, and every single indigenous inhabitant had to be converted to Christianity. In hand with the extermination of indigenous people and the dehumanization of African slaves, came the missionary movement, the making of Christians, and the planting of churches. The conquered population was humiliated in the name of God.

Some Caribbean theologians identify this current as the 'theology of imposition', which meant that the Caribbean understanding of faith, liturgy, creeds, and beliefs do not represent their real and everyday life, their hopes, and struggles. In the same vein, William Watty identifies the major theological current in the Caribbean as the theology of imposition followed by a theology of imitation.[9] The Caribbean inherited a notion of a European God, a Western theology, liturgy, and forms of ministry, architecture, ethos, and church government. Theologian Robert Moore conceives the task of a Caribbean Theology to be a 'theology of exploration' in order to reflect critically about Caribbean reality in the light of the Christian faith.[10]

Caribbean people have suffered the pervasive consequences of colonialist and neocolonialist enterprises. In addition, they have struggled with problems of dependence, racism, and exploitation. It is in this context of colonialism that we can talk about the features of a Caribbean Theology of Emancipation.

It is a contextual theology, and like other global Christians, Caribbean people are seeking new ways of articulating their faith: a response made in the Caribbean context, by Caribbean people, and for Caribbean people. Idris Hamid and Kortright Davis call it a decolonizing and emancipatory theology.[11] It is a theology that allows the oppressed and marginalized to express their experience of God today and over the years. It seeks the transformation of the unjust structures of society. It is multidisciplinary in the sense that it uses disciplines such as social sciences and history to interpret reality.

The sources of this contextual theology are real-life stories, testimonies, and autobiographies. During the colonial period, the Bible was used in the Caribbean to support the *status* quo. It was an ideological instrument to sanction the cultural values of the colonial powers. However, Caribbean Emancipatory theology affirms the Bible as a source for its reflection, and more than a reflection, it is praxis for liberation. In the Caribbean, the Bible is re-read in the light of a hope for the emergence of a new and more just world order. Renewed emphasis on Bible study has been observed, suggesting some new ways of re-reading the Scripture, mainly narrative ap-

---

[9] W. Watty, *From Shore to Shore: Soundings in Caribbean Liberation Theology* (Barbados: Cedar Press, 1981).

[10] Robert Moore, 'The Historical Basis of Theological Reflection', in Idris Hamid (ed.), *Troubling of the Waters* (San Fernando, Trinidad: St Andrew's Theological College, 1973), pp. 37-48.

[11] Hamid (ed.), *Troubling of the Waters*, pp. 49-54.

proaches. This 'calypso' exegesis, suggested by George Mulrain, has as its subjects the poor, power, the kingdom, glory, peace, and development.[12] Concomitantly with the Bible, the history of the people of the Caribbean, the writings of Caribbean sociologists and economists, as well as the history of the Church in the region are sources for this emancipatory theology.

The foundations of this contextual theology are also genuine Caribbean socio-cultural and historical ones. Its methodology takes its point of departure from the Caribbean reality. As a liberation theology, it reflects on praxis, and its concerns are concrete realities. This reality includes an intensive participation in the life of the people, specifically their sufferings. This method requires a radical assessment of the needs of the Caribbean constituency, which is seeking to interpret the meaning of the Gospel in the Caribbean context. Thus the inclusion of Caribbean folk wisdom, songs, dreams, testimonies, sermons, myths, dance, movements, domestic customs, music, and cultural history is essential.

Davis identifies at least six major manifestations of Caribbean crisis experiences that inform Caribbean Theology: persistent poverty, migration, cultural alienation, dependence, fragmentation, and drug trafficking and narcotics abuse.[13] The historical reality of these experiences provokes a theological reflection that aims answers to questions raised by these present challenges. Most of Caribbean theologians agree that the major concerns are decolonization, integration, education, and development.

Adolfo Hams asserts that the theological task in the Caribbean demands the recognition that the independence of some Caribbean nations and the abolition of slavery did not mean total decolonization.[14] The Caribbean has not achieved a total decolonization in other dimensions of their life, namely, personally, collectively, polit-

---

[12] George Mulrain, 'Is there a Calypso Exegesis?', in S. Sugirtharajah (ed.), *Voices from the Margins: Interpreting the Bible in the Third World* (Maryknoll, NY: Orbis Books, 1995), pp. 37-47. See also Eliseo Pérez Alvarez, *The Gospel to the Calypsonians: The Caribbean Bible and Liberation Theology* (México: Publicaciones El Faro, 2004).

[13] Kortright Davis, *Emancipation Still Comin': Explorations in Caribbean Emancipatory Theology* (Maryknoll, NY, USA: Orbis Books, 1990), pp. 32-40.

[14] Adolfo Hams, 'Caribbean Theology: The Challenge of the Twenty-First Century', in Howard Gregory (ed.), *Caribbean Theology: Preparing for the Challenges Ahead* (Kingston, Jamaica: United Theological College, 1995), pp. 1-6.

ically, economically, ideologically, or psychologically. This step is the first in the affirmation of the full humanity of the Caribbean people who have been created in God's image.

The challenge of identity demands working dialectically in each Caribbean country independently and as a unique region of communities as a whole. There is a common vision for a united Caribbean and the desire for an emergence of a Caribbean identity in all areas of life. To gain a better quality of life for all Caribbean people is one of the tasks of development in the region. Kathy McAfee proposes a development that must feature being ecologically, psychologically, economically, and socially sustainable.[15] She recognizes that this development must rescue Caribbean culture and identity, empower the region's poor majority, and hence build the basis for a more genuine democracy.

The aim of a Caribbean theology is to help Caribbean people understand their situation in order to change it through a process of reflection and action. To reach this goal, the academy and the church must intentionally point out the history of the Caribbean and its culture through the lens of sociology, politics, and economics, to give relevance to popular readings of the Bible as well to popular religion, native churches, contextual theology, and interculturality.

In Caribbean theology, the word 'Emancipation' is used for liberation, evoking the history of slavery lived by the region. In this context 'sin' is defined as racism, classism, self-contempt, lack of responsibility, exploitation, as well as sexism. To include the experience of women in the theological agenda is part of the creative approach that would contribute to the transformation of persons and structures. Women are struggling to envision the values of integrity, inclusion, collaboration, and mutuality that promote the just interdependence of women and men who seek a holistic liberation which is at the core of the Gospel's demands.[16]

Caribbean theology asserts that the North Atlantic world does not have a monopoly on Christianity. God must not remain a stranger in the Caribbean. God lives in the midst of the Caribbean

---

[15] Kathy McKafee, *Storm Signals: Structural Adjustment and Development Alternatives in the Caribbean* (London: Zed, 1991).

[16] Cf. Elsa Tamez (ed.), *La sociedad que las mujeres soñamos: Nuevas relaciones varón-mujer en un nuevo orden económico* (Costa Rica: DEI, 2001).

reality and must be interpreted with Caribbean categories. God is the Supreme Being who is free and wants everyone to be free as well. Every human being was created in God's image and called to live in a world of justice and freedom.

In terms of a Caribbean Christology, Caribbean theologians insist that a recontextualization of the person of Christ is imperative. Christ must reflect the Caribbean reality. A rupture with the traditional Christology (which only sees the Caribbean as a land of mission) is necessary. The people of the Caribbean region recognize the praxis of Jesus Christ as one of justice in the social, political, and economic arena. The Caribbean is the geographic space where the Gospel can be lived. Here, Jesus Christ is the Son called from Egypt, Africa, as well as the great ancestor.

As Kortright Davis convincingly argues, 'God's emancipatory work in the Caribbean is still "comin"'.[17] The beauty of the Caribbean will be fully appreciated by the whole world when the fruits of justice become a concrete reality of peace. How does the church insert itself as a messenger of good news for Caribbean people? I do affirm that this process of emancipation, decolonization, and liberation must be part of the church agenda, specifically in the Pentecostal church, in accordance with the strong claim of liberation with its Holy Spirit's doctrine.

According to the historian Samuel Silva Gotay, Roman Catholicism and Protestantism arrived in Puerto Rico through Spanish colonization and North American invasion respectively.[18] This marriage between church and violence brought economic, social, cultural, and theological consequences.[19] Interestingly, in his research, Silva Gotay is oblivious to the fact of the arrival of Pentecostalism.[20]

I suspect that it is easier to identify the link between Catholicism/colonization and Protestantism/Americanization than to rec-

---

[17] Davis, *Emancipation Still Comin'*, p. 1.

[18] See Samuel Silva Gotay, *Protestantismo y Política en Puerto Rico 1898-1930: Hacia una historia del protestantismo evangélico en Puerto Rico* (San Juan, PR: Editorial Universidad de PR, 1997); and *Catolicismo y Política: Bajo España y Estados Unidos, siglos XIX y XX* (San Juan, PR: Editorial de la Universidad de Puerto Rico, 2005).

[19] For a deep and revelatory work about this violence see Luis Rivera Pagán, *Evangelización y Violencia: La conquista de América* (San Juan: Ediciones Cemí, 1992).

[20] In the presentation of his recently published book, *Catolicismo y Política*, at the Seminario Evangélico de Puerto Rico in San Juan, PR (2007), Gotay was asked about this silence regarding Puerto Rican Pentecostalism. He limited his answer to: 'let the Pentecostals deal with that'.

ognize that Pentecostalism has, in many ways, affirmed our identity as Puerto Rican and Caribbean people more consistently than other Christian traditions. The Pentecostal message in Puerto Rico is not refractory: it includes in our worship and language the cultural elements that identify us as Puerto Ricans. It is precisely the peasants, the menial workers, and even important segments of society who have been the most enthusiastic in accepting the Pentecostal theology.

According to Juan Sepúlveda, to understand the effectiveness of Pentecostalism as an offer of liberation among popular sectors of society it is important to point out some clues. First, Pentecostalism proposes not a new doctrine or new beliefs but the possibility of a particularly intense religious experience. This intense experience is shown literally in testimony through expressions that point out the emergence of a radical reorientation in people lives, indeed providing a new way of life. Second, there is an emphasis in the Pentecostal message of an access to God without mediation. Traditionally this mediation occurs through priests or by the clergy, who usually do not come from the same social class or do not speak the language of people.[21] Pentecostal church life occurs in the streets, as in the Loíza popular feast, opening the access to this religious experience to everybody without the need of 'qualified agents'. Through the singing, dancing, prayers offered aloud, and the different ways of participation, all the faithful participate as legitimate speakers of the religious message.[22] However, Sepúlveda recognizes that even while the Pentecostal message is different from the popular Roman Catholic tradition, it borrows many forms of expression from it. For example, Pentecostalism refuses processions in honor of the saints but maintains the idea that in religion, the parade has a central place. Pentecostalism is against the promises to the saints but ap-

---

[21] Juan Sepúlveda is a former president of the Chilean Confraternity of Churches. He, in cooperation with Manuel Canales, Samuel Palma, and Hugo Villela, formed the Amerindia Study Team, which is responsible for a research project on Pentecostalism. Their results have been published under the title, *La subjetividad popular y la religion de los sectores populares: El campo pentecostal* (Santiago, Chile: SEPADE, 1987).

[22] Juan Sepulveda, 'Pentecostalism as Popular Religiosity', *International Review of Mission* 309 (January 1989), pp. 80-88.

plies the same type of communication with what is sacred to the relationship with God.[23]

As in the Loíza popular feast, in Pentecostal worship emotion plays an important role, and it is expressed by means of a non-verbal language, through the body and the senses, dimensions that are repressed by a modern culture marked by rationalism and intellectualization. In addition, it is important to point out that in the Caribbean context there are social and historical reasons for that body language, as a mean of protest and rejection of the 'official codes' imposed by those who exercise power.[24] In the Caribbean, this non-verbal language had a protective function. It was like a secret code only understood by those members of the community and unintelligible by the oppressor.

As mentioned previously, the three groups that met from the sixteenth to nineteenth centuries in the Caribbean (pre-columbian native indigenous people, Africans, and Iberian people) are responsible for the *mulato* character of our culture and religion. This *mulatez* is more palpable among peasants and poor people. These groups had in common cultural, social, and religious principles that were characterized by festivity, a strong and harmonious relationship with nature, the celebration of sensuality, eating, equal relationships between women and men, and a communitarian model of living. The body was not strange to the divine. Bodies danced for gods and goddesses expecting better health, good harvest, or simply as an act of gratitude.[25]

The conquest and colonization imposed the abstention of pleasures and consequently, eating, drinking, or celebrating.[26] The intolerance and racism of the civilizatory model of the European elites

---

[23] Sepulveda, 'Pentecostalism as Popular Religiosity', p. 88.

[24] See Edenio Valle, svd., 'Psicología Social y Catolicismo Popular', *Revista Eclesiástica Brasileira* 36.141 (March 1976), pp. 154-71.

[25] Maximiliano Salinas Campos, *Gracias a Dios que comí: El cristianismo en Ibero-América y el Caribe Siglos XV-XX* (México: Ediciones Dabar, 2000), pp. 86-107.

[26] Anthropologist Mary Douglas, *Natural Symbols: Explorations in Cosmology* (New York: Pantheon Books, 1970), points out: 'The physical experience of the body ... sustains a particular view of society' (p. 93). The body is a micro-cosmos that reflects the social order. Closed and hierarchical societies control the bodies, the dressing, how to comb, and behaving. It is the method to build a strict group conscience of these norms. Rafael Aguirre, *La mesa compartida: Estudios del Nuevo Testamento desde las ciencias sociales* (Santander, España: Editorial Sal Terrae, 1994), pp. 26-34.

during the sixteenth to eighteenth centuries, followed by the North American one of the nineteenth and twentieth centuries were based on a Greco-Roman political model called *the perfect white.* This *perfect white* was primarily a European man created in God's image. To accomplish this model required practicing aristocratic ascetics that punished dance, food, and sensuality.[27] The bodies of these ethnic groups were bent in their daily life and through an imposed religiosity.

A Caribbean or Puerto Rican Pentecostal church must be conscious of the exposed reality and as a community empowered and gifted by the Spirit must witness to the world how these gifts help them to be more faithful to the gospel of Christ. In this context, a word of wisdom, a message of knowledge, a prophetic action, a discernment of where the Spirit of God is and where are the 'demonic' forces is more than relevant. In addition, the gift of healing is necessary to cure the pain caused by poverty, racism, sexism, or any other kinds of discrimination. The miracle of Pentecost is necessary in our Caribbean countries. The Pentecostal church, which understands Pentecost as its constitutional event, through its affirmation of speaking in tongues as a gift of the Spirit, must continue affirming this miracle of languages and communication that facilitates understanding. As on the Day of Pentecost, the gift of tongues could help the church to be understood by people in its own language. There was no need to learn another language or to be colonized or assimilated because everybody could understand the good news within its own culture, in its own skin (Acts 2).

The Roman Catholic and Protestant churches in Puerto Rico have been denounced as being too silent regarding the social evil of racism. According to Ebenecer López Ruyol, the Roman Catholic Church from the beginning of the process of colonization imposed its beliefs over native and African people, arguing for the existence of a white god, white angels, white priests, and white virgins. The religious expressions coming from black culture were called pagan and heretical. In the biblical history there was no presence of negritude. The history of the papal successions does not consider the presence of black popes like Pope Victor, who in 196 CE held a

---

[27] Eduardo Galeano, *Las venas abiertas de América Latina* (México: Siglo XXI Editores), p. 65.

council in Rome. The Church is silent regarding the racial identity of Jesus, Augustine, Monica, Benedict, Moses, or Saint Martín de Porres.[28]

López Ruyol also denounces the same attitude in what he calls 'the Protestant silence'. More than a century of Protestant presence has been reinforced by a whitened vision of the divinity. He argues that even when the Scripture is central in this tradition, there is no mention of the black wives of Abraham and Moses. There is no emphasis on the fact that Moses' father-in-law, Jethro asked Moses to delegate leadership to others in order to attend to the complaints that the recently liberated people from slavery brought him. In López Ruyol's analysis, this omission is detrimental in the struggle for a more just society because it dispossesses black man and black woman from a dignified place in Christian history.[29]

The Puerto Rican-Caribbean Pentecostal church can find in the wisdom of our African heritage an epistemological source for its vision and mission. It is not enough to include in its worship and language the elements that are part of our roots. To be inculturated is to help people organize their communal life and express their identity. Theologically, we might say that culture is what people have made of God's good creation. Taking the Loíza feast as a case study is to affirm a strong sense of community, the inclusion of everybody, the relevance to maintain the connections with our family and country people no matter how far we live, the joy of celebration in spite of difficult times, the resistance to assimilation, the recognition of being created in God's image, the edification and care of people, the practice of justice, and the recognition of being an agent of proclamation and reflection.

---

[28] Ebenecer López Ruyol, *El racismo nuestro de cada día* (San Juan, Puerto Rico: Editorial ITS Inc., 2005), p. 116.

[29] Ruyol, *El racismo nuestro de cada día*, p. 120.

8

PENTECOSTALISM AND THE INFLUENCE OF PRIMAL REALITIES IN AFRICA

J. KWABENA ASAMOAH-GYADU[*]

This chapter examines Pentecostal spirituality from an African perspective. We will first refer to the work of early twentieth-century indigenous charismatic prophets and the African initiated churches that their activities brought into being. These were the precursors of modern African Pentecostalism. Harvey Cox provides a methodological clue to the study of such experiential movements by noting that religion is an invaluable window into understanding human behavior because people live 'according to patterns of value and meaning without which life would not make sense'.[1] African Pentecostal religion makes sense when viewed against the backdrop of the resilience of primal religious ideas even in the face of modernity, technology, and scientific development. For example, non-Africans may find it amazing that African Christians in the search of breakthroughs in life – health, promotion, travel visas, employment opportunities, and the like – simply inveigh against enemies and call upon Pentecostal fire of God to destroy them.

---

[*] J. Kwabena Asamoah-Gyadu (PhD, University of Birmingham) is Professor of Contemporary African Christianity and Pentecostal/Charismatic Theology in Africa at the Trinity Theological Seminary, Accra, Ghana, where he is also Director of Graduate Studies. He has served as visiting scholar to Harvard University (2004); Luther Seminary, Minnesota (2007); and the Overseas Ministries Study Center, New Haven, CT (2012). Kwabena Asamoah-Gyadu is a member of the Lausanne Theology Working Group.
[1] Harvey Cox, 'Foreword' to Allan H. Anderson and Walter J. Hollenweger (eds.), *Pentecostals after a Century: Global Perspectives on a Movement in Transition* (JPTSup 15; Sheffield: Sheffield Academic Press, 1999), p. 11.

Harvey Cox's book *Fire from Heaven*, published in 1995, was well received as coming from the stable of a theologian who was not known to be associated with Pentecostal Christianity.[2] In relation to Africa, the strength of the material lay in the strong affinity it creates between Pentecostalism and African religious worldviews or the primal imagination. *Fire from Heaven* recognized that primal spirituality constituted the substructure of Pentecostal religion in Africa and gave it a distinctive quality. In other words, Pentecostalism as a world religion may have the same theological foundations, but in non-Western contexts such as Africa it has acquired characteristics influenced by traditional religious worldviews and modes of spirituality. That is why we can talk about both African Pentecostalism and Pentecostalism in Africa in the same breath. Pentecostalism in Africa would refer to the global phenomenon and African Pentecostalism refers to the distinctive modes of being Pentecostal that have come about as a result of African religio-cultural values. The primal imagination, as it is understood in this chapter, encapsulates a certain culturally-innate sense of a world of transcendence and how this encroaches upon the human world; it involves belief in a sacramental universe in which the physical is indicative of spiritual realities and the assumption that we live in an 'intentional world' in which nothing happens by chance. In the primal worldview, events have causes, and this explains the constant resort to imprecatory prayers or curses and vengeance against enemies, whether real or imaginary, in African Pentecostalism. Further, the primal imagination, constantly affirms the non-rational aspect of the *Holy* and hence its strong orientation towards experiential spirituality.

These features, which are particularly evident in the non-literate cultures of the southern continents, are not mutually exclusive. In indigenous religions and cultures such as those of Africa, sacred and secular realities are usually inseparable. As a religion that is at home with the supernatural, Pentecostal Christianity and its more recent progenies – the various charismatic movements – share the orientation of primal religions towards experience of the supernatural and its transformative influence on the natural order. The truth is that cursing the enemies on the road to success in libation prayer has

---

[2] Harvey Cox, *Fire from Heaven: The Rise of Pentecostal Spirituality and the Reshaping of Christianity in the Twenty-first Century* (Reading, MA: Addison-Wesley Publishers, 1995

always been a part of indigenous religiosity. In taking it on, Pentecostalism simply invokes and works within familiar idioms and discourses. It does not justify indigenous practices, rather it betrays a penchant for Old Testament religion with its undeniably close proximity to primal religious ideas. African salvific goals are often evident in libation prayers which focus on 'material blessings'.[3] The clue to this spirituality in relation to the Christian faith lies in the fact that Africa first accepted Christianity in terms of her traditional worldviews and in relation to traditional goals.[4] Here we examine the synthesis between primal imagination and African Christian religious innovation through a number of themes picked up through interactions with Pentecostal religion. They include the Pentecostal/charismatic theological distinctive of speaking in tongues and experiential worship as the ultimate means of religious expression, the reinvention of prophetism as a means of diagnosis and communication, salvation as an existential reality including material prosperity, healing and deliverance as the two most important ministries that draw people into Pentecostalism, leadership as sacred office, and the gender inclusiveness of Pentecostalism made possible by its emphasis that God indeed does pour out his Spirit upon all flesh. Sacrifice lies at the heart of primal religions and we will note how tithes and offerings are understood to serve similar purposes as gifts offered to shrines and deities in African cultures.

Pentecostalism and the Restoration of Primal Spirituality

This essay is guided by the understanding that although African Pentecostalism does not intentionally seek to articulate a Christian spirituality that is decidedly indigenous, it functions within contexts in which its worldview resonates strongly with familiar ways of being religious. Pentecostalism has become popular in Africa partly because it offers forms of spirituality that are relevant in terms of what Africans consider important in religion. In the 1960s it was thought that God would be edged out of public space by the forces

---

[3] E. Bolaji Idowu, *Olodumare: God in Yoruba Belief* (New York: Frederick A. Praeger, 1963), p. 116.
[4] Andrew F. Walls, *The Missionary Movement in Christian History: Studies in the Transmission of Faith* (Maryknoll, NY: Orbis Books; Edinburgh: T&T Clark, 1996), pp. 86, 90.

of secularism. Having been proven wrong by the global spread of Pentecostalism, Cox revised his thesis and concedes that 'it is secularity, not spirituality, that may be headed for extinction' and that Pentecostalism has contributed immensely to the process of reshaping of spirituality in the twenty-first century.[5] Pentecost, as an experience of the outpouring of God's Spirit and as a religion that takes spirit possession seriously, has never been alien to the African experience. Not only are pilgrims from Lybia and Egypt listed among the beneficiaries of the original Pentecost in Acts 2, but also one of the first respondents to the mission of the early church was the Ethiopian eunuch ministered to and baptized by Philip under direct instruction from the Holy Spirit (Acts 9). Africa has become a major heartland of Christian presence and its religions are predominantly religions that take the spirit realm seriously. It is thus not surprising that most African initiatives in Christianity have had a pneumatic orientation.[6] Ogbu U. Kalu, for example, explains how the pneumatic Christianity of early twentieth-century prophets of Africa was closer to the grain of African culture in their responses to the gospel and so felt the resonance between the charismatic indigenous worldviews and the equally charismatic biblical worldview.[7] To that end, the sub-title of Cox's book, *The Rise of Pentecostal Spirituality and the Reshaping of Religion in the Twenty-first Century*, aptly summarizes the contribution of Pentecostalism to the global spread of Christianity. Indeed non-Western Christianity, including its African expressions, has appeared in Western contexts and almost entirely in the form of Pentecostalism. In the context of this discussion, the attraction to *Fire from Heaven* lies in the profound admission by Cox that 'Pentecostals have touched so many people because they have indeed restored something'.[8] This is where the primal imagination gains significance. Against the grain of Enlightenment mindset, religious innovation in Africa restored expressions of the faith in ways that resonated directly with the primal imagina-

---

[5] Cox, *Fire from Heaven*, p. xv.

[6] See for instance: Allan Anderson, 'Pentecostal Pneumatology and African Power Concepts: Continuity or Change', *Missionalia* 19.1 (1990), pp. 65-74.

[7] Ogbu U. Kalu, *African Pentecostalism: An Introduction* (Oxford: Oxford University Press, 2008), p. x.

[8] Cox, *Fire from Heaven,* p. 81.

tion. [9] Thus for our purposes, Cox and Bediako both demonstrate that this form of spirituality is original to African cultures, and that observation partly explains why Pentecostalism does so well in our context. In Pentecostalism, theology matters, but as with primal religiosity, experience is paramount.

Black Roots of Pentecostal Spirituality

Walter J. Hollenweger, the doyen of the academic study of Pentecostalism, consistently draws attention not just to the oral nature of Pentecostalism but also to the Black roots as being 'responsible for the unprecedented growth' of the movement in the Third World.[10] Hollenweger contends that Pentecostalism is the only worldwide church that was initiated by a black person, namely William J. Seymour who led the 1906 Azusa Street revival in Los Angeles, USA. Today, the claim by some scholars that global Pentecostalism originated from North America is largely contested, but the influence of Seymour remains significant. The influence of his black spirituality, particularly the oral nature of that theology on the movement he led, is widely acknowledged. Oral theology has been singled out as the medium through which primal piety is communicated, and Hollenweger gives Seymour credit for that development: 'Through Seymour's mediation black (African and pre-Christian) oral means of communication became part and parcel of Pentecostalism'.[11] Following Hollenweger, Cox reiterates the affinity between Pentecostal spirituality and primal piety as seen in the spirituality of the movement Seymour led:

> Under Seymour's deft hand, long-suppressed currents of archetypal human religiousness had resurfaced in a new form and under explicitly Christian auspices. Seymour had grown up in a southern black religious culture in which an extraordinary synthesis of indigenous African elements had already been incorporated into Protestant Christian worship. Trance, ecstasy, visions,

---

[9] Kwame Bediako, *Christianity in Africa: The Renewal of a Non-Western Religion* (Edinburgh: Edinburgh University Press, 1995), p. 106.

[10] Walter J. Hollenweger, 'The Pentecostal Elites and the Pentecostal Poor: A Missed Dialogue?', in Karla Poewe (ed.), *Charismatic Christianity as a Global Culture* (Columbia, South Carolina: University of South Carolina Press, 1994), pp. 200-14.

[11] Hollenweger, 'Pentecostal Elites', p. 201.

dreams and healings were not foreign either to the slaves or to their descendants. Furthermore, they did not retain these primal practices merely as heirlooms. In keeping with the typical African respect for spiritual power wherever it is found, they adapted and transformed their African spirituality in the new environment.[12]

In Africa this type of religion as part of Christian expression was first seen in the ministries of the African independent/indigenous/initiated churches (AICs) and the prophets which Kalu spoke about above. Thus although they are not usually classified as 'Pentecostal', there is some merit in Cox's reference to the older independent churches as constituting 'African expressions of the worldwide Pentecostal movement'.[13]

Aladura Spirituality

The AICs are the trail blazers in the reformation of Christianity on the continent, and they did so through a synthesis of biblical thought as they understood it and the African religio-cultural reality.[14] This innovative approach to Christianity, which distinguished the AICs from their historic mission denomination forebears, is discussed in Benjamin C. Ray's very important work, 'Aladura Christianity: A Yoruba Religion'. He comes to the revealing conclusion that 'Aladura Christianity among the Yoruba is a distinctive form of Christianity that bears the full imprint of Yoruba traditional religion'.[15] Ray adduces evidence to support his conclusion that Aladura Christianity constitutes 'a unique synthesis of biblical belief, Christian liturgical forms, and Yoruba religious and ritual concepts'.[16] In adopting Christianity, which in the context of the article is described as a 'foreign religion', Aladura Christians drank from

---

[12] Cox, *Fire from Heaven*, p. 100.
[13] Cox, *Fire from Heaven*, p. 246.
[14] Kwesi A. Dickson, *Theology in Africa* (London: Darton, Longman and Todd, 1984), chapter 2.
[15] Benjamin Ray, 'Aladura Christianity: A Yoruba Religion', *Journal of Religion in Africa* 28.3 (1993), pp. 266-91 (267).
[16] Ray, 'Aladura Christianity', p. 267.

their own wells of indigenous culture by 'creatively' transforming Christianity 'into a religion of their own'.[17]

The creative transformation of Christianity into an African faith took place through the retention of two major elements in African religious culture which informs independent church Christianity in Africa. These are 'the belief in invisible spiritual forces, especially malevolent spiritual powers, and the belief in the efficacy of ritual action'.[18] The benevolent spirit world of Africa is essentially a source of life, strength, and protection. It is generally held that in order to be able to plow one's way through this dark terrain, as Kwame Bediako notes, human beings are wont to 'enter into relationship with the benevolent spirit-world and so share in its powers and blessings and receive protection from evil forces by these transcendent helpers'.[19] While Western Christianity has largely abandoned belief in malevolent powers in particular, indigenous churches sustained African traditional beliefs in the powers of evil that constantly interfere in human destinies for ill.

Regarding Aladura belief in ritual action, Ray explains that most rituals are assumed to have an efficacious effect: 'prayers and offerings not only say things, they are supposed to do things'.[20] The point of ritual is to attract benevolent powers and repel the malevolent ones: 'prayers, offerings and sacrifices require the construction of sacred space, where the forces of the invisible "other" world can be brought into this world and effectively controlled'.[21] Here Ray speaks generally for traditional Africans when he notes that the Yoruba go to their shrines 'to seek cures for their ills, answers to their questions, and guidance in their lives'.[22] For many Africans who had to turn away from these resources of supernatural succor, the AICs and the Pentecostal/charismatic churches offer alternative locations within which help may be solicited from the God of the Bible through Jesus Christ and the power of the Holy Spirit. It is the ability to operate within this worldview that endeared the older independent churches to African Christians.

---

[17] Ray, 'Aladura Christianity', p. 267.
[18] Ray, 'Aladura Christianity', p. 268.
[19] Bediako, *Christianity in Africa*, p. 94.
[20] Ray, 'Aladura Christianity', p. 268.
[21] Ray, 'Aladura Christianity', p. 268.
[22] Ray, 'Aladura Christianity', p. 268.

Indeed Birgit Meyer, in her work *Translating the Devil*, illustrates how among the Ewe of Ghana the choice between mission Christianity and the independent churches was determined by how successful they were able to fill the gap in dealing with evil as traditional religion did. In each case the independent churches proved more and more relevant until the mission churches were forced into emulative action by introducing charismatic renewal movements into their structures. Lamin Sanneh is forthright on how the AICs achieved this:

> A process of internal change was thus initiated in which African Christians sought a distinctive way of life through mediation of the Spirit, a process that enhanced the importance of traditional religions for the deepening of Christian spirituality ... Biblical material was submitted to the regenerative capacity of African perception, and the result would be Africa's unique contribution to the story of Christianity.[23]

In Africa today, the older AICs may be declining quantitatively, but their qualitative impact on African Christianity continues through an enduring religious and theological heritage. In other words, their diminishing presence has not erased their unique contribution to Africa's Christian story as outlined by Sanneh above. This heritage is alive in contemporary charismatic Christianity. On the reinvention of traditional religious worldviews and goals in the theological orientation of these religious innovators, Christian G. Baëta reaches this conclusion:

> As the needs, cravings and hopes remain unchanged, so also the basic ideas regarding the character of the universe, of its forces, their possibilities and the modes of their operation, have been preserved intact. In point of fact, this turning away 'from idols to serve a living and true God' does not appear to be essentially different from the usual practice in African religion whereby a god or fetish which has plainly failed the requirements of its suppliants, is abandoned in order that another one, believed to be more effective, may be embraced.[24]

---

[23] Lamin Sanneh, *West African Christianity: The Religious Impact* (Maryknoll, NY: Orbis, 1983), p. 180.
[24] Christian G. Baëta, *Prophetism in Ghana* (London: SCM, 1962), p. 135.

The AICs belong to a different generation. However, they have left an enduring heritage on African Christianity through their innovative synthesis of traditional cultural and biblical beliefs in the search for relevance in the appropriation of Christianity.

Reinventing Indigenous Worldviews in Neo-Pentecostal Christianity

Religious innovation in Africa entered a new phase towards the end of the twentieth century with the rise of African neo-Pentecostal or charismatic churches. But these charismatic churches are new only in the sense that the demographic composition of the membership, their almost entirely urban centered mega-sized congregations, relatively better educated leadership (not necessarily in theology), innovative appropriations of modern and sophisticated media technologies, attraction for Africa's upwardly mobile youth, international outlook, transnational networks, and emphasis on material wealth as indices of God's blessing, mark them out as physically different from the AICs. Theologically however, the new charismatic churches share continuities with their older compatriots.[25] The continuity of the primal imagination in the Christianity of the older AICs and the new Pentecostals may be illustrated by their approach to the problem of barrenness. In Africa barrenness, like ill-health, is a spiritual issue for which the affected search for solutions at the shrines. Prophets and pastors of independent and charismatic churches have become the Christian equivalent of shrine priests in response to this problem. They create ritual contexts within which to fight devils, demons, and witches that disturb the normal biological functions of women in particular to prevent them from giving birth. In such situations the woman is said to have come under a 'curse', or a witch could be said to have spiritually dislocated or even 'removed' her womb in order to steal from her the 'glory' of motherhood. The two sets of churches develop 'solution centers' for such problems and this may be illustrated by the following cases.

First, consider the case of a 38-year old client of an African independent church. She was a typist with four children from a previ-

---

[25] Walls, *Christian History*, p. 92.

ous marriage who was seeking to bear a child with her present spouse:

> I wanted a child ... I went to the Ark of Noah Spiritual church but the prophetess there could not help me, so I came to this church. I have conceived before, but the stomach was as it was [that is the pregnancy could not mature] ... The [prophet] ... told me it was witchcraft and that the [witches] had sat on my stomach. I myself know it is witchcraft. It is not one person. There are several in my family ... who have joined together. My present husband's previous wife is a notorious witch, and she is collaborating with a member of my *ebusua* [extended family]. I did not go to hospital because I knew very well that it was a spiritual matter ... It is all witchcraft and nothing else. I have faith that *Osofo* [Pastor] Quartey through the power of God will destroy the witchcraft.[26]

Second, in December 2006, Pastor Enoch Aminu the Nigerian founder of the Ghana-based charismatic church, Pure Fire Miracle Ministries, held a 3-day program dubbed 'Operation 10,000 Babies'. The program attracted about eight thousand people, a majority of them women, who were looking for what the charismatics refer to as 'fruit of the womb'. Pastor Aminu very constantly during his sermons over the period referred to witchcraft and family members as being the cause of people's barrenness. Several times he claimed to have seen visions of 'black pots' being broken, old ladies in the village tying up wombs, family members consulting medicine men to destroy relations, and so on and so forth. These are the symbols of witchcraft in traditional religion.

The medicines of witches are kept in black pots; they are usually family members, and up to ninety percent of all those accused of witchcraft are very old women. Indeed, as part of this annual three-day program hosted by the Pure Fire Miracle Ministries, those who had been there the previous year and have had their dreams of childbirth fulfilled were also present in their numbers. The women were all dressed in white, which in African color symbolism speaks of victory. They had come first, as concrete testimonies of the cred-

---

[26] Bridget Levitt, 'A Case Study: Spiritual Churches in Cape Coast, Ghana', in Asempa Publishers (ed.), *The Rise of Independent Churches in Ghana* (Accra: Asempa Publishers, 1990), p. 62.

ibility of the pastor and the power of God to deliver from shame. Secondly, they had come for the babies to be anointed with oil for 'spiritual protection' just as Hannah presented Samuel to the Lord. Charismatic Christianity, as Patrick Claffey establishes from the context of the Republic of Benin, shares with the AICs an emphasis on solutions to personal problems:

> the narrative is almost always of a personal *problem* (a recurring illness, mental or physical, impotence, infertility, possession or other problems arising from occult practices) and the fruitless search for a *solution*, until the *satisfaction* is found in the Church in which the person is presently a member.[27]

In the hermeneutic of contemporary indigenous African Christianity, Hannah's rival has survived as the witch that rejoices in bringing shame upon her family members. So childbirth is an opportunity to celebrate God's victory and give him thanks for shaming one's physical and spiritual enemies. These examples from barrenness and childbirth from the two African Christian traditions amply illustrate the fact that there are continuities between the theological focus of the old and new forms of Christian innovation in Africa. The charismatic churches are new and taking a more sophisticated and technological approach to their Christianity. However, at deeper levels the sorts of worldviews within which they operate and the theological paradigms with which they work actively engage with traditional worldviews within contemporary African settings. I illustrate the point by discussing the relevant themes from here.

Speaking in Tongues

Andrew Walls notes that generally it is impossible for any of us to take in a new idea except in terms of an idea we already have.[28] This is how Pentecostal 'tongues' may be understood in traditional African religious terms. We have identified a sense of transcendence as a hallmark of the primal imagination and 'speaking in tongues' or *glossolalia* is a form of transcendental experience. Thus it is instructive that Cox refers to the phenomenon as a rediscovery of 'a pow-

---

[27] Patrick Claffey, *Christian Churches in Dahomey-Benin: A Study of the Socio-Political Role* (Leiden: Brill, 2007), p. 261.

[28] Walls, *Christian History*, pp. 86, 90.

erful and primal form of religious expression'.[29] Those familiar with the experience would concede that 'speaking in tongues' constitutes a symbol of divine intervention in the limits of human communication with the divine. From the Pentecostal viewpoint, the critical text is Rom. 8.26,

> In the same way, the Spirit helps us in our weakness. We do not know what we ought to pray for, but the Spirit himself intercedes for us with groans that words cannot express.

Similarly, in many African traditions, the gods do not communicate in human languages, they do so in 'primal tongues' as a sign of the limitations of human languages. It lies in the power of religious functionaries with access to the language of the supernatural realm to relate to suppliants what the gods may be saying. Again Cox is relevant here:

> I believe that the inner significance of speaking in tongues or praying in the Spirit can be found in something virtually every spiritual tradition in human history teaches in one way or another: that the reality religious symbols strive to express ultimately defies even the most exalted human language. Virtually all the mystics of every faith have indicated that the vision they have glimpsed, though they try very desperately to describe it, finally eludes them.[30]

It is within this context of the human inability to capture and express adequately the deep things of the spirit that Paul describes Pentecostal tongues as 'groans' or 'sighs' that are 'too deep for words' (Rom. 8.26). It is obviously striking that between the two spiritualities – primal and Pentecostal – we find ourselves within worlds where the power of transcendence could be manifested in languages that do not belong to the human realm. Thus whether we are talking about Pentecostal tongues or primal tongues, the principle is that God or the gods are not approachable in 'mere human languages'.[31] In Pentecostalism therefore, speaking in tongues, is particularly prized as a medium for the oral expression of God's

---

[29] Cox, *Fire from Heaven*, p. 88.
[30] Cox, *Fire from Heaven*, p. 92.
[31] Cox, *Fire from Heaven*, p. 96.

greatness and majesty during worship, whether we are referring to personal or corporate worship.

Worship as Experience

Worship is the context within which a religious community's sense of awareness of transcendence is most evident. In the African traditional religious context, it is built around an ardent desire to encounter the felt presence of the supernatural. Its key emphases are spirit possession and communication, spontaneity, and spirit-inspired prophetic utterances. When a deity possesses a person in Akan religious traditions with the intent of conscripting him or her into religious service for example, what follows is an intimate relationship between possessor and the possessed. This high calling is what qualifies a person as mediator of divine communication. African religions, we have noted, pay a great deal of attention to the search for divine intervention in a precarious environment of perilous spirits and witches. Through the act of possession and consultation, the needs of the people are presented to the deity for action.

On that score, Pentecostalism has proven popular in Africa because by integrating prophecy, healing, and exorcism into worship through what is called 'ministration', it provides the Christian ritual contexts within which people may experience God's presence and power in forceful and demonstrable ways. Music plays a critical role in this therapeutic and edifying process of Pentecostal/charismatic worship. In many of the local Pentecostal/charismatic choruses the Holy Spirit, *Sunsum Kronkron,* comes to 'work' among his people when they gather for worship. In one song, he brings *ayaresa* (healing), *ogyee* (deliverance), and *enuonyam* (glory) to those who wait upon him. In another locally composed Pentecostal chorus, the Holy Spirit, in keeping with the biblical imageries of him, is *ogya* (fire), *mframa* (wind), and *adom nsu* ('water of life'). As 'fire' he purifies, as wind he fills, and as living water, he restores life to dry deserts and lands resulting from drought.[32]

Pentecostals worship in expectation that in the midst of the singing and prayer, the Holy Spirit will visit and that people will en-

---

[32] J. Kwabena Asamoah-Gyadu, '"Signs of the Spirit": Worship as Experience in African Pentecostalism', *Journal of African Christian Thought* 8.2 (2006), pp. 17-24.

counter his presence as he does so. It is a mode of religious expression that appeals to African religious sensibilities because of its experiential and therapeutic nature. In the words of Hollenweger 'it should be clear to the theologian that the place where wholeness and healing may be expected ... is the Christian community. Health and sickness are not private; they belong to the realm of public liturgy and for those who need help'.[33]

Prophetism

Current developments in African Christianity show that Christian Baëta was very 'prophetic' in predicting that the element of 'prophetism' associated with the AICs was also likely to re-emerge in new forms of African initiated Christianity. There is a very thin line between prophecy and divination. Writing more than four decades ago, he noted that prophetism appeared to be 'a perennial phenomenon of African life' and that individuals endowed with the requisite charisma and claiming 'inward illumination, a sense of divine vocation' and with the ability to evoke a sense of spontaneous enthusiasm from people would, from time to time, emerge and secure a following due to the effects such charismatic vocations have on African society.[34] In his book *Ghana's New Christianity*, Paul Gifford has also marshaled substantial evidence to prove that 'prophetism' has re-emerged with the new charismatic churches, and it has done so with fuller force.[35]

Prophetism has truly been reinvented, and many individuals, whether they cast themselves as prophets or not, operate within charismatic churches, healing camps, with some really large ones administered under the auspices of classical Pentecostal churches such as the Church of Pentecost. In these places, people driven by the fears and insecurities of life proceed in search of religious solutions to their predicaments. They bring their problems, they bring their tithes and offerings, and they bring their prayers to the courts of the prophets. It then falls on the prophet, like the diviner in the traditional world, to look into happenings in the supernatural world

---

[33] Hollenweger, *Pentecostalism,* p. 229.
[34] Baëta, *Prophetism,* pp. 6-7.
[35] Paul Gifford, *Ghana's New Christianity: Pentecostalism in a Globalizing African Economy* (Bloomington and Indiana: Indiana University Press, 2004).

to diagnose and prescribe solutions to the problems. The reinvention of the prophetic element in charismatic Christianity is very evident in this enterprise. In many charismatic churches and healing settings, 'a man of God is now able through his special anointing to identify and destroy your blockage and ensure your blessed destiny without you speaking'.[36] The new charismatic prophets flourish in places like Ghana because they claim to have the answers to the existential problems of Ghanaians. These are the same problems that take people to shrines and the courts of diviners in search for answers to mysterious destinies and for abundant life or salvation.[37]

Salvation and Prosperity

The ultimate aim of religion is to mediate salvation/liberation. This is what the Akan of Ghana refer to as *nkwa*, 'abundant life' or life in its fullness. E. Kingsley Larbi in a study of Ghanaian Pentecostalism comes to the conclusion that salvation or 'abundant life' in the Christian understanding as it translates in the vernacular, 'manifests continuity with Akan traditional religious aspirations. Salvation here is a religious process in which health, prosperity, dignity, fertility, security, vitality, and equilibrium within the cosmos are dominant'.[38] Traditional African thought links such salvation with the existential and ultimate destiny of the human person. In other words, we are in this world to fulfill given destinies. In the traditional understanding, destiny which is of divine origin is potentially positive. However, in the midst of powerful malevolent forces, auspicious destinies could be thwarted through sickness, incapacitating accidents, failure, infertility, womanizing, drunkenness, or other such negative occurrences and emotional disorders that bring shame and disgrace to people and their families. Many of these are inflicted upon their victims by human and supra-human agents. Thus if a person is a drunkard, for example, the popular interpretation is usually sought for it in witchcraft activities. In that case witches may have placed a 'mystical pot' in the person's stomach and since the pot is mystical it means it never gets filled up irrespective of the quantity of alcohol con-

---

[36] Gifford, *Ghana's New Christianity*, p. 89.
[37] Gifford, *Ghana's New Christianity*, p. ix.
[38] E. Kingsley Larbi, *Pentecostalism: The Eddies of Ghanaian Christianity* (Accra: CPCS, 2001), p. xii.

sumed. The drinking habit only continues until life comes to complete ruin.

The constant search for advancement, protection, and prevention, explain the proliferation of Pentecostal/charismatic healing camps, all-day prayer vigils, and the re-emergence of prophets in charismatic Christianity. The prophets, like traditional diviners, specialize in dealing with the powers of evil in order that negative destinies may be brought back on course. Ray explains that in both contexts, engaging with the world of transcendence requires the construction of sacred spaces 'where the forces of the invisible 'other' world can be brought into this world and effectively controlled'.[39] On the significance of such spaces, Ray notes further:

> It is prayer that engages God and directs his power against the evil forces of this world. Gaining access to God, however requires the proper ritual context, namely, the construction of sacred space, which the foundation for contact between this world and God in the heavenly realm.[40]

In Accra, the capital of Ghana, there are now replications of prayers services variously dubbed: 'Hour of Deliverance', 'Hour of Restoration', 'Hour of Grace', 'Hour of Divine Favor', and 'Hour of Divine Intervention'. These new prayer centers serve the same purposes as the 'mercy ground' and the 'garden' associated with the older AICs. They all constitute sacred spaces where the power of the Spirit may be invoked to intervene in human affairs.

Healing, Deliverance, and Vengeance

Cox observes, 'Whenever primal piety re-emerges the link between health and spirituality emerges with it'.[41] If destinies remain unfulfilled after wrestling with God in prayer, then certain 'supernatural blockages' must be removed, hence the popularity of the ministry of healing and deliverance in contemporary charismatic ministries. In the African imagination, sickness can easily change the course of a promising life. Generally, we have noted, African traditions answer questions of cause and effect by attributing illness and misfor-

---

[39] Ray, 'African Christianity', p. 268.
[40] Ray, 'African Christianity', p. 270.
[41] Cox, *Fire from Heaven,* p. 108.

tune to supra-human agents. Persistence and austerity, particularly in the case of ill-health, is critical to interpretation and hence determines the choice of therapeutic action. The passage of time is important because misfortunes which may initially be interpreted as 'naturally caused' may later be attributed to mystical sources.[42] Thus Akan philosophical thought differentiates between *bonè* (sin), normally used in reference to 'ordinary' moral evils, and *mbusu*, both of which have the potential to bring misfortune to the whole community and disturb destinies.[43] *Mbusu* is removed only through ritual action. 'To remove' is to *yi*. *Mbusuyi* therefore means 'deliverance' and is used in relation to the 'ritual removal' of curses, misfortune, and sicknesses resulting from sin or breaches of the cosmic order. The philosophy here is not dissimilar to the Old Testament idea of covenant, in which a breach or sin endangers the harmonious relations between God, his people and the created order (Exod. 34.6; Psalm 85).

This worldview coheres with that underlying diagnosis in healing and deliverance situations. When several problems are present or when a particular one recurs repeatedly, the likelihood is that there is a curse in operation. The belief is that patterns of frustration may be evident in one's business, career, relationships, financial affairs, or health. In the African traditional context, divinatory practices are necessary in human situations where answers to decisions, which are not to be taken lightly, are sought. People may resort to divination to find out the cause of an illness or the person responsible for a particular conjunction of events that causes an unhappy destiny.[44]

Gifford explains that in this Christianity, spiritual forces are at work everywhere and have brought about the petitioner's predicament; and 'although human responsibility is not ignored, this fate allotted by God is a kind of predestination, and it is against that background that these prophets can be seen as manipulators of people's destinies'.[45] Although he cautions against seeing the new

---

[42] Steven Feierman, 'Struggles for Control: The Social Roots of Health and Healing in Modern Africa', *African Studies Review*, 28.2/3 (1985), pp. 73-147 (77).

[43] For detailed discussion, see Kwame Gyekye, *African Philosophical Thought: The Akan Conceptual Scheme* (Philadelphia: Temple University Press, rev. edn, 1995), pp. 131-35.

[44] Kofi Asare Opoku, 'African Mysticism', *Trinity Journal of Church and Theology*, 2.2 (December 1992), pp. 32-54 (44).

[45] Gifford, *Ghana's New Christianity*, p. 108.

type of Christianity as simply traditional religion with a Christian overlay, Gifford sustains our argument that the typical charismatic church 'preserves many of the preoccupations, concerns and orientations of the traditional believer transposed into the modern setting'.[46] Names, for example, may possess mystical connotations, and Pentecostal/charismatic 'healing and deliverance' theology affirms this worldview through the belief that inappropriate names could affect the lives of the bearers.

That is why the 'prayer of Jabez' that God will free him from pain and enlarge his territory, for example, has such a forceful impact in African Pentecostalism. His mother had named him Jabez meaning, 'I gave birth to him in pain' (1 Chron. 4.9-10). In Pentecostal/charismatic hermeneutic, it is thought that this name may have brought Jabez misfortune, hence his prayer to God to reverse those misfortunes and enlarge his territory. In a case involving the relationship between names and spirit possession dealt with by Archbishop Milingo, spirits claimed that the victim had been 'pledged to them' at birth. In his ministry to the girl who had come under 'demonic influences', therefore, Archbishop Milingo operated within the framework of certain African traditional beliefs. In this vein, Kwame Bediako writes of the ministry of Milingo in relation to the African context:

> It is clear from Milingo's ministry and writings that he develops his theological ideas on healing, exorcism and pastoral care consciously in relation to the thought-patterns, perceptions of reality and the concepts of identity and community, which prevail within the primal worldview of African societies. He does this, however, not as a mere practical convenience, but because he considers that the spiritual universe of the African primal world does offer valid perspectives for articulating Christian theological commitment.[47]

The same principle underlies the belief in ancestral curses, which constitutes a major reason why people look for deliverance. The Ghanaian Pentecostal concept of 'ancestral curse' is underpinned by the belief that 'the consequences of the sins committed by the pro-

---

[46] Gifford, *Ghana's New Christianity*, p. 108.
[47] Bediako, *Christianity in Africa*, pp. 19-23.

genitors are recurrent in their family lines'.[48] The effects, it is believed, are to be seen in the prevalence of chronic and hereditary
diseases, emotional excesses and allergies, and frequent miscarriages
and deaths, suicidal tendencies, and persistent poverty within one's
family.[49] Where they are administered, deliverance questionnaires
are meant to help trace the ancestry of victims and of any physical
or spiritual contacts leading to 'demonic contamination'. Pentecos-
tal/charismatic Christianity, with its emphasis on the immediacy of
God's presence, is believed to provide an alternative ritual context
within which generational curses may be dealt with. There is therefore much in the theological worldview underlying African neo-
Pentecostal healing and deliverance hermeneutics that coalesces
with African cosmological views. In other words, 'healing and deliverance' take on added poignancy in the Ghanaian context where
salvation connotes deliverance from evil and all misfortunes 'for an
unrestrained enjoyment of material prosperity in all its forms'.[50] It is
the effective implementation of a healing and deliverance procedure
that paves the way for prosperity and the fulfillment of divine destiny.

Leadership: 'Touch not the Lord's anointed'

Mediation in African religion has everything to do with personalities
and leadership, and in the Pentecostal context it is persons who
embody charisma. We therefore need to touch on the nature of
charismatic leadership and its continuity with concepts of leadership
in traditional societies. In African societies generally, religion and
politics tend to be interwoven together. Not only are traditional religious priests held in awe on account of their privilege status as
mouthpieces of the divine but like traditional chiefs, their very personalities are considered sacred. Sacredness commands loyalty. It is
thus interesting that the critical word in how members relate to the

---

[48] Opoku Onyinah, 'Deliverance as a Way of Confronting Witchcraft in Modern Africa: Ghana as a Case History', *Asian Journal of Pentecostal Studies* 5.1 (2002),
pp. 109-36 (119).
    [49] Onyinah, 'Deliverance as a Way of Confronting Witchcraft in Modern Afri-
ca', p. 119.
    [50] Christian R. Gaba, 'Man's Salvation: Its Nature and Meaning in African
Traditional Religion', in Edward Fashole-Luke *et al.*, *Christianity in Independent Africa*, p. 394.

prophet or charismatic pastor is also 'loyalty'. These pastors are held in very high regard as mediators of divine power and those familiar with the nature of chieftaincy in Africa cannot fail to appreciate how charismatic concepts of leadership appear similar to those of indigenous cultures. The credentials of the African traditional ruler are 'mystical and are derived from antiquity'.[51] The 'mystical credentials', Bediako notes, derives from the critical roles ancestors play in African societies as the custodians of traditional political authority.[52]

One implication of this is that traditional rulers acquire a certain sacral status sustained by taboos. The authority of the traditional chief emanates from his status as the representative of the ancestors. Similarly, as Abraham Akrong points out, the medium/prophet, as distinct from the chief and priest, is the mouthpiece of the divine and hence his/her authority:

> is believed to possess charisma – the divine mandate – which sets him apart from all the others ... The sacred nature of kingship is based on the belief that the king's divine status as the mediator of divine power enables him to perform the necessary rituals capable of sustaining and protecting society from chaos. ... The temptation of royal power is that the sacred power can be abused and corrupted and become a demonian exaltation of human power against the divine, which becomes evil or can also mediate divine power for the good.[53]

The call of the pastor as being of divine origin has virtually become akin not simply to the religious installation of the chief, but like the chief, the pastor is treated, and so sees himself, as possessing a sacred personality and with the power to even bless and curse. The favorite text is taken from the words of David: 'touch not the Lord's anointed' (1 Chron. 16.22; Ps. 105.15).

Pastor Mensa Otabil has preached on this topic and his thoughts summarize our point. His understanding of leadership is partly based on an Old Testament theology of sacral leadership found in

---

[51] Meyer Fortes and E.E. Evans-Pritchard (eds.), *African Political Systems* (London: KPI in Association with the International African Institute, 1987 [1940]), p. 16.

[52] Bediako, *Christianity in Africa*, p. 239.

[53] Abraham Akrong, 'Religion and Traditional Leadership in Ghana', in Irene K. Odotei and Albert K. Awedoba (eds.), *Chieftaincy in Ghana: Culture, Governance and Development* (Accra: Sub-Saharan Publishers, 2006), p. 194.

the story of King Saul and David in 1 Samuel 24. Saul had pursued David with the intent of killing him, but when David had the opportunity to take the king's life, he spared it on the grounds that 'the Lord's anointed' must not be touched (v. 6). Leaders, according to charismatic theology, are 'anointed' and appointed to the 'throne' by God. This is an understanding of leadership often supported with the literal interpretations of Rom. 13.1-2:

> Let every person be subject to the governing authorities; for there is no authority except from God, and those authorities that exist have been instituted by God. Therefore whoever resists authority resists what God has appointed and those who resist will incur judgment.

Although their intention is to be biblical, the charismatic view of leadership is also present in African indigenous culture and has crept into modern politics as well. What I have in mind here is how primal religions and new initiatives in African Christianity seem to be virtually operating within comparable paradigms rather than any conscious attempt to be African in the understanding of leadership. A church member may disagree with leaders or even loathe them, but irrespective of their failures, the principle is that their interest must be protected because they lead by divine ordination, approval, and consent.

Gender

A key feature of primal religion is its gender inclusiveness when it comes to the custodianship of spiritual power. When mission Christianity first arrived in Africa, for example, it encountered indigenous faiths in which women served prominently as shrine priestesses and mediums of deities. The most powerful custodians of supernatural power in Africa are often females. African traditional societies are quite patriarchal, and traditional taboos are used to exclude women from certain socio-political functions and sacred spaces; but women, particularly post-menopausal women, seem to acquire a certain uncanny quality that makes it easier for them to be touched and used by spirits in ways that men are not. For example, until her demise in the early 1990s, Nana Oparebea of the Akonnodi Shrine at Akwapim Larteh had established a reputation as one of the most powerful traditional priestesses in sub-Saharan Africa. Her fame and that of her shrine spread as far as the America's, and people interested in African religious culture travelled across the seas to Larteh to consult with and study the Akonnedi brand of traditional religion. Thus one could argue that the innovative gender ideology of the AICs beginning with women like Grace Tani, a powerful convert from traditional priesthood and associate of Prophet William Wade Harris, only reinvented within a Christian context something that was already an important part of primal religiosity. For primal religions, what was important as far as spiritual power and mediation were concerned was not gender but profound religious experiences validated by authentic prophecy and the manifestations of various therapeutic abilities.

Pentecostalism operates within a similar religious mindset. It is a religion that is very conscious of its biblical heritage, including the specific reference to 'maidservants' and 'daughters' in Joel as equal beneficiaries of the outpouring of God's Spirit upon 'all flesh' in the 'last days'. Against the backdrop of its ability to respect the religious experiences of women, Cox describes Pentecostalism as a religion that cherishes racial and gender inclusiveness.[54] Indeed, as he notes further, 'Pentecostalism is unthinkable without women'.[55] Bediako and Philip Laryea have both demonstrated in separate articles and reflections the very deep and profound theological insights with which the late Afua Kuma, an illiterate Pentecostal woman of Ghana's Church of Pentecost (CoP), brought the Christ event and its holistic salvific implications to the church through her 'prayers and praises' using traditional cultural symbols and idioms.

In modern Pentecostalism, one of the most noticeable personalities in any church is the 'first lady', that is, the wives of the pastors. Some have been ordained, but generally they occupy powerful positions in the various ministries, bringing women together and challenging them to make their contributions to the life of the church. Lamin Sanneh did not speak amiss when he suggested that it is women who have saved Christianity from suffering a moribund fate in Africa. The contribution that women make to the lives African Pentecostal/charismatic churches as visionaries, prophetesses, heal-

---

[54] Cox, *Fire from Heaven*, p. 126.
[55] Cox, *Fire from Heaven*, p. 121.

ers, and composers of chorus affirms a certain understanding of supernatural power that is also familiar to traditional religiosity.

Conclusion

The theological themes discussed here uphold worldviews that are solicited both from the Bible (especially the Old Testament) and African philosophical thought. In *Christianity in Africa*, Bediako establishes that primal religion, the indigenous faith of Africa, has proven a fertile soil for Christianity. One of the reasons, as he notes, is that 'it is this life, this existence and its concerns, its cares, its joys which are the focus of African primal religions'.[56] We have illustrated, for example, that childbirth fits into this worldview because it is an existential need. As Bediako argues, the primal imagination can surface anywhere, and in the present time it has surfaced most forcefully in the innovative Christian movements established by Africans in response to the intellectualized and over-rationalize forms of Christian expression inherited from western missions. In the words of Bediako: 'it is in African Christianity that the primal heritage in Africa is most likely to acquire a more enduring place in African religious consciousness'.[57] The spirituality of African independent Christianity, both old and new, has proven that when people appropriate new faiths, they do so by drinking from familiar wells, and that is how the faith acquires relevance in its new contexts.

[56] Bediako, *Christianity in Africa*, p. 100.
[57] Bediako, *Christianity in Africa*, p. 262.

9

PENTECOSTALISM IN FRANCOPHONE WEST AFRICA: THE CASE OF BURKINA FASO

PHILIPPE OUÉDRAOGO[*]

Introduction

The purpose of this chapter is to survey the Pentecostal movement in Francophone Africa and especially in Burkina Faso.[1] The global movement of Pentecostalism experienced in the USA, UK, and other parts of the world did not take long to reach West Africa. Some of the actors in the Pentecostal movement were of African origins. William J. Seymour from the Apostolic Movement (1906) is one important example.[2] About the same time there were some signs of the pouring of the Holy Spirit among indigenous Africans.

For example, William Wade Harris (c. 1865-1928), who originated from Liberia, came to Ivory Coast and founded an indigenous church. He was the leader of a mass movement to Christianity in Africa that inspired creation of an African Christian Church. The prophet Harris created the largest mass movement to Christianity in the history of the African continent and revolutionized the religious life of the southern Ivory Coast. He paved the way for the growth

---

[*] Philippe Ouédraogo (PhD, Oxford Centre for Mission Studies) is the Executive Director of the Association Evangélique, d'Appui au Développement, Senior Pastor of Boulmiougou Assemblies of God Church in Ouagadougou, Vice President of Burkina Assemblies Of God Church, and President of the Alliance of Evangelical Schools and Universities of Burkina Faso.

[1] Assemblies of God Burkina was first to be planted in West Africa Sub region.

[2] Pierre-Jean Laurent, *Les pentecôtistes du Burkina Faso* (Paris: IRD-Karthala, 2009), p. 30.

of the Catholic Church and the establishment of the Protestant Church and for the creation of several indigenous religious institutions. Most significant among these is the Harrist Church of Côte D'Ivoire, which institutionalized his teachings. His impact was unique among the movements to Christianity led by African prophets in that it reflected a totally indigenous initiative in a population not previously Christianized by missionaries.[3] Harris visited countries along the coast such as (Gold Coast) Ghana and founded churches. Other countries like Burkina received missionaries that came as the result of the Pentecostal revival in the USA and became the center from which Pentecostalism grew in West Africa.[4]

Pentecostalism in Francophone West Africa

The Pentecostal movement spread like fire out of the mainline churches and later became denominational itself. However, it migrated across denominations among the evangelicals, eventually reaching the Roman Catholic Church through the Charismatic movement thus affecting the entire Church. This phenomenon affected members of the evangelicals who then moved into Pentecostalism because the traditional/mainline churches found them out of order. This movement reached other evangelical churches and created new ones, both from the missionaries and also with indigenous believers who were led by the Holy Spirit where expatriate missionaries did not reach. This is illustrated in William Harris's case.

Harris's strong awareness and expression of the power of the Holy Spirit and the Spirit's gifts (foresight, prediction, healing, exorcism, tongues, trance-visitations, empowerment of the word, wonders) was his own appropriation of an important biblical and apostolic reality that had been nurtured by a deep biblical culture begun under the influence of the Methodist John C. Lowrie.[5]

Some Francophone countries located inland in the former French Sudan were largely Muslim populated (Burkina, Mali and Niger, Guinea Conakry, Mauritania, Senegal) together with those in

---

[3] See <http://www.bookrags.com/research/harris-william-wade-eorl-06/> (accessed May 18, 2012).

[4] For an in-depth study see Laurent, *Les pentecôtistes du Burkina Faso*.

[5] See <http://www.dacb.org/stories/liberia/legacy_harris.html> (accessed May 18, 2012).

North Africa (Algeria, Morocco, and Tunisia). The same situation applies in North Ghana, Nigeria, Togo, Benin, and Ivory Coast. Due to access and language barriers, among others, these countries were less visited by Western missionaries; however, by God's sovereign Grace, God sent messengers (men and women) to plant churches among them. In Burkina Faso the majority of evangelical denominations are of Pentecostal origins. Along the coast are found also the mainline churches such as the Baptists, Methodists, Presbyterians, Roman Catholic, and Church of England, who are also experiencing the baptism of the Holy Spirit with the speaking of tongues as evidence.

The Case of Burkina Faso

For the case of Burkina Faso, which I know personally, the Assemblies of God (AOG) is the largest denomination among the evangelicals. Fourteen churches and missions came together to form The Federation of Churches and Evangelical Missions (FEME). Newly planted and independent churches still have to apply to become members. They too are of Pentecostal origins. All evangelical churches (together with the Roman Catholic Church) who profess the Lordship and saving grace of Jesus Christ experience the movement of the Holy Spirit, drawing people to a special relation with and service of Christ Jesus. All evangelicals cooperate, and the fastest growing are the Pentecostals. They have joint ministry ventures and share similar liturgies. The works of the Holy Spirit and the manifestations of the gifts draw people to Christ. The Charismatic movement is very active in evangelism and prayer. That network meets for specific renewal programs such as all night prayer meetings, healing, evangelistic outreaches, and leadership training.

In 1996 the AOG celebrated its 75th anniversary in Ouagadougou, Burkina Faso. To record the history, a team of six missionaries were sent by the AOG of the USA to establish a mission in Upper Volta, now Burkina Faso. There were two couples: Mr Harry and Mrs Grace Wright and Mr and Mrs Leeper, as well as Margaret Peoples and Jennie Farnsworth. They came through Mali, crossing the river Niger to Mopti, then by horse and bicycles and on foot made their way through the north Burkina to reach the capital Ouagadougou on January 1, 1921.[6]

The purpose of the missionaries was to announce the Good News of salvation through Jesus Christ to the local populations. Very soon they started learning the local language in order to be able to communicate directly with them. Most of the first codification of the Mooré language was done by Margaret Peoples. She became very familiar with the women, relating to them in their daily domestic duties and with a good ear phonetically transcribing the language afterward. The work of the Gospel started timidly due to the handicap with the language and reached those that were near, such as the domestics of the missionaries, and from there spread its nets wider in the country in the coming years.

In October 1926, Arthur E. Wilson opened the first interior mission in north east region in Kaya after three years of evangelism, while planting a mission base. The new believers were now able to read the Bible and were soon to evangelize in turn the neighboring towns and villages. Others were sent with or without the missionaries to other regions, thus promoting the native missionary venture as led with the help of the Holy Spirit. It is obvious that such ventures go with their own risks, attacks, and breakthroughs. The second mission compound opened in Yako in the North in 1928 by M. Shirber. To consolidate the work, two Burkinabe (nationals) named M Ba Zapa and Sana Compaoré were sent from Ouagadougou. The missionary Vivan Smith also reached there in 1929. In the east a national by the name of Dengtoumda Nizemba first went to Tenkodogo, followed by the missionary Glenn Johnson. Three years later there was the mission in the north Ouahigouya where the missionary was the first to reach the center of the country that later received the auxiliary Wentègda Zabré and then the missionary Vivan Smith.

The Good News went from the center among the Mossé peoples to reach other ethnic groups of the country. In 1935-38 the Gourounsi and the Mossé of the Centre-West Koudougou, Zoula, received the Gospel again by native missionaries such as Zida Bingassida and Salou Dimvia. Mr and Mrs Harold Jones opened the

---

[6] *75eme Anniversaire des Assemblées de Dieu du Burkina Faso* (Ouagadouogu: Editions Flamme, 1996), p. 6.

mission there in 1938. A similar experience happened in Pô with the Kasena, with the missionary Flaterry in the South. The Tenado region in the West was opened in 1952 by Mr and Mrs Howard Fox. In 1948 the American missionaries were followed and assisted by the French, such as Mr and Mrs Pierre Dupret with their team who invested themselves in more holistic ways, such as education and basic health.[7] They all fought to protect the women from all abuses, especially in relation to gender issues. That vision was then shared by a Pentecostal missionary from Sweden who set up a Bible and pastoral School in the West, a rehabilitation center for troubled youth, building many schools colleges and medical centers, as well as assisting in food security, among other interventions. These programs have been overseen since 1976 by Pastor Bertil Johanson and his wife in collaboration with the national church.

With such foundations, the AOG in Burkina, even in the context of socio-economic challenges due in part to its geographical location, were able to send their own missionaries to the neighboring regions of Côte D'Ivoire, Ghana, Togo, Benin, Niger, Mali, Guinea Conakry, Senegal, Tchad, Switzerland, Belgium, Luxembourg, the USA, and to the interior of Burkina Faso. The church runs eight Bible schools across the land, media ministries with radio, television and press, and a proven education program among others activities, with over 3000 churches and 4000 pastors. The challenges remain constant, but the vision of the church is to reach as many nations as the Holy Spirit leads. Since the early stage of their implantations in the country in January 1921, the AOG, followed by others such as the Christian Alliance Church (EAC/BF), the Sudan Interior Mission (SIM/EE), Eglise Evangélique, the World Evangelical Crusade (WEC), Eglise Protestante Evangélique (EPE), the Southern Baptists, the International Centre for Evangelism (CIE), the Apostolic Church of Pentecost, the Mennonites, and newly independent churches have a vision to reach the whole country and continue to send their own missionaries to the neighbor countries and the rest of the world.

---

[7] See P. Ouédraogo, 'Overcoming Obstacles to Female Education in Burkina Faso' (PhD, Oxford Centre for Mission Studies, 2010), section 2.7.

Burkina Faso and the Global Movement of Pentecost

The AOG Burkina is part of the Global Movement of the Decade of the Holy Spirit (2010-2020) with objectives geared to praying for people to be filled with Holy Spirit and leading thousands to accept Jesus as Lord and savior. A short term objective for 2010-2012 is to see 60,000 believers baptized in the Holy Spirit. There are churches in Burkina that for over three decades have called for regular revival prayer meetings and healing ministries. Such a vision has led them to organize a yearly week of prayer similar to a convention. where believers and non-believers come from different parts of the surrounding nations to worship, pray, and teach the word of God. These practices are widely implemented by many churches to the point that the national leaders of AOG invite every local church to organize a week of prayer each year. This is becoming a mega movement among the Pentecostal churches in Burkina Faso, and all-night prayer meetings are happening every week where miracles are taking place. God urged the leadership of AOG Burkina to call a monthly all-night prayer meeting to live more fully the experiences of the early church. The first meeting took place on the April 28, 2012 at the 75th anniversary hall in Ouagadougou where thousands came and experienced power ministries.[8]

Pentecostals in Burkina are involved in the socio-economic sectors of the nation. They are key actors in education, health, media, peace building, community development, and relief among others. They have strategies for leadership development, and they run different levels of Bible training, going from certificate and diploma to degree levels. Some of the leaders have completed doctoral programs. One can say that the Pentecostal churches make a point to uphold Christian moral values that influence the whole nation. Along with these achievements, however, there are areas where they need to work more to maintain the unity, the holistic vision for their mission, and to find the best ways to reach other ethnic groups in the less evangelized areas of West Africa and the rest of the world.

The churches in West Africa that believe in the person and work of the Holy Spirit find themselves united in what most binds them.

---

[8] See *75 eme Anniversaire des Assemblées de Dieu du Burkina Faso.*

From April 23-27, 2012 in Accra Ghana, the West Africa Regional Alpha Conference took place. The participants experienced a common interest in this discipleship tool that unites all Christians who believe and want to experience the baptism in the Holy Spirit. Christians from different denominations and traditions studied and prayed together in unity and in the Holy Spirit. That conference was a visual illustration of an experience of Global Pentecostalism in West Africa.

Conclusion

Pentecostalism is currently experienced in Francophone West Africa, and churches such as the Assemblies of God Burkina Faso are playing a key role. Believers from different walks of life bring their contributions to the socio-economic sectors of the nations. They work alongside their governments in a more holistic way as a result of the movement of the Holy Spirit. It involves the Charismatic movement and the Roman Catholic Church. It is a biblical and unique experience that is lived among the body of Christ in the region.

10

OLD WINE AND NEW WINE SKINS: WEST INDIAN AND THE NEW WEST AFRICAN PENTECOSTAL CHURCHES IN BRITAIN AND THE CHALLENGE OF RENEWAL

CLIFTON R. CLARKE[*]

Introduction

Immigration, transnationalism, and globalization have fanned the flames of Pentecostalism into a worldwide movement. The global spread of Pentecostalism bears the hallmarks of a 'bottom up' movement and not one that emanated out of a unified global strategy, as was the case for Catholic and Protestant missionary movements precipitated by the Berlin conference of 1884. Research has often emphasized the particularities of the movement (ethnographic, sociological, religious, and otherwise) and not the overarching and more holistic features that bear the hallmark of a global movement. Thus, one of the challenges for Pentecostal scholars is to recognize the global theological synergies and emerging historiographical features that are distinctive to the movement as a whole as it unfolds on a global stage.

---

[*] Clifton Clarke (PhD, University of Birmingham) is Associate Professor of Global Missions and World Christianity at Regent University in Virginia Beach, Virginia and Director of the Center for Global Missions. He is an ordained bishop in the Church of God (Cleveland TN) and worked as a mission educator in Ghana for ten years (1997-2007), teaching at Good News Theological College, Pan African Christian University College, and Akrofi Christeller Center for Contextual Theology. Clarke is also a member of the USA Cabinet for Empowered 21 and has been a part of the Asia and USA global conferences.

In Britain, the growth and development of black Pentecostalism over the last fifty years has been an important part of the global Pentecostal kaleidoscope. The emergence of black Pentecostalism in Britain is linked to migration patterns and fluctuating economic factors. Migration and transnationalism in Europe are inextricably linked to centuries of European trade advancement and colonial conquest.[1] The globalizing tendencies of colonialism and the vicissitudes of international division of labour, labour policies, trade relations, and the formation of political alliances have contributed to mass migration. The growth and development of black Pentecostalism in Britain is a corollary of these historical trajectories. Migrants to Britain have therefore contributed to a new religious reality, which is no longer a monochrome but, as Akindunde Akinade states in referring to the American context, 'a rainbow of many religions and congregations from all over the world'.[2]

In this essay, I juxtapose and bring into critical dialogue two streams of black Pentecostalism in Britain that have exploded onto the British religious landscape: the 1950s and 1960s wave of black Pentecostals from the Caribbean and the proliferation of the new African migrant churches from Nigeria. I contend that while research on black British Pentecostalism in Britain has a tendency to emphasize local identities and historiographies, researchers must also recognize the need for a more holistic, unified, and global Pentecostal historiography. In examining black Pentecostalism in Britain, I will proceed by briefly noting the global appeal to Pentecostalism and then go on to examine what lessons may be learnt from the old and new waves within black Pentecostalism as experienced by the African Caribbean and the more recent proliferation of new African churches. I am particularly interested in the missiological question of contextualization and the theological challenges of renewal for future generations.

---

[1] An important book that discusses the link between migration and colonialism is P.C. Emer (ed.), *Colonialism and Migration: Indentured Labour Before and After Slavery* (New York: Springer, 1986).

[2] Akintunde E. Akinade, 'Non-Western Christianity in the Western World: African Immigrant Churches in the Diaspora', in Jacob K. Olupona and Regina Gemignani (eds.), *African Immigrant Religions in America* (New York: New York University Press, 2007), p. 89.

The Global Pentecostal Canopy

Walter Hollenweger divides the global Pentecostal movement into three streams: the classical Pentecostal denominations (including their mission churches); the Charismatic movement within all traditional churches (including their mission churches); and a new type of emerging non-white Christian church.[3] Hollenweger associates the appeal of Pentecostalism's phenomenal growth to the moorings of its black roots. These include orality of liturgy; narrativity of theology and witness; maximum participation at the levels of reflection, prayer, and decision-making (thereby becoming a community that is reconciliatory); inclusion of dreams and visions into personal and public forms of worship; and an understanding of the body/mind relationship that is informed by experience of correspondence between body and mind (the most striking application of this insight is the ministry of healing).[4] Robert Beckford defines the hallmarks of black Pentecostalism in Britain in three distinctive theological categories: the experience of God, a dynamic spirituality, and empowering worship.[5] Steven J. Land has described the heart of Pentecostalism as 'a passion for the kingdom'. He adds that it was the confluence of African-American and Wesleyan spiritualities that gave rise to this movement of participation in the Spirit.[6] Allan Anderson notes that the central theme in Pentecostal and Charismatic theology is the work of the Holy Spirit.[7] Russell Spittler has noted the otherworldliness, orality, and biblical authority as among the key values of the movement.[8] The appeal of black Pentecostalism in Britain is due in part to these endearing Pentecostal distinctives as well as its appeal to other aspects of western postmodern culture.

---

[3] Walter J. Hollenweger '"After Twenty Years" Research on Pentecostalism', *International Review of Mission* 75.297 (January 1986), p. 3-12 (3).

[4] Hollenweger, 'After Twenty Years', p. 7.

[5] Robert Beckford, *Dread and Pentecostal: Political Theology for Black Churches in Britain* (London: SPCK, 2000), p. 171.

[6] Steven J. Land, *Pentecostal Spirituality: A Passion for the Kingdom* (JPTSup 1; Sheffield: Sheffield Academic Press, 1993), p. 52.

[7] Allan Anderson, *An Introduction to Pentecostalism: Global Charismatic Christianity* (Cambridge, NY: Cambridge University Press, 2004), p. 187.

[8] Russell P. Spittler, 'Implicit Values in Pentecostal Mission', *Missiology: An International Review* 16.4 (1988), p. 409.

Old Wine and New Wine Skins

As researchers shift their empirical attention to the new predominantly Nigerian churches in Britain, the opportunity for a generational analysis afforded by over fifty years of African Caribbean Christianity in Britain necessitates a pause for critical reflection. What are the lessons that the experience of the African Caribbean churches, such as the New Testament Church of God (NTCG), could teach the new African churches in Britain, and what is the lesson for the global Pentecostal community? What can they teach us about the challenges of holding together transnational and national identities with regard to renewal beyond the first pioneering generation and the initial move of the Spirit? What about the ongoing struggle of creating appropriate space for the white indigenous population within their church and community? What of the challenges of adjusting to new ways of communication and the use of technology in ministry? These and other pertinent questions must form part of a broader discussion and dialogue with the emerging proliferation of new African churches in Britain. Interpreters of black Pentecostalism in Britain must resist the ethnographic, sociological, and anthropological attempts to fragment its historiography and begin to conceive the movement as a whole.

Roswith Gerloff, who is among the scholars who have undertaken extensive research on African Caribbean churches in Britain, makes an important observation when she notes that 'research into the relationship between black Pentecostalism on the one hand and the African initiated churches on the other still remains to be undertaken'.[9] Although the more recent developments of the new African Pentecostal churches in Britain has overshadowed the earlier African initiated churches, research into African Caribbean streams of Pentecostalism and the new African streams still remain an important area. Migration, diaspora, and globalization studies have detracted from the broader missiological (contextual) implications and theological questions raised by the advent of the new black Pentecostal churches in Britain. The survival and renewal of black Pentecostal churches in Britain lies in part in its ability to recognize

---

[9] Roswith Gerloff, 'Pentecostalism in African Diaspora', in Afe Adogame, Roswith Gerloff, and Klaus Hock (eds.), *Christianity in Africa and the Africa Diaspora: The Appropriation of a Scattered Heritage* (New York: Continuum, 2008), p. 67.

this broader canopy described by Leslie Newbigin, following Van Dusen, as the 'Third Force of Christendom'.[10] Philip Jenkins goes even further by describing it as the next Christendom and the coming of global Christianity.[11] It is in this broader framework, or what Ogbu Kalu calls in another context 'global Pentecostal historiography'[12] that black Pentecostalism in Britain must be located. I want to proceed therefore by assessing the African Caribbean Pentecostal wave and then look at the new African Pentecostal churches.

African Caribbean Church in Britain and the Challenges of Renewal

In 2003, the New Testament Church of God (NTCG), the largest African Caribbean denomination in Britain, celebrated fifty years of ministry; and on Tuesday February 28, 2006 the Rev. Dr Oliver Lyseight, the founder and first National Overseer of the New Testament Church of God in England and Wales (NTCG), passed away. These milestones provided a rare opportunity for serious national reflection of the church's mission and purpose for the twenty-first century.[13]

The 1960s and 1970s saw major church planting and evangelistic efforts to reach out to the African Caribbeans who flocked to the UK as economic migrants. The heyday of the African Caribbean church in Britain was undoubtedly the 1980s, during which the churches peaked in growth. The acquisition of church buildings and the establishment of Bible schools and social initiatives for their members were signs of an increasing confidence in effective Christian outreach missions. In 1982, the NTCG, for example, purchased a large property in Northampton to house its new Bible school and

---

[10] Paul A. Pomerville, *The Third Force in Missions* (Peabody, MA: Hendrickson, 1985), p. 20.

[11] Philip Jenkins, *The Next Christendom: The Coming of Global Christianity* (New York: Oxford University Press, 2002). The term 'next Christendom' as one describing global Pentecostalism has been challenged by Ogbu Kalu on account of its colonial overtones and expansionist motif. See Ogbu Kalu (ed.), *Interpreting Contemporary Christianity: Global Processes and Local Identities* (Grand Rapids: Eerdmans, 2008), p. 5.

[12] Ogbu Kalu, *African Pentecostalism* (Oxford: Oxford University Press, 2008), p. 3.

[13] The BIGMOVE initiative and the Gideon Project are two examples of efforts to modernize the NTCG in recent years. See <http://www.ntcg.org.uk/bigmove.html>.

church national headquarters. The failure, however, to read the writing on the wall as British immigration policies tightened and as a new black British generation emerged would become a significant loss of opportunity for renewal a decade ahead. William Kay observes that congregational splits, doctrinal differences, a widening generation gap between young and old, dissension over moral norms, and the allure of high profile technologically savvy ministries (which created discontentment for many members who felt these leaders seemed closer to God than their own pastors) have all contributed to Pentecostal woes.[14] Beckford notes that the context of the African Caribbean diaspora in Britain has produced a distinctive black-British expression of Pentecostalism.[15] The challenge for African Caribbean churches such as the NTCG, particularly over the past twenty-five years, has been negotiating between continuity and change in the search for new relevant identity. Nicole Toulis's research, which maintains that the black church enabled the first generation of Caribbean immigrants to carve out their transnational identity as African-Caribbean-British, highlights the difficulty of living between two cultures.[16] How Pentecostal churches renew the message and spirituality for subsequent generations is an important area of research for the future of the movement. Robert Beckford's 'Dread Pentecostalism' is a creative and innovative attempt to fuse both old and new identities to bring about renewal within African Caribbean Christianity in Britain. Although Beckford represents a far too radical attempt for many conservative black churches – to whom Rastafarian ideology represents the very antithesis of their beliefs and practices – any attempt at serious renewal will not come without critical points of departures from well-established norms. Factors surrounding the rise of the African Caribbean church particularly have been a matter of much scholarly research over the past forty years and need not be reiterated in detail here.[17] Suffice it

---

[14] William Kay, *Pentecostals in Britain* (Carlisle, Cambria, UK: Paternoster Press, 2000), pp. 37-38.

[15] Beckford, *Dread and Pentecostal*, p. 171.

[16] Nicole Toulis, *Believing Identity: Pentecostalism and the Mediation of Jamaican Ethnicity and Gender in England* (New York: Berg, 1997), pp. 170-75.

[17] A good summary on the major works along with bibliographical references is presented by Robert Beckford, *Jesus is Dread: Black Theology and Black Culture in Britain* (London: Darton, Longman & Todd, 1998). *See also* M.J. Calley, 'Pentecostal sects among West Indian migrants', *Race* 3.2 (1962), pp. 55-64; *God's People:*

to say that traditional black Pentecostalism in Britain has reached a critical juncture in its history in which the conundrum of reform and renewal without isolating its traditional base is at its heart.

Within the African Caribbean Pentecostal churches in Britain, I have identified five critical areas wherein renewal is desperately needed. The first of these is within the area of leadership. The absence of a denominational 'personal retirement scheme' and financial planning on the part of first generation leaders forced many leaders to remain in the pastorate long after their prime. In 1999, 75% of the pastors in the NTCG were over fifty-five year of age. This created a disincentive for younger leaders to ascend the ecclesiastical ranks and created a 'back home' orientation which had little meaning for British born blacks. The second is the neglect to plant new vibrant churches that reflected the black British experience. Ninety-five percent of the NTCG churches in Britain today were planted more than thirty years ago.[18] Third, the church has not responded effectively to the challenges of black urban youth subcultures and deviance. The high profile racial killings, such as the murder of the black teenager Stephen Lawrence, have not evoked sufficient public outcry from the rank and file of black churches. Fourth, the neglect to redefine the place and importance female leadership in the life of the church cannot be underestimated. Fifth, the lack of socio-political involvement, what Robert Beckford calls 'political quietism,' has reinforced the notion of the church being

---

West Indian Sects in England (London: Oxford University Press, 1965); Roswith Gerloff, *A Plea for British Black Theologies* (Frankfurt: Peter Lang, 1992), pp. 23-48; C. Hill, *Black Churches: West Indian and African Sects in Britain* (London: Community Race Relations Unit of the British Council of Churches, 1971); *idem*, 'From Church to Sect: West Indian Sect Development in Britain', *Journal for the Scientific Study of Religion* 10 (1971), pp. 114-23; Nicole Toulis, 'Beliefs and Identity: Pentecostalism Among First Generation Jamaican Women in England' (PhD, University of Cambridge, 1993).

[18] In a dialogue conducted between Grant McClung and Donald McGavran in McClung's book *Global Believer.Com,* McGavran was asked what would be his admonition to denominational groups and ministries today. His answer is very pertinent to the black church movement. He said 'I would urgently stress … [that they] fear – even as they fear death – getting "sealed off" into respectable churches that grow only by biological and transfer growth. This is the kiss of death.' Secondly he said he would advise them to 'spend 2 percent of [their] annual income to research church planting and development'. See Grant McClung's, *Globalbeliever.Com: Connecting to God's Work in Your World* (Cleveland, TN: Pathway Press, 2000), p. 198.

too heavenly minded to be of any earthy good. This list is by no means exhaustive but highlights the need for black Pentecostals to re-contextualize and re-appropriate their initial appeal. The issue of contextualization is given very little attention within Pentecostalism and is an area in need of further research. The challenge for the older African Caribbean classical black Pentecostal churches (as with white Pentecostal churches) according to William Kay, is how to retain existing members while continuing to attract new members and subsequently to integrate the two.[19] These and other issues are important ones not just for the African Caribbean church but also to the new migrant African churches to which I now turn.

New African Churches in Britain

At a time when the black Pentecostal churches (and the predominately white middle class independent and denominational charismatic churches) have genuinely stagnated or declined, Stephen Hunt notes, 'the emerging new African Pentecostal churches in Britain offer a 'measure of optimism for the future of the wider Pentecostal movement'.[20] It is my contention that the emergence of this new black Pentecostal movement in Britain must be tied into the broader black Pentecostal movement in Britain. Ogbu Kalu underscores the importance of weaving the African story into the global and Western historiography.[21] The African Caribbean and the new African migrant churches are distinct, and yet they are an important part of the black Pentecostal historiography in Britain. Stephen Hunt who has conducted extensive research on the Redeemed Christian Church of God (henceforth RCCG) points out this distinction. He notes:

> By way of belief, practices and cultural orientation, these West African churches are in many regards a very different ilk from the black Pentecostal congregation that has been present in Britain for well over fifty years. Indeed, this stark contrast, not only in terms of theological preferences, but in social composition,

---

[19] William Kay, *Pentecostals in Britain*, p. 52.
[20] Stephen Hunt, 'The "New" Black Pentecostal Churches in Britain' (Paper Presented at CESNUR 14th International Conference, Riga, Latvia, August 29-31, 2000), p. 1.
[21] Kalu, *African Pentecostalism*, p. vii.

mark them out in such away as to challenge long accepted sociological framework regarding the origin and functions of these
churches. [22]

Although, as Hunt attests, the new African migrant churches are
of a different genre from the older African Caribbean churches,
they do nonetheless share much in common. Hunt's sociological
observation is useful in its delineation of the socio-economic difference of the constituents of these churches; it however pays little
attention to the interconnections between African and Caribbean
Pentecostalism and the broader framework of Global Pentecostalism. In order for black Pentecostal denominations to develop beyond the life span of its initial revival there is a need for interchange
and mutual learning. David Daniels, in addressing the impact of the
immigrant churches in the North American context, maintains that
it requires a reconceptualization of what constitutes the black
church in America. He states:

> [A] reconceptualization of the Black Church is required, and this
> reconceptualization entails a critical dialogue between the histo-
> riography of African Christianity and the historiography of Afri-
> can American Christianity in order for the incorporation of Afri-
> can immigrant religion to be performed with intellectual integri-
> ty.[23]

This idea of reconceptualization is a useful one when considering the black church scene in the UK. There is a need to continually
reconceptualize black Pentecostalism in Britain as a whole as it unfolds in various waves through global processes and local identities.

The novelty surrounding the emergence of the new African migrant church in Britain is in many ways reminiscent of the African
Caribbean churches in the 1970s. In the same way it has captured
the attention of researches and the popular media alike. According
to a report conducted in 1999 by the Council of African Christians
Living in Europe, there are over three million African Christians

---

[22] Hunt, *The New Black Pentecostal Churches*, p. 1.
[23] David D. Daniels, 'African Immigrant Churches in the United States and
the Study of Black Church History', in Jacob K. Olupona and Regina Gemignani
(eds.), *African Immigrant Religion in America* (New York: New York University
Press, 2007).

living in Europe.[24] In recent years, these figures have increased significantly. In a recent *Newsweek* article entitled 'A Pentecostal
preacher from Nigeria has made big plans to save your souls', Bishop Adebayo – the leader of the RCCG – boasts of having 14,000
churches in Nigeria (4,000,000 members) and 350 churches in Britain and America respectively, as well as churches in other European
countries. He also reiterated his vision to plant churches 'like *Star-
bucks*': fifteen minutes' walk for the developing world and fifteen
minutes' drive for the developed world. In spite of one's opinion on
these new migrant churches their impact cannot be ignored.

In relation to the African Caribbean churches in the UK, the
new African churches have provided valuable lessons of renewal
and rebirth. The leadership is often youthful, professional, and
globally aware. There is a strong appeal for young adults. Hunt's
research into *Jesus House* in London, a branch of RCCG, noted that
93% of its membership was under forty and 79% worked in higher
and lower professional employment. Unlike the earlier West Indian
churches who came over expecting to stay for five years and then
return home, these new migrants possess a more permanent mindset which fosters social political involvement. The aggressive church
planting program exemplified by Bishop Adebayo also attests to the
importance of church planting as part of a continuing renewal process. Their global approach which blends worship and preaching
styles, songs and theology with western Pentecostal churches has
added to their wider appeal.

In spite of these and many other successes however, research
shows that these new African churches have failed to integrate the
indigenous population into their membership and still only appeal
mainly to Nigerian migrants to Britain.[25] The lack of indigenous
white members within the New Testament Church of God has
been an ongoing concern and discussion. After over fifty years of
ministry, the church is still 95% African Caribbean. It is an example
of such issues related to white integration and the overall issue of

---

[24] Report of the Council of African Christian Communities in Europe (CAC-
CE) at the 1999 meeting in Belgium, quoted in Roswith Gerloff, 'Religion, Culture and Resistance: The Significance of African Christian Community in Europe', *Exchange* 3.3 (2001), pp. 276-89.
[25] Hunt, *The new Black Pentecostal Churches*, p.16.

inclusivity, in which both African and Caribbean Pentecostal churches in Britain could have fruitful exchange.

Pentecostal Renewal

The issue of renewal is a pertinent one for Pentecostals. Pentecostal revivalism is strongly experience based and it is often linked to key personalities and cultural change. This has been the case for the African Caribbean churches, and it will soon become a challenge for the new African migrant churches as a new generation of adherents emerges with changing needs and expectations. As in the case of the NTCG, the form in which the original revival took shape concretized into a sacred tradition impervious to change. No doubt there is something within the black Pentecostal experience which has a much broader appeal beyond the particularity of black expression. Capturing this theological heart of black Pentecostalism and being able to contextualize it through the vicissitudes of cultural change and global shifts will determine whether Pentecostalism, black or otherwise, has longevity. Amos Yong's Pentecostal distinctives for a world Christian theology is perhaps helpful here towards our understanding of the unifying elements of black Pentecostalism in Britain. He argues that a distinctive Pentecostal theology should be biblically grounded with an approach to Scripture through a hermeneutical and exegetical perspective informed explicitly by Luke-Acts. Secondly, he notes that the heartbeat of Pentecostal spirituality is the dynamic experience of the Holy Spirit; and thirdly he maintains that a distinctive Pentecostal theology would also be confessionally located, in the sense of emerging from the matrix of the Pentecostal experience of the Spirit of God.[26] In addition to Yong's key distinctives, I would suggest a further five areas that a black British Pentecostal theology should have as its core distinctives:

1. Pentecostal Cooperation

In spite of past efforts to forge cooperation between the various strands of black Pentecostalism in Britain, they still remain essentially fragmented. There is a need for African Caribbean and the new migrant African Pentecostal churches in Britain to discover

---

[26] Amos Yong, *The Spirit Poured out on All Flesh: Pentecostalism and the Possibility of Global Theology* (Grand Rapids: Baker Academic, 2005), pp. 27-29.

their commonality and shared Pentecostal experience and theology. A distinctive black Pentecostal theology for a British context will only be born through cooperation among the various strands of black Pentecostalism.

2. Pastoral Care

The pastoral care of black Pentecostals should go beyond its adherents and extend across to the poor and downtrodden in society of all races, colors and creeds. Robert Beckford describes the Black Church as a 'shelter' or 'rescue', a place of radical transformation, driven by the Spirit and family. The idea of shelter, according to Beckford, should also express concern for what happens outside the church in Black communities as well as being concerned with the 'saved' inside the church.[27]

3. Prophetic Leadership

The pneumatological emphasis should also inspire leaders to confront oppressive structures and systems which bear down upon their constituents drawn from minority communities. The black British experience is often one of racial prejudice and exploitation and social injustice, and black Pentecostal leadership needs to speak to this existential reality of black life.

4. Experiential

The emphasis on experience over against pure dogma has broad appeal within a postmodern context. This feature is pertinent for both Caribbean and new African Pentecostalism. These experiences include baptism in the Holy Spirit and the speaking with other tongues, healing and deliverance, corporate worship and prayer. Allan Anderson observes that 'the emphasis on "freedom in the spirit"' has rendered the Pentecostal movement inherently flexible in different cultural and social contexts worldwide. This flexibility has made the transplanting and assimilating of its central tenets easier.[28]

5. Biblical Hermeneutics

Significant changes in the social context of black British experience will influence the reading of Scripture. Negotiating these changes effectively represent a great challenge to the future of Black Pente-

---

[27] Beckford, *Dread and Pentecostal*, p. 5.
[28] Allan Anderson, 'The Gospel and African Religion', *International Review of Mission* 89.354 (2000), pp. 373-83.

costalism in Britain. Postmodernism is one area in which black British Pentecostal hermeneutics must contend. Postmodern Britain requires of Black churches a new hermeneutics that will speak to a multicultural environment.

Wonsuk Ma points out the strange irony that exists between Pentecostalism and postmodern contexts. He notes: 'Postmodernism is particularly appealing to Pentecostals because it provides legitimacy for their intuitive reading of the Scriptures'. He states further:

> Developing a spirituality rooted in God's word found in Scripture and nurtured by the Holy Spirit is greatly needed if Pentecostals are going to successfully negotiate effective ministry in [the] Post Modern world. Such biblically-based spirituality will empower Pentecostals to address the issues of the institutionalization for Pentecostalism, the engagement of [with] Pentecostals' social concern, inclusion of women in Pentecostal ministry, the continued vibrancy of the church's global mission, the necessity of racial reconciliation, and the renewal of the vision held by early Pentecostal pioneers for a healthy ecumenical relationship with other Christians.[29]

Conclusion

In this essay, I have sought to explore a black Pentecostal historiography in Britain as a global movement of the Spirit which is manifesting itself through different historical waves or revivals. I have contended that although there are crucial differences within the new African Pentecostal churches and the older African Caribbean churches there is the need for Pentecostal cooperation and mutual learning. The challenge of renewing black Pentecostal traditions within a British context is one that will face all immigrant churches at one time or another. Discovering the essence of black Pentecostalism through interaction and integration will help define the essential theological distinctives that will enable the contextualization of the black Pentecostal experience from one generation to the next. The congruence of black Pentecostalism's prevailing distinctiveness

---

[29] Wonsuk Ma, 'Biblical Studies in the Pentecostal Tradition', in M.W. Dempster, B.D. Klaus, and D. Petersen (eds.), *The Globalization of Pentecostalism: A Religion Made to Travel* (Oxford: Regnum, 1999), p. 64.

and black British culture will involve many challenges of contextualization, requiring Pentecostals to reassess their worship forms, socio-political attitude, hermeneutical stance, attitudes to women in leadership, theological training and prophetic leadership.

11

THE CRISIS OF IDENTITY OR ANTHROPOLOGY AT RISK

OLGA ZAPROMETOVA[*]

Christianity is a global reality; however, we must keep in mind that it is best served when all voices are heard. The challenges of the twenty-first century are relevant to all of us. Change is constant, yet the way we engage with it will define our future: the future of our theological institutions; their faculties, students, graduates; and their involvement in secular society.

This essay addresses the concerns that have grown out of my years of lecturing and teaching at Pentecostal theological schools, including the Eurasian Theological Seminary and Moscow Theological Institute. I have taught at St Andrew's Biblical Theological Institute, which was founded by the prominent Russian Orthodox priest, theologian, and biblical scholar Fr Alexander Men.[1] Other places include various community centers that are Pentecostal, Russian Orthodox, and Jewish – in Russia, Belarus, Ukraine, Armenia, and Latvia in addition to tutoring at the Open University of Israel through its affiliate center that operates in the Russian language.

---

[*] Olga Zaprometova (PhD, Moscow State University) is a senior lecturer at the Eurasian Theological Seminary, Moscow (where she served as academic dean from 1998-2011) and St Andrew's Biblical Theological Institute, Moscow. She served as director of Mission Possible (1991-1995) and was in charge of the correspondent program in Christian Education (1995-1998).
[1] Alexander Men (1935-1990) is famous for his missionary and evangelistic efforts. He wrote dozens of books, opened one of the first Sunday schools in Russia, founded an Open Orthodox University (1990), and was one of the founders of the Russian Bible Society (1990). Fr Alexander was murdered with an axe on his way to the church and is considered by many to be a martyr.

The social changes taking place within the churches of Russia reflect the crisis of contemporary society that is often considered to be a result of secularization and is particularly apparent within theological educational institutions. We have to accept the fact that, as elsewhere in the world, many Russian Christians nowadays feel themselves 'homeless', moving from one church to another as religious institutions become marketing agencies and religious traditions become consumer commodities. Feeling and being 'at home' in this sense, is a gift and a call from God. We are immersed in a postmodern[2] identity crisis.[3] Russian Christian analysts report the decline of the first wave of religious enthusiasm that appeared in the post-Soviet territory and the aspiration for a second wave yet to come.[4] Religion, however, has not disappeared from the social stage. Religious experience reflects the multiplicity of transformations and every human being's way of life. The godless way of life, implanted by mass media, does not leave us without any perspective concerning secularism and religion. Quite the opposite, the deconstruction of traditional dispositions and beliefs taking place now gives a chance for a new social search for religious truth.[5]

The Torah and Jewish Hermeneutics of Late Antiquity

Let me compare the challenge of postmodernity with the challenge of Hellenism for the Jewish tradition and lift up the achievements of the Jewish intellectual/spiritual elite. Two well-known tendencies present among Jews since fifth century BCE are as follows: first, a *search for cosmopolitanism* – a society is drawn to mix with other socie-

---

[2] In this essay the author is referring to postmodernity and postmodernism as the terms generally used to describe the aspects of contemporary culture that are the result of the unique features of late twentieth century and early twenty-first century life.

[3] The round table that was organized in St Petersburg (March 12, 2010) to discuss the question: 'What type of culture is forming in today's Russia?' testifies to the urgency of the problem. See *Voprosy Kul'turologhii* [Questions for Cultural Studies] 8 (2010), pp. 93-120.

[4] P. Levushkan, 'Tzerkov I Google world' [The Church and the Google World], *Mirt* [The Myrtle] 1 (2009), pp. 12-13

[5] A.S. Vatoropin and K.M. Olkhovikov, '*Perspeltivu Sekularisma I Relighii v Epokhu Postmoderna'* [The Perspectives of Secularism and Religion in the Postmodern Era], *Socialnuje Nauki I Sovremennostj* [Social Sciences and Modernity] 3 (2003), pp. 136-45.

ties (intermarriages helped to spread Judaism and not everyone considered this a negative development) – and second, a *tendency to separatism* (the idea of preserving 'the holy remnant'). After the three Jewish revolts, the destruction of Jerusalem and its Temple, which was at the center of the Jewish religious life, the nation's history seemed to come to its end. A major national tragedy called for a new orientation, which became possible through the development of new hermeneutics, which in their turn led to the formation of a theology (Rabbinic Judaism). In their deconstructed world, the Jewish scholars (the sages of Mishnah and Talmud) were creative in placing the Torah in its true context as a cornerstone – what was later known as *normative Judaism* (the new religion) started with scriptural interpretation. In a sense the same was true for the emerging Christianity – Jesus Himself was the first exegete and had been teaching his disciples the new (as we call it the Christological) interpretation of Scripture. In a sense, for Christianity, Jesus Christ is the New Torah,[6] the end of the old Torah era, and the new revelation for the fullness of time (Rom. 10.4; Gal. 4.4).

Biblical interpretation – making God's truth relevant to our world(s) and seeking him most of all – has been the way of faithful ministry for many prominent figures in the course of history. Their biblical scholarship was the handmaiden of theology. For Jewish thought, the end of the first century BCE is considered to be the beginning of the growth of new worldviews (later formed into the traditions known as Christianity and Rabbinic Judaism). For Rabbinic Judaism the Torah was becoming the new unifying symbol and center of the new ideology, transferring the text of the ancient (biblical) culture to a new cultural level with new meanings. The different approaches of Alexandrian and Palestinian exegesis (newly developed traditions of scholarship) were meeting the needs of contemporary society by bridging the gap between the traditional (literal) biblical meaning and the system of philosophical categories of Hellenistic culture.

In this exegetical process of the Second Temple period we are witnessing the emergence of 'Judaism' as *an idea* with the law con-

---

[6] Matthew 5; Gal. 6.2. See also: G.F. Moore, *Judaism in the First Centuries of the Christian Era: The Age of the Tannaim* (Cambridge: Harvard University Press, 1927), I, pp. 269-70.

cept as one of its foundational principles.[7] Alexandrian Jewish exegesis, following the tradition of the interpretation of the Holy Scripture that originated during the Persian period, reached its climax in the writings of Philo, preparing the foundation for all subsequent biblical hermeneutics. Interpretation becomes the priority; the foundational concept of Judaism and one of the main symbols of the Jewish culture, namely the Torah, gets a new reading in the context of the changing culture. According to pseudo-Aristeas, it was the Law of Moses (the Torah) given to the Jews with all its scrupulous prescriptions that fenced the Jews off from the sinfulness of other nations.[8] Torah is no longer a mere historic memory of the nation of Israel, it is one of the constituents of the multinational empire. In the writings of Philo (*De Opificio Mundi* 1.3) we see how the Torah, conformed to the ethical (moral) law of the world (cosmos), allows its followers to be citizens of the world (cosmopolitan).[9] In our contemporary language it might be defined as the answer of Alexandrian Jewish thought and its concern with the Jewish identity crisis to the process of globalization. According to the Palestinian tradition of exegesis witnessed by the Qumran texts (CD IV. 6-12; VI.2-11), it was the interpretation of the founders of the community of believers, not the Torah itself, that was considered to be the fence, as in the Alexandrian. It was this idea that was later developed by Rabbinic Judaism – to build a fence around the Torah (Avot 1.1; 3.13). Thus different traditions of interpretation have been building their fences around the main body of the same sacred text, confronting each other in seeking the Truth, developing their own worldviews in dialogue. Later, the concept of *Law* will appear at the center of the discussion within Judaism and within Christianity, functioning, according to Lotman, as 'semiotic condenser', step-

---

[7] P.R. Davies, '"Law" in Early Judaism', in J. Neusner & A.J. Avery-Peck (eds.), *Judaism in Late Antiquity*, Part Three, Where we stand: Issues and Debates in Ancient Judaism (Leiden: Brill, 2001), pp. 3-33.

[8] O.M. Zaprometova, 'Ideya Atemporal'nosty Toru v Ravvinisticheskykh Textakh: Svidetel'stva *Bereshit Rabbah*' [The Idea of the Atemporality of the Torah in the Rabbinic Texts: The Testimonies of *Bereshit Rabbah*], *Vestnyk Moskovskogo Universyteta* [Bulletin of Moscow State University], Ser.13, *Oriental Studies* 4 (2008), pp. 117-31.

[9] Zaprometova, 'The Idea of the Atemporality of the Torah in the Rabbinic Texts'.

ping forward as the mediator between textual synchrony and cultural memory.[10]

It is a well-known fact that texts in general perform at least two major functions: adequate conveying of meaning and creation of new meanings. It is the Torah that has become the symbol[11] which transfers the text of the ancient (biblical) culture with its plot patterns and its traditions from one cultural level to another. This example of the Torah concept development is given to demonstrate how the Jewish scholars (sages) of late antiquity (via biblical hermeneutics) have been 'constructing the context' (making sense of history): *first* through the construction and perpetuation of collective identity, *second* through the reconstruction of patterns of orientation after catastrophes and events of massive destruction, *third* through the challenge of given patterns of orientation presented through the confrontation with radical otherness, and *finally* through the general experience of change and contingency.[12]

Pentecostal Hermeneutics and the Identity Challenge of Postmodernity

The last decade has witnessed numerous declarations of the end of history in general and of Christian history in particular. Some scholars define our time as postmodernity, others as the post-Christian era. We have to admit the sad fact that in the hands of at least some ministers (preachers, teachers, and theologians are among them) the Bible means whatever they want it to mean.[13] That is why it is so

---

[10] Y. Lotman, 'Symvol v SystemjeKul'turu' [Symbol in the System of Culture], in *Statji po Semiotikje Iskusstva* [Articles on the Semiotics of Art] (St Petersburg: Academic Project, 2002), pp. 211-25.

[11] Symbol – a semantic morphosis that represents a universal way of the reality explanation – steps forward as a process and as a result of the spiritual activity of a human being. One of the main features of Cassirer's symbolic forms is their representation as the living, untwisting systems that in turn accumulate and translate the spiritual experience of a human being. See E.A. Tsareva, 'Symvol v SystemjeKul'turu' [Symbol in the System of Culture], in *Statji po Semiotikje Iskusstva* [Articles on the Semiotics of Art], pp. 211-25.

[12] See also J. Ruesen (ed.), *Meaning and Representation in History* (New York: Berghahn Books, 2008), p. xi.

[13] Olga Zaprometova, 'Ghermenevtika, Praktixheskoye Bogosloviye I Mezhkonfessional'nyj Dialog' [Hermeneutics, Practical Theology, and Interconfessional Dialogue] in V.A. Alikin (ed.), *Analyz Texta: Metodu I Podkhodu v Biblejskykh Issledovanyjakh, Istorii Tzerkvi I Bogoslovii* [Text Analysis: Methods and Ap-

important for biblical scholars and theologians to cooperate in their efforts to discern the meaning of the Bible for our time and our place. By losing the centrality of the Torah, of Jesus (the new Torah), and of the Cross, we are losing the foundational Christian truths and the meaning of our life itself. The reality is that our understanding of the Bible is related to our doctrine of God and doctrine of humankind (which in turn depends on the tradition we are in).

With its recent changes of leadership, the Russian Orthodox Church (the traditional Christian body of Russia) is turning anew to biblical studies.[14] The main Russian Orthodox schools work on developing the liturgy and strengthening historical memory, with special attention given to the last century. Worthy of particular note are their new educational and research programs linked to the formation of new departments and new faculty bodies. This response of the Orthodox Church to the cultural changes of contemporary society demonstrates its realization of the need for intellectual and spiritual awakening. By contrast, Russian Pentecostalism, in its search for recognition in the same society, is gradually losing its self-identity and its strength, which was mainly derived from the central role it gave to experiential theology.[15]

The recent volume of 'European Pentecostalism' (the seventh volume in Global Pentecostal and Charismatic Studies published by Brill) provides us with a brief review of Pentecostal history in Russia and Ukraine.[16] According to Cecil M. Robeck, by 1909 Eleanor

---

proaches in Biblical Studies, Church History, and Theology]. Proceedings of the International Conference, April 19-20, 2012 at St. Petersburg Christian University (St Petersburg: St Petersburg's Christian University Press, 2013), pp. 115-28.

[14] The author serves as a secretary of the Russian board of the Institute for Bible Translation (<http://www.ibt.org.ru>) and is aware of the recent developments in the sphere of biblical studies and Bible translation. See also A. Desnizky, '"Novaya Germenevtyka" I Perspektovy Pravoslavnoy Bibleistyki' ["New Hermeneutics" and the perspectives of the Orthodox Biblical Studies'] at <http://bogoslov.ru>.

[15] O. Zaprometova, 'Losing the Identity: On Pentecostal Theological Education in Russia', *Acta Missiologiae* 3 (2011), pp. 97-105. See also: Homer G. Rhea (ed.), *Living the Faith* (Cleveland, TN: Pathway Press, 2001); P. Alexander, *Signs and Wonders: Why Pentecostalism is the World's Fastest Growing Faith* (San Francisco: Jossey-Bass, 2009).

[16] Pavel Mozer and Oleg Bornovolokov, 'The Development of Pentecostalism in Russia and the Ukraine', in William K. Kay and Anne E. Dyer (eds.), *European Pentecostalism* (Leiden: Brill, 2011), 416 pp.

E. Patrick, a missionary who followed German immigrants to Estonia and Latvia, had reached Belarus and then eventually went on to Russia itself where she worked from 1911 until 1916 founding Pentecostal congregations.[17] The information provided by Pavel Mozer and Oleg Bornovolokov in the chapter entitled 'The development of Pentecostalism in Russia and the Ukraine' should be compared with secular sources, according to which the Norwegian-American Gerhard Olsen Smidt introduced Pentecostalism to evangelical communities in Helsinki (which in 1911 was a part of Russian empire).[18] To his monograph dedicated to the analysis of the Azusa street mission and revival,[19] which was translated into Russian and published in 2012, Robeck added an extra chapter entitled 'The Azusa Street Message Comes to Eastern Europe'. He proves there that the impact of Azusa Street was felt in Russia as early as 1907,[20] although most known accounts of Russian Pentecostalism begin in 1920 with the return of Ivan Voronaev from the United States to his motherland.[21] According to Robeck, the first sign of the Azusa Street Mission impact came through the Baltic area. For instance, the Reverend William Fetler, a Baptist pastor from Latvia and a graduate of the famous Spurgeon's College in London, who in 1907 was serving as a pastor in St Petersburg, had open doors for visiting Pentecostal preachers from Western Europe and USA. The other means by which the Pentecostal message arrived in Russia were those locals who, seeking the deeper things of God, visited Wiborg [Vyberg], Finland [now in Russia], which was at that time ruled by Russia (details are outlined in the writings of Frank Bartleman). A

---

[17] Mozer and Bornovolokov, 'Russia and the Ukraine', p. 261. See also Cecil M. Robeck, *Azusa-Srit: Missiya I Probuzhdenije. Zarozhdenije V semirnogo Pyatidesyatnicheskogo Dvizhenija*, [*The Azusa Street Mission and Revival*] (trans. M. Pavlov; Alexandria: Ezdra, 2012), pp. 351-89.

[18] <http://personal.inet.fi/koti/rossi/hellu.html>; <http://erkki.wordpress.com/category/finland/> (in Finnish). See also O.Y. Vasiljeva and N.A. Trofimchjuk (eds.), Istoriya Relighyj V Rossii. Uchebnik. [The History of Religions in Russia. The Study Book] (Moscow: RASS, 2004), pp. 432-33; <http://www.gumer.info/bogoslov_Buks/protestant/VozrPatides.php>.

[19] Cecil M. Robeck, *The Azusa Street Mission and Revival: The Birth of the Global Pentecostal Movement* (Nashville, TN: Thomas Nelson Publishers, 2006), 342 pp.

[20] Beginning in 1905 (the edict of religious tolerance was proclaimed on April 17), Russia enjoyed several years of religious freedom. See I.S. Prokhanov, *V kotle Rossyi. Autobiographia Ivana Stepanovitcha Prokhanova* [In the Cauldron of Russia] (Chicago, IL: World Fellowship of Slavic Evangelical Christians, 1992), p. 127.

[21] Mozer and Bornovolokov, 'Russia and the Ukraine', pp. 261-89.

third source came through the endeavors of Eleanor E. Patrick, whom I mentioned earlier. Robeck also points out that another group of Russian churches came into being through the work of Andrew bar David Urshan, the Iranian immigrant to the United States, who was baptized in the Spirit at the tent meeting of William Durham, pastor of the North Avenue Mission in Chicago. Convinced that his own people also needed to hear the Pentecostal message, Urshan left the USA and arrived in Iran in 1914. Due to the outbreak of the First World War, he was later forced to flee, though on his way Urshan preached and founded Pentecostal congregations throughout Iran, Azerbaijan, Georgia, and Russia, from south of the Caucasus mountain range to St Petersburg in the north (where he arrived in 1916). Thus, according to Robeck, the Pentecostal message came to the Baltics by 1908, to Poland and Russia by 1910, to the Caucasus by 1916, to Ukraine and Bulgaria by 1921, and a year later to Romania. The Pentecostal movement was clearly present within the territories of the Russian empire before the Bolshevik Revolution of 1917-18; and because of its minimal contact with the Western Christianity until after 1989, it may be considered an indigenous work.

It was from the northwest of the country that the first wave of Pentecostal revival reached Russia. The second wave came from the south: Voronaev's return to his homeland from the USA in 1921 is an outstanding example of many early Pentecostal converts who were faithful to God's calling. The story of Russian Pentecostalism is still untold, especially in regards to the formation of its doctrinal views. The multiple format of the young movement, which experienced persecution and was deprived of theological education, resulted in the two tendencies constantly struggling with each other: striving for unification with those who are of the same Spirit and striving for independence, underlying the uniqueness of its orthodoxy and orthopraxy.

As I mentioned earlier, there is a difference between a Western and an Eastern understanding of 'doing' theology. For the East, theology starts with the *orthodoxy*, understood as proper worship.[22]

---

[22] Olga Zaprometova, 'Bitter and Sweet Tears: Exploring the Spirituality of the Eastern Church Fathers in the Light of Postmodern "Enthusiastic Christianity" in Russia', in Rolf Olsen (ed.), *Mission and Postmodernities* (Oxford: Regnum Books, 2011), pp. 191-203.

For the West, *orthodoxy* is related more to the correct understanding of doctrinal statements (taking a different meaning of the Greek word *doxa* which underlies the second element of the word 'orthodoxy'). It is a rational way of thinking. In other words the difference is in the emphasis put on the experiential versus the rational way of doing theology. It does not mean that Western theology excludes the spiritual life of the believer nor that Eastern theology excludes a correct understanding of doctrine.

In Christianity, as in Judaism, the experience of God's Spirit awakens new expectations about life, giving a reason for the eschatological longing for the completion of salvation and the new creation of all things. Eastern churches insist that humanity was created in the image of God, and despite its Fall, it is the Almighty's purpose to restore humans to original perfection, and it is by the power of the Spirit that the true relationship between God, humankind, and nature is restored.[23] Experiential (mystical) theology aims at being a category of wisdom drawn from the experience of knowing God rather than a doctrinal wisdom. Mysticism and discipleship belong together and are of vital importance for a church which calls itself by the name of Christ. We often perceive more with our senses than we realize, or than was intended by a writer or speaker. This is the reason why experiencing God must not be restricted to controlled religious forms of expressing these experiences. Contemporary Pentecostal theologians have observed that the movement, which at its dawn was open for others to join, and only later in its history preferred exclusivism, is now turning back to its own origins. Some Pentecostals are appealing for a new era, in which Pentecostals rediscover their 'identity'.[24] Pentecostalism itself with all its intercultural diversity is presented by Paul van der Laan as a paradigm shift in classical theological thinking.[25]

Some Russian pastors do realize the importance of biblical and theological studies (including hermeneutics) for practical Christian

---

[23] S.M. Burgess, *The Holy Spirit: Eastern Christian Traditions* (Peabody: Hendrickson Publishers, 1989), p. 2.

[24] P.N. Van der Laan, 'Catching a Butterfly – The Identity of Pentecostal Theology', *Journal of the European Pentecostal Theological Association* 2 (2009), pp. 33-48.

[25] Van der Laan suggests the application of a quadrilateral Pentecostal methodology (experiential, scriptural, prophetic, and intercultural) to a systematic theology. I hope he will succeed.

ministry, but they are few (mostly they are Presbyterians and Baptists, well-educated themselves). The majority of Pentecostal leaders prefer to turn to secular institutions for programs in Religious Studies of Philosophy to secure better recognition in society. It is a paradox: those who complained that they were deprived of education during the persecution, in the time of 'new freedom' preferred emigration to the USA, Israel, and Germany with all its challenges for their traditional faith; those who decided to stay had to face the other challenges (secularization, freedom for everything, the crisis of postmodernity), and for them theological education was not and still is not the priority.

As far back as 1996, Kenneth J. Archer pointed to the dialogical and dialectical essence of Pentecostal hermeneutics that 'will speak with a liberating voice accented by postmodernity'[26]. It is obvious that multiculturalism gives more freedom for plural interpretations. It was a challenge for twentieth-century religious philosophical thought, and it is even a greater challenge for us today.

Anthropology at Risk

Let me turn from history to the current problem of ministerial professionalism, especially with regard to the future of theological education and to the emerging problems of the new 'informational anthropology' in Russia.[27] We are finding ourselves in a completely new environment that requires from us a certain adaptation as well and results in certain changes in our physiology, psychology, and social skills. It is of special interest that alongside the general speeding up of information technology, a shift to 'close reading' and 'slow reading' is taking place that is connected to post-structuralism and postmodern philosophy.[28] The other well-known fact is that

---

[26] Archer underlined the interdependence between the Scripture, Spirit, and reader(s). See K.J. Archer, 'Pentecostal Hermeneutics: Retrospect and Prospect', *Journal of Pentecostal Theology* 8 (1996), pp. 63-81.

[27] See the recent publications of Prof. Konstantin K. Kolin (Principal Researcher of the Institute of Informatics Problems of the Russian Academy of Sciences): *Filosofya Informaztii. Struktura Real'nosti I Fenomen Informaztii* [Philosophy of Information. Structure of Reality and Phenomenon of Information] and others. <http://www.inion.ru/index.php?page_id=472>

[28] See the works of Jacques Derrida (1930-2004) that are so influential for the contemporary, cultural memory studies (J. & A. Assmanns, J. Ruesen), Jewish studies (D. Boyarin, A. Kovelman and others), etc.

philosophy, the traditional dialogue partner with theology, has today been replaced by sociology – Orthopraxis replaces Orthodoxy.[29] The scholars consider that we are giving birth to a new civilization and are concerned with the formation of a new type of personality – *homo informaticus*. Does this, one must ask, bother the Pentecostals as well?

The voluntary sufferings that were so common among Russian and other Eastern European Christian communities under Communist regimes are still an important mark for Asian Pentecostals (in China, North Korea, Vietnam, and other countries). I have been asked by one of the Russian Orthodox priests (Fr Alexander Borisov, the successor of Fr Alexander Men) on many occasions why the Pentecostals who were faithful and were the example of a true Christian faith in the time of sufferings emigrated in such great numbers when freedom to preach the Gospel arrived in Russia? Those of you who are from Palestine and other countries will understand that it is not easy to persevere. Who are we to blame these brethren and their children who mostly acted in their turn for the sake of their own children? But when we begin to consider the very large numbers of church leaders from the Ukraine, Moldova, and Rumania, as well as Russia, who left their congregations for the sake of a better life abroad, we find ourselves facing a serious and troubling question about pastoral responsibilities.

At one of the recent academic conferences at Moscow State University ('Lomonosov's Readings – 2011') a paper on contemporary Chinese Christianity was presented in a session entitled 'Religions of the countries of Asia and Africa: History and Modernity'.[30] The author referred to the 'house group' movement as 'homebred (primitive)' or undeveloped Christianity. When I asked for the reasons for such a definition, I received the explanation that there is

---

[29] J. Tipei, 'Communicating the Gospel to Postmodernity: Practical Guidelines', in Alexandru Neagoe & H.E. Zorgdrager (eds.), *Postmodernity – Friend or Foe? Communicating the Gospel to Postmodern People: Theological and Practical Reflections from Central and Eastern Europe* (Utrecht: Kerk in Actie, 2009), pp. 159-85.

[30] See A.B. Zakharyin, 'Buddhism I Khristianstvo v Kitaje. Relighija I Vlast'. Istoriya I Sovremennost' [Buddhism and Christianity in China Китае. Religion and Authority. History and Modernity], *Vestnyk Moskovskogo Universyteta* [Bulletin of Moscow State University], Ser. 13, *Oriental Studies* 4 (2011), pp. 50-65. A note on the conference may be found at <http://www.msu.ru/science/lom-read/2011/ vostok.html>.

no professionalism and there is no theological education among the ministers of these fast growing congregations. This is just an example of how the secular world of Russia today estimates the quality or the professional level of the Christian ministry in China. Indeed, the same is true in relation to national Christianity – in today's world professionalism and specialization are considered crucial in every area of social life. It is even more important for those who are responsible for 'constructing the context' (see earlier section 'The Torah and the Jewish Hermeneutics'). It is Pentecostal hermeneutics that are 'constructing' our self-identity as a Christian body/church.

Here is the shift that obviously taking place in Russian Pentecostalism (at least it is true for those who are within the 'fence' of the RUCEF): success versus suffering, marriage and counseling versus pastoral care, comparative religion versus theology, organizational-activity games versus *theosis*[31]/fellowship with God (seeking the Lord and his will) – these are just a few examples. I believe it is more vital than ever today for Russian Pentecostalism to claim our roots in Patristic tradition, especially in the writings of Gregory the Theologian, Isaac of Nineveh, and Simeon the New Theologian. Their theology, as is all Eastern spirituality, was rooted in spiritual experience, which in turn traditionally has been rooted in the Holy Scriptures. One of the great saints of the Russian church, Seraphim of Sarov (1759-1833), considered prayer, fasting, and works of mer-

---

[31] According to Plato, and the principle as old as Greek philosophy itself, the like is only known by the like, the νοῦς, the superior part of the soul, would not be able to see the ideas if the soul were not 'related to the divine, to the immortal, to the intelligence, to the simple, to the indissoluble, and to the immutable' (*Phaedon*, 80a-b). The result of this relationship between the individual and divinity is that human duty and happiness consist in absolute submission to universal reason, to follow the dictates of the divine order. Platonism remained the root of Stoicism that may be defined as a religious philosophy with its thirsting for purification, for salvation, and for divinization through personal union with God. The Pauline concept of 'deification' or *theosis* (Greek: 'making divine') – the unification of a human being with God, the theology and mysticism of the apostle, presents divinization as the direct effect of the assimilating union with the Holy Spirit. The development of this concept has been shown by the French scholar Jules Gross who has attempted to investigate the New Testament roots of this doctrine that developed in a uniquely Christian form from the time of Irenaeus onward. See J. Gross, *The Divinization of the Christian according to the Greek Fathers* (Anaheim: A&C Press, 2002), p. 44-83.

cy to be only the means, not the goal, of the Christian life, which he saw as *the acquisition of the Holy Spirit.*[32]

Conclusion

The search for a more solid and constructive dialogue between followers of Eastern and Western Christian traditions is one of humankind's most urgent tasks, especially in the light of changing cultural contexts and globalization. There is a need to remind ourselves that no Christian tradition is sufficient in itself. We have to explore ways of enhancing mutual understanding and co-operation. Exploring the spirituality of the early Church Fathers and Mothers can serve as a helpful way for Pentecostal and Charismatic believers in Russia to overcome the postmodern crisis of self-identity. It may help find in Church history answers relevant to the contemporary Russian context. The experience of the closeness of God and his intimate presence is infinitely greater for secularized society than mere theological proofs of God's existence.

There were always and there still are those who are not afraid to go beyond the fence of their own tradition. It is always a risk, and one must be well rooted in the Trinity, the Scriptures, and in a theology that is built primarily on the interpretation of Scripture and the history of its tradition. However, there is much to be learnt from all kinds of ecumenical encounter! We must not forget that theology was born and developed in dialogue. If we are to enter into any sort of dialogue with secular society, culture, and with the academic world, we must be better equipped! Theological education could and should be seen as a mission of the Church to the secular world. In our pluralistic society it is important to be open to ecumenical dialogue and to learn to hear the voices of others, other traditions of interpreting the Scripture, and other spiritual experience. We must find time and space in our busy lives for reflection, stimulation, and discussion with others who are asking similar questions in seeking the meaning of life. The task of interpreting the Bible requires also that we know ourselves in our changing contexts. This is the task that demands much from us, but also offers us hope and is worthy of all our utmost efforts.

---

[32] Burgess, *The Holy Spirit: Eastern Christian Traditions*, pp. 79-83.

SECTION III

THE GLOBAL NORTH

12

DIVINO COMPAÑERO DEL CAMINO: THE STAKES FOR LATINO PENTECOSTAL THEOLOGY IN PENTECOSTALISM'S SECOND CENTURY

DANIEL RAMÍREZ[*]

As theologians and other scholars train their sights on the possible course of global Pentecostalism in the twenty-first century, the Oxford 2012 Consultation on Global Pentecostalism affords a too rare opportunity to compare notes from different points of the compass. The geographically expansive conversation represents a welcome development. That the language of the conversation is English, however, reminds us of our continued captivity and epistemic limitations. While the diasporic people of many ethnicities who gathered around the Upper Room in Jerusalem (Acts 2) reported hearing of God's work in their own tongues, the scholarly interpretation of the new Pentecost continues to be filtered through the lingua franca – its lexicon and its epistemologies – of our time. This essay seeks to weigh the price of that paradox.

---

[*] Daniel Ramírez (PhD, Duke University) serves as Assistant Professor, North American Religious History, in the Departments of American Culture and History at the University of Michigan. He is an active member of the Red de Investigadores del Fenómeno Religioso en México and the Comisión para el Estudio de la Iglesia en Latinoamérica. He serves as Co-Chair of the History of Christianity Section of the American Academy of Religion and as History Interest Group Leader of the Society for Pentecostal Studies (2009-2012). In 2011, Ramírez was invited as an Observer to the Sixth Quinquennium of the International Catholic-Pentecostal Dialogue in Rome, Italy, under the auspices of the Pontifical Council for the Promotion of Christian Unity. He also participated as an Observer at the 2010 Centenary World Missions Conference in Edinburgh, Scotland.

To accomplish this the essay turns from the universal to the particular, in this case to the borderlands experience of Latino/a populations in the United States and their kin in Latin America. The 'borderlands' I reference entail a more elastic concept and experience that stretch beyond the geographical swatch that runs from the California Pacific to the Gulf of Mexico. 'Borderlands' also refers to a positionality, to paraphrase the nineteenth-century Cuban American writer (the exiled – to New York – father of Cuban independence) José Martí, within 'the entrails of the beast'. Such a vantage point or, as cultural theorist Walter Mignolo calls it, locus of enunciation can provide a clearer space to hear the emerging Latino/a Pentecostal theological discourse.[1] That discourse carries a special resonance at the interstices of two societies. It also reflects a long-overdue attention to corporeal, sonic, and musical spheres. Following an illustrative vignette, I will trace briefly the course of US Latino Pentecostal thought through the last two decades, offer some methodological considerations, and then return to the matter of the high stakes at play in the exchange between Pentecostalisms of the global North and South.

November 1993, Hotel Fénix, Guadalajara, Mexico – The first question from the floor was directed to the US and Canadian members of the plenary roundtable, all leading lights of the Society for Pentecostal Studies: '¿Cual es su opinion sobre los peligros del neoliberalismo para el bienestar de la miembresía de nuestras Iglesias latinoamericanas, y qué pueden hacer la Iglesias norteamericanas para frenar su expansion?' The convener, Dr Manuel Gaxiola, a Fuller Seminary and University of Birmingham trained theologian, Apostolic church leader, and professional translator of academic texts, ably translated the challenge: 'What is your opinion of the dangers that neoliberalism poses for the welfare of our church members in Latin America, and what can the North American churches do to slow its expansion?' From the response, however, it was obvious that something more than expert translation was needed. 'We should be wary of all currents of liberalism that can sway the Church. Perhaps we in North American can do a better job of publishing materials to help the Church in Latin America mature

---

[1] Walter D. Mignolo, *Local Histories/Global Designs: Coloniality, Subaltern Knowledges, and Border Thinking* (Princeton: Princeton University Press, 2000).

theologically and be on her guard.' While my recollection of the exact phrasing of the reply may not be precise, it does capture the gist of the exchange. I do recall clearly the looks of astonishment in the faces of the several Latin American and Latino scholars and church leaders, the embarrassment of the translator, and my own bemusement at yet another squandered opportunity for dialogue between the Pentecostal global North and South.

For its 20th annual meeting, the Society for Pentecostal Studies (SPS), in an unprecedented move, owing of course to Manuel Gaxiola's leadership (he was the Society's first non-US president), had convened in a city whose royal charter as Nueva Galicia predated by a century the founding of New England. With the best of intentions, no doubt, SPS regulars gathered to compare notes with an unprecedented number of Latin American scholars. However, the separate siting of parallel language tracks made for little meaningful contact between the delegations. The English-language sessions were held in the conference hotel and the Spanish ones at a Congregational church in another part of the city; hence, the heightened importance of the plenary and worship sessions. But even in the shared *site* of the plenary, folks' *sight* of the looming future (and present) proved vastly different, as evidenced in the multivalence of the above *cites*.

Why the urgency of the matter in the minds and hearts of Latin American Pentecostals? At that moment, further south in Mexico, a revolt was smoldering, threatening to smudge the ink on the still-drying North American Free Trade Agreement. On January 1, 1994, the very day of NAFTA's implementation, indigenous and mestizo rebels rose up in armed protest against late capitalism's exclusionary new paradigm and wrapped their struggle with the revolutionary mantle of Emiliano Zapata, the long-ago champion of agrarian reform and land redistribution. President Salinas de Gortari dispatched the federal army and state and local police. The armed skirmishes and long aftermath evoked a hemispheric and global chorus of criticism against the processes and exigencies of economic globalization enshrined in the NAFTA accord, one of economic neoliberalism's charter documents. In the face of the economic onslaught, Latin American church leaders and scholars pondered with alarm the consequences for their flock, especially in the vulnerable countryside. There, the erasure of protectionist arrangements (owing to NAFTA's rules), the flood of heavily subsidized corn from the United States (in contravention of NAFTA's rules), and the dismantling of agrarian reform communities (a parallel neoliberal reform of President Salinas) threatened to overwhelm and uproot subsistence farmers into a transnational pool of cheap labor. 'Free trade' between a Goliath and a David did not ensure *fair* trade.

Clearly, a more prophetic challenge could not have been put forth to the SPS roundtable. Indeed, in the NAFTA period, as predicted, rural migration, especially from southern Mexico and Central America, intensified. Among the desperate peasantry-turned-migrating proletariat were thousands of Pentecostals. Of course, lacking the social and economic capital of more elite countrymen – the advocates and beneficiaries of NAFTA and neoliberalism – and given the tiny legal funnel, their entry into the US labor force took place by irregular means via channels set in place over many decades. Once in the US, they replenished and reinvigorated Pentecostal congregations, especially Latino ones and including many in the flagship denominations like the Assemblies of God and the United Pentecostal Church International.[2] The vast majority of labor migrants, of course, were Catholic; thus, the American Catholic Church also gathered in many sheaves. At the same time, the new immigration wave, especially the one coursing through Arizona toward new places of destination in the Southeast, Midwest, and Northeast, revived or reinforced xenophobia among certain sectors of the US electorate. The events of 9-11 and economic turmoil later in the last decade intensified those sentiments.

From their comfortable perch in North American Zion, Canadian and US Pentecostals could only imagine the danger being alluded to in Guadalajara was coming from an as yet unknown (to them) theological current swirling somewhere in the hemisphere. A second-generation liberation theology perhaps? More importantly, who was minding orthodoxy's store? And how could Springfield and Cleveland help arrest the allure of heterodoxy? Obviously, the incommensurabilities stretched further than mere differences in lexicons. They also included differences in loci of enunciation and ep-

---

[2] Sammy Alfaro reports estimates by denominational leaders of a 91.2% growth in Latino adherents in the Assemblies of God from 1980 to 1997 versus a 7.7% growth in Anglo geographical districts. Sammy Alfaro, *Divino Compañero: Toward a Hispanic Pentecostal Christology* (Eugene: Wipf and Stock, 2010), pp. 2-3.

istemic-experiential prisms. The Pentecostal South, whose theological reflection and religious practice were shaped by economic exigencies, was decrying inequitable arrangements in the production and consumption of food. The Pentecostal North, in response, pledged to produce better food for thought. Put simply, these were ships passing in the night.

Clearly, disparate (and desperate) existential circumstances (sites) can make for vastly different ways of seeing (sights) the world and one's place and vocation in it, as well as for different questions (cites) that one sees fit to pose to it. A shared religiosity does not necessarily mitigate this problem; indeed, it may blind us to it. Scholars are not exempt from this epistemological constraint.

In the same period as the SPS Guadalajara meeting, new theological voices began to issue clarion calls out of that captivity. The publishing of what we might call Latino Pentecostal academic theology began with Eldin Villafañe's 1992 *The Liberating Spirit: Toward an Hispanic American Pentecostal Social Ethic* and his 1995 *Seek the Peace of the City: Reflections on Urban Ministry*.[3] Both works built upon Villafañe's long tenure as founding director of Gordon-Conwell Theological Seminary's Center for Urban Ministerial Education (CUME) in Boston. CUME at that time was, except for Fuller Seminary's Hispanic program in Pasadena, California, the only such seminary-tied program with a broad Latino church constituency in the United States. While both institutions emerged out of the US Fundamentalist-to-evangelical and Reform continuum or matrix, Latino Pentecostals excavated out in each important leadership roles. Villafañe, a product of the historic Juan 3:16 church in New York City and doctoral student at Boston University, led CUME for over a decade-and-a-half, at times co-teaching with Harvey Cox of Harvard Divinity School. Another Asambleas de Dios minister, Harvard Divinity-trained Issac Canales, headed up Fuller's program from 1992 to 1999. In 1998, Samuel Solivan (also Asambleas de Dios) published *The Spirit, Pathos and Liberation: Toward an Hispanic Pentecostal Theology*.[4] At that time he served as Professor of Christian Theology at Ando-

---

[3] Eldin Villafañe, *The Liberating Spirit: Toward an Hispanic American Pentecostal Social Ethic* (Lanham, MD: University Press of America, 1992); *idem, Seek the Peace of the City: Reflections on Urban Ministry* (Grand Rapids: Eerdmans, 1995).

[4] Samuel Solivan, *The Spirit, Pathos and Liberation: Toward an Hispanic Pentecostal Theology* (JPTSup 14; Sheffield: Sheffield Academic Press, 1998).

ver Newton Theological School, having succeeded his mentor, the late missiologist Orlando Costas.

That succession was not accidental. The early Latino Pentecostal theological corpus was trenchant with proto-liberationist themes common to Costas's and others' work. Villafañe chose as his *locus theologicus* the setting and process of the Latino Pentecostal church service, carefully noting the tentativeness of his search for an implicit theology. Echoing Costas and Brazilian liberationist Leonardo Boff (with whom Villafañe was in conversation), Villafañe observed that the Latino Pentecostal church's:

> mere *presence* in the barrios is a prophetic testimony concerning:
> 1) the principalities and powers, viewed as institutions and/or persons that dehumanize the children of God; 2) the other churches and denominations that have abandoned our barrios or refused to enter them; 3) the very inhabitants of the barrios, who are challenged and called to forgiveness, hope and community; and 4) the believers themselves, who are challenged and called to not accept their status quo.[5]

For Villafañe, Latino Pentecostal congregations evidenced a multidimensional theology: contextual, spiritual, personalist, existential, liberative, charismatic, and democratic. Then, borrowing from sociological theory on conflict, anomie and structure, and church-sect, and building on theological critiques of 'principalities and powers', he urged Latino Pentecostals to attune themselves to the grieved and brooding Spirit over creation and to widen their theological vision to encompass the social and institutional dimensions of the 'mystery of iniquity'.[6] The prophecy and liberation ar-

---

[5] Eldin Villafañe, *El Espíritu libertador. Hacia una ética social pentecostal hispanoamericana* (Buenos Aires and Grand Rapids: Nueva Creación and Eerdmans, 1996), p. 112. I translated the passage from this Spanish version of the earlier English book (1992). Villafañe (pp. 216-17) references an exchange with Leonardo Boff at a Petrópolis, Brazil, gathering of Latin American liberation theologians, wherein the latter responded with four positive attributes of Pentecostal churches in his country's *favelas*: 1) at the very least a rescue of dignity; 2) religious resistance; 3) spiritual liberation; and 4) a launched challenge to society.

[6] Among the authors engaged by Villafañe: Walter Wink, *Naming the Powers: The Language of Powers in the New Testament* (Philadelphia: Fortress Press, 1984); idem, *Unmasking the Powers: The Invisible Forces that Determine Human Existence* (Philadelphia: Fortress Press, 1986; John H. Yoder, *The Priestly Kingdom: Social Ethics as Gospel* (Notre Dame: University of Notre Dame Press, 1984); Stephen C. Mott, *Etica bíblica y cambio social* (Buenos Aires: Nueva Creación, 1995). Importantly,

ticulated in Latino Pentecostalism, then, should match the deep and broad field of sin in which creation finds itself enmeshed.

Like Villafañe and anticipating Sammy Alfaro's later work (see below), Samuel Solivan posited the Latino religious experience as one important point of departure:

> In the face of what some may see to be hopelessness, the Hispanic church sings. In the face of oppression, it proclaims liberty to the captives, and in the absence of medical care, it engages in healing. In the presence of the collapse of family in our society, it welcomes dysfunctional families into community. The Hispanic church lives subconsciously and at times consciously in the eschatological hope of the not-yet. It dares not forget the memory of its suffering. Furthermore, it does not allow the sufferings of the past to define the expectations of mañana.[7]

Solivan offered several striking insights, including the understanding of Latino inner diversity as a cultural glossolalia that equips a borderlands people for a role as mediators and interlocutors between cultural, linguistic, and epistemic systems. Latino Pentecostals, in particular, could serve as interlocutors between different wings of Christian thought and practice: the evangelical and liberationist. Along this latter line, his most innovative idea was that of orthopathos, a recovery of the sensibility of the brooding Spirit – especially from the vantage point of the poor – and a recovery of the liberative understanding of truth ('the truth shall set you free') in the Church's expression of orthodoxy and orthopraxis:

> *Orthopathos* seeks to correct the absence of human pathos in most orthodox theology by pointing to how the Holy Spirit works in and through our brokenness to bring us to benefits of Christ.
>
> *Orthopathos* seeks to be the third leg of a new theological triad, a bridge or link between orthodoxy and orthopraxis, a living link

---

Villafañe distances his argument from John Wimber's notion of spiritual warfare, which Villafañe views as too individualistic and mismatched to the geography of evil, that is, social structures of sin and evil. Villafañe, *El Espíritu libertador,* p. 173. John Wimber, *Power Evangelism* (San Francisco: Harper and Row, 1986).

[7] Solivan, *The Spirit, Pathos and Liberation,* p. 135.

that witnesses to the liberating power of the Holy Spirit in and through the lives of suffering people.

Orthopathos seeks to raise a different set of questions, to bring a different perspective to doctrinal construction and to revitalize and ground orthopraxis and orthodoxy in the soil of the pain and suffering of the people. Orthopathos seeks to remind orthodoxy of its humanity and the pathos of God and to call orthopraxis back to the place of its much needed incarnation.[8]

Again, it is notable that both writers imbedded their analysis in the setting and practice of Latino churches in the US Northeast, from New York to Boston. In moving from the practice to theory and back to practice, the exemplified one of the central insights of liberation theology: praxis. That both Villafañe and Solivan marked out dialogical territory with currents and methods of liberationism should not surprise us, especially when we consider their intellectual mentors and interlocutors: Orlando Costas (Baptist), Justo Gonzales (Methodist), Carmelo Alvarez (Disciples), and others from historic Protestant traditions, as well as Catholic thinkers such as Enrique Dussel, Gustavo Gutiérrez, Leonardo Boff, Virgilio Elizondo, Ada María Isasi Diaz, Juan Luis Segundo, and Andrés Guerrero. Both New York and Boston also afforded dialogical opportunities with Black theology, including, of course, the work of James Cone of Union Theological Seminary.

In other words, Latino Pentecostal theology has represented as much, if not more, a conversation with other Latino and Latino American Christian theologians including René Padilla and others from the Fraternidad Teológica Latinoamericana, the Consejo Latinoamericano de Iglesias, and the Seminario Biblico Latinoamericano in Costa Rica, as with other (i.e. white) US Pentecostals. To be sure, they have engaged such vanguard thinkers as Steven Land, Cheryl Bridges Johns, Doug Peterson, and Murray Dempster.[9]

---

[8] Solivan, *The Spirit, Pathos and Liberation*, p. 148.
[9] Steven Land, *Pentecostal Spirituality: A Passion for the Kingdom* (JPTSup 1, Sheffield: Sheffield Academic, 1993); Cheryl Bridges Johns, *Pentecostal Formation: A Pedagogy among the Oppressed* (JPTSup 2, Sheffield: Sheffield Academic, 1993); Douglas Peterson, *Not by Might, Nor by Power: A Pentecostal Theology of Social Concern in Latin America* (Oxford: Regnum, 1996); Murray Dempster, Byron Klaus, and Douglas Peterson, *The Globalization of Pentecostalism: A Religion Made to Travel* (Irvine: Regnum, 1999).

The SPS and its journals have provided a valuable venue for this. But this is only half of the story. The contemporaneous emergence in the last two decades of such networks as the Asociación para la Educación Teológica Hispana, the Hispanic Summer Program, and the Hispanic Theological Initiative have allowed for a purposeful cross-fertilization of theological thought across confessional boundaries, including the all-important Pentecostal–Catholic one. In the case of the latter two programs, the collaborative trust of founders Justo Gonzalez and Virgilio Elizondo has modeled a remarkable ecumenical equanimity, setting a bar that many younger theologians and other scholars have been challenged to emulate.

Finally, for the purpose of discussion, the work of Pentecostal-raised but Mainline-trained and identified prodigals has introduced Pentecostal sensibilities into the broader theological guild. If continuity rather than rupture is our guiding principle, then a modest Pentecostal claim can still be made on the important work of Efrain Agosto, a New Testament scholar, Daisy Machado, a historian-theologian and Dean of Union Theological Seminary, and Benjamon Valentín, an emerging public theologian who currently occupies the Orlando Costas chair at Andover-Newton Theological Seminary.[10] Valentín has challenged Latino/a theologians to de-ghettoize (or de-barrioize) their thought, in order to make it more accessible to a broader public – to engage the particular with the universal. The title of Valentín's 2002 book is telling: *Mapping Public Theology: Beyond Culture, Identity and Difference* (2002). Given his willingness to take on certain sacred cows, namely important pioneering notions such as mestizaje, teologia en cunjunto (theology as a collective enterprise), and mujerista (Latin womanist) theology, Valentín's trenchant critique marks a point of maturation in Latino/a theology generally.

The final two and more recent theological voices to consider come to us from a different point on the US regional and denominational compass.[11] Notably, Daniel Castelo and Samuel Alfaro

---

[10] Efraín Agosto, *Servant Leadership: Jesus and Paul* (Chalice Press, 2005); *idem*, 'Paul vs. Empire: A Postcolonial and Latino Reading of Philippians', *Perspectivas* 6 (Fall 2002), pp. 37-56.

[11] This discussion does not include a more recent entry, Nestor Medina, a University of Toronto trained Guatemalan-Canadian theologian (Pentecostal Assemblies of Canada) at Regent University. Medina's work has focused on Catholic theology.

emerge out of the Sonoran-Arizona Church of God borderlands. The former, a Duke trained ethicist, has engaged the work of Stanley Hauerwas and Will Willimon on Christian alienation from the world, and has upped the ante. While Hauerwas and Willimon describe Christians as 'resident aliens' voluntarily living out their countercultural faith in 'colonies' (church) in the world,[12] Castelo emphasizes the double-alienation experienced by folks who are at once both Christian (voluntary alienation) and excluded non-citizens of the nation-state in which they reside (imposed alienation). For Castelo, their testimony from the shadowy margins of society reminds American Christians of the tentativeness of their ease and comfort in Constantinian Zion. What the nation-state gives the nation-state can take away. The illegal alien presence also demands a welcoming hospitality too rarely seen in our current xenophobic moment.[13]

Castelo's musings are not far removed from (or far ahead of) the actual practice of Latino Pentecostal churches. He has merely fleshed out theologically what Pentecostals of the Southwest and Midwest (and now elsewhere throughout the country) have been practicing for over a century: a pre-critical but biblically informed hospitality toward the sojourner. In other words, a gut-level solidarity. With few exceptions, Latino Pentecostals throughout the twentieth century saw their churches as divine altars and doorways to heaven, or, to mix metaphors, as salvation vessels in the stream of a migrating humanity. We can find traces of this practice in the songs of Zion they sang to each other, songs that undergirded and informed their practice. The current moment of interdisciplinary sensibility has allowed for a scholarly retrospective on that praxis. (I will return to this point below).

Today, US Latino Pentecostals remain at the front seeking and practicing justice for the stranger. Two leaders, in particular, have acquired notoriety for their brokering of political dialogue between major presidential candidates and *evangélicos*: Samuel Rodriguez, President of the National Hispanic Christian Leadership Confer-

---

[12] Stanley Hauerwas and William Willimon, *Resident Aliens: Life in the Christian Colony* (Nashville: Abingdon Press, 1989); *idem, Where Resident Aliens Live: Exercises for Christian Practice* (Nashville: Abingdon Press, 1996).

[13] Daniel Castelo, 'Resident *and* Illegal Aliens', *Apuntes* 23.2 (Summer 2003), pp. 65-77.

ence and Hispanic National Association of Evangelicals and Gabriel Salguero of the National Latino Evangelical Coalition. The former, an Assemblies of God pastor in Sacramento, California, has made comprehensive immigration reform the deal-breaker between Republicans and their ostensibly conservative allies: Latino evangelicals. Salguero, who pastors a Nazarene church in New York City, has brought a Pentecostal fire to gatherings of the Christian Community Development Association and to the conclaves of progressive Evangelicals (Sojourners/Call to Renewal). Interestingly, both leaders are Nuyorican, as is the most prominent congressional advocate for comprehensive immigration reform, Representative Louis Gutierrez of Chicago.[14] Puerto Ricans, of course, hold US citizenship; their advocacy for Mexican and Central American undocumented immigrants stands in stark contrast to Cuban American political and religious leadership. Below the radar of most political commentators, several Pentecostal bishops and pastors and many laypersons could be found in pro-immigrant marches of 2006. In May 2010, Chicago-area Apostolic pastor Martin Santellano, striken over the family disintegration caused by ICE (Immigration Control and Enforcement) raids, initiated a fast call to moratorium of such deportations. In this he lifted a page from farmworker leader Cesar Chavez and, for that matter, the ancient Hebrew agitator Mordecai, Esther's troublesome uncle. Santellano's life-endangering actions

---

[14] To be sure, Latino/a Pentecostals and ex-Pentecostals have long been active in the social and civic sphere, as seen in the career and rhetoric of land grants advocate Reis López Tijerina (Arizona and New Mexico), the early support of Apostolic farmworkers for Cesar Chavez (central California), and the urban ministries of Leoncia 'Mama Leo' Rosado Rousseau, Ana Villafañe, Aimee García Cortese, and Rosa Caraballo (New York City). The latter context drew admiring comments from Nuyorican writer Piri Thomas, who, like James Baldwin a generation earlier, was a prodigal of the movement. Piri Thomas, *Savior, Savior, Hold my Hand* (New York: Doubleday, 1972), pp. 19-20, cited in Villafañe, *El Espítu libertador*, pp. 112-13. Recent scholarship in history, sociology, anthropology, ethnomusicology, and political science has begun to excavate these stories. See Elizabeth Rios, 'The Ladies are Warriors: Latina Pentecostalism and Faith-Based Activism in New York City', in Gastón Espinosa, Virgilio Elizondo, and Jesse Miranda, *Latino Religions and Civic Activism in the United States* (Oxford: Oxford University Press, 2005), pp. 197-217; Daniel Ramírez, 'Public Lives in American Hispanic Churches: Expanding the Paradigm', pp. 178-95; *idem*, 'Borderlands Praxis: The Immigrant Experience in Latino Pentecostal Churches', *Journal of the American Academy of Religion* 67.3 (Fall, 1999), pp. 573-96; Rudy Busto, *King Tiger: The Religious Vision of Reies López Tijerina* (Albuquerque: University of New Mexico Press, 2005).

(his sons joined him) eventually attracted Mainline support. Catholic, Episcopalian, and Methodist clergy (who had harbored the notorious undocumented activist Elvira Arellano and her son) and even Jesse Jackson took up the fast chain. Within months, the Obama administration declared a halt to the raids. The new federal directives targeted more criminal elements among the undocumented migrant population and afforded more administrative discretion to ICE officials in the case of deleterious family outcomes. In other words, mercy, and justice kissed briefly. As Pentecostals, of course, Santellano and others possessed the insouciance to believe that their prayers for heavenly succor would be answered. The Antorcha Guadalupana movement, an annual Catholic-inspired relay of a torch from the Basilica of the Gualdalupe in Mexico City to St Patrick's Cathedral in New York City declares a similar hope.

This activism brings us to the theological project of Sammy Alfaro, who calls for an emphatic shift to pneumatic Christology as both a more accurate reflection of Latino Pentecostal experience and, importantly, as a bridge for that most intractable intra-Pentecostal divide of all, the Trinitarian-Oneness one.[15] Alfaro notes that the early doctrinal rupture within (White) American Pentecostalism not only pushed the Assemblies of God into a hyper-creedal reactive mode but also locked in Christological positions that exacerbated the divide. Ironically, these positions squandered the very pneumatic sensibility that the new Pentecost offered and disdained the hyper-Christology offered by the Oneness camp. From a century's distance, Alfaro offers a Spirit-Christology, one that is less refracted through contextual Chalcedonian lenses (he does not discount Chalcedon's Logos Christology, but rather recognizes its contingency)[16] and one that is more illumined through,

---

[15] Sammy Alfaro, *Divino Compañero: Toward a Hispanic Pentecostal Christology* (Eugene: Wipf and Stock, 2010). I estimate that Oneness Pentecostals comprise about one-half of Mexican and Mexican American Pentecostals, a proportion much higher than that seen in White and Black US Pentecostalism. See my pessimistic assessment – owing in part to the lack of representation or recognition of this important difference – of the SPS-sponsored Trinitarian-Oneness Pentecostal Dialogue in Daniel Ramírez, 'A Historian's Response: Final Report of the Trinitarian-Oneness Pentecostal Dialogue', *Pneuma* 30.2 (2008) pp. 245-54.

[16] Alfaro engages with, among others, the Spirit-Christological projects of Geoffrey Lampe, Paul Newman, and James Dunn. Geoffrey W.H. Lampe, *God as Spirit* (Oxford: Clarendon, 1977); Paul Newman, *A Spirit Christology: Recovering the Biblical Paradigm of Christian Faith* (New York: University Press of America, 1987);

well, Pentecostal experience of the borderlands. He also takes square aim at Prosperity Gospel schemes. Alfaro offers a hint of where he is headed in his discussion of liberation Christology:

> Building on the concept of Jesus as the liberator of the poor and the oppressed, Christology takes on a different form. Instead of simply hypothesizing about what exactly happened at the incarnation, how one can understand the nature of the person of Jesus, or what theories of atonement make the most sense, liberation Christology turns to the ethical demands the historical Jesus made and continues to make. Given that the historical Jesus committed his life to the service of those in need of liberation, all theologizing about his life should inevitably be aligned with the convictions he held. Through the lens of the marginalized, thus, the Jesus of history becomes the focal point in which God expresses his solidarity with the victims of every kind of injustice. In short, the understanding of the salvific work of Jesus – his life, death and resurrection – take on new meaning for those suffering all types of oppression.[17]

Like his predecessors, Alfaro dialogues freely with Latino/a and Latin American theologies. Even more than these, he proposes a deep exploration of the theological notions evident in Latino/a Pentecostalism's own musical archive of the twentieth century.[18] Given my own work in history and ethnomusicology, I welcome this interdisciplinary turn. Given the thin textual archives of the first decades – migrating and farmworker Pentecostals had little time to systematize their understanding of God but plenty of time declare in word and song the mighty works of God – scholars would do

---

James D.G. Dunn, *The Christ and the Spirit: Collected Essays of James D.G. Dunn* (2 vols.; Grand Rapids: Eerdmans, 1998).

[17] Alfaro, *Divino Compañero*, p. 104.

[18] Samuel Solivan anticipated this methodological turn: 'The orthopathic work of the Holy Spirit is grounded in love and seeks out reconciliation among us all. This is one of the early fruits of the presence of orthopathos in our lives. Music and song are probably the most powerful tools for expressing and maintaining our sense of community. In song and music we bear witness to our diversity and our commonality in knowing the peace of God among us. What we sing is often more telling about who we are as a people and what we believe and hope for than any other single piece of data. Only as we join others different from ourselves will we come to know a fuller and richer experience of the orthopathic work of the Spirit' (Solivan, *The Spirit, Pathos and Liberation*, p. 144).

well to expand their analytical toolkits to consider artefacts of musical culture.

Appropriately, Alfaro titles his monograph with an old borderlands *himno* that appropriates (and collapses) the Emmaus Road post-resurrection story, the Jericho Road parable, and the account of the Sea of Galilee storm-calming to convey the existential melancholy and hope of migrating faith:

Divino Compañero	Divine Companion
Divinio compañero del camino,	Divine companion of the way,
tu presencia siento yo al transitar.	I feel your presence as I walk
Ella ha disipado toda sombra.	It has dissipated every shadow.
Ya tengo luz, la luz divina de	I now have light, the divine light of
tu amor	his love.

Coro	Chorus
Quédate, Señor, ya se hace tarde.	Stay, Lord, it's getting late.
Te ofrezco el corazón para morar.	I offer you my heart to stay.
Hazlo	
tu morada permanente. Acéptalo,	Make it your permanent dwelling.
acéptalo, mi Salvador.	Accept it, accept it, my Savior

La sombra de la noche se aproxima.	The shadow of the night is nearing.
Y en ella el tentador acechará.	In it the temptor will waylay.
No me dejes sólo en el camino.	Don't leave me alone on the road.
Ayúdame, ayúdame hasta llegar.	Help me, help me until I arrive.

Contigo la jornada se hace corta.	With you the road seems short.
No habrá sed ni sol fatigará.	There'll be no thirst and no tiring sun.
Si en el mar las olas amenazan,	If on the sea the waves threaten,
tú sobre ellas majestuoso andarás.	You will stride majestically on them.

Alfaro finds the song particularly resonant, owing to his own immigrant experience and to the hymn's provenance. Like almost one-third of the original Spanish-language corpus of Latino Oneness Pentecostalism, the song displays a traveling or sojourning motif. When sung in corporate worship, whether as a solo affirmed by a weeping congregation or as a weepy congregational song, and when wrapped in a common *ranchera* musical genre, 'Divino Compañero' articulates a vision of accompaniment, of solidarity, of bread breaking and solidarity. This allows Alfaro to argue, not for a substitution of prior Pentecostal theological schemas, but rather for their expansion:

In part, the road toward a holistic Pentecostal theology has already been paved, but we need to expand it. By this, I mean that we need to reinterpret our christocentric fivefold gospel from a corporate and not merely an individualistic understanding. For Jesus is not just our personal Savior; he is the Redeemer of the world. Jesus is not just our personal Sanctifier; he yearns to bring corporate sanctification to the church and society. He is not just our personal Healer, but also the One who can deliver all people from every social evil. He does not baptize us with his Spirit for our own personal enjoyment; he does so to send us out on a Spirit-led mission to the poor and the oppressed. Lastly, Christ is not just our Coming King; but the Proclaimer of God's reign among us – a reign that does not operate only in the spiritual dimensions, but that denounces injustice and demands a praxis of love and justice. I believe that such a vision can be undertaken and put to practice as we wrestle with the meaning of life and mission of Jesus in the power of the Spirit.

As Pentecostal leaders and thinkers map out the course of this young century, it will be interesting to see whether they chart a disempowering (in the sense of emptying out of oneself so that the Spirit can take charge) or a triumphalistic trajectory. The case of the Edinburgh World Missions Conference of 1910 should be instructive. When the global (read US and European) leaders of Protestant missions agencies met to take stock of the previous one hundred years and to project the following one hundred ones, their prodigious organizing skills and privileged location atop the Anglo-American empire blinded them to the nascent Pentecostal revivalism sprouting up in far-flung corners and niches. As we all now know, their assumptions skewed their vision. During the ensuing century, Christianity's center of gravity was blown southward by pneumatic winds.

Certainly, Alfaro and others in his guild do not discount the significance of numerical growth; there is much to celebrate here. Their caution is over the fidelity of the Pentecostal witness in the midst of that success. That witness can be seen and heard in the Emmaus and Jericho roads of our globalizing time, the roads and seaways that lead from the global South to the global North and back. Like Paul and Silas, Latino Pentecostals exercise their prerogatives of citizenship in a powerful nation to move about freely in the world. But like Paul writing to the Philippians, they also are mindful of protecting the anonymity of the brethren who live as second-class citizens or as non-citizens in Ceasar's household, under the very nose of power. This consciousness makes for an ambivalent patriotism and for a critical stance vis-à-vis the allure of Constantinian cooptation, whether economic or political. It also makes for a witness to the broader Church, as Samuel Solivan notes in his conclusion:

> Hispanic Americans are a boundary people, a people on the margins. As such we can potentially serve as interlocutors between various communities and cultures. As a multi-racial, multi-ethnic and multilingual community, the Hispanic American church can serve as a model for Christian unity and diversity. This is a difficult task because we too have learned well the lessons of our oppressors. Yet we dare to believe and hope that the pathos of God in Jesus Christ, in the power of the Holy Spirit, that has transformed our pathos and alienation into liberation, will give us the discernment to act in love and justice for all people, the poor and all those who suffer.[19]

A Historical and Ethnomusicological Postscript

It is gratifying to engage in an interdisciplinary conversation with theologians of the early twenty-first century. As a historian, I hesitate to conjecture about the future course of Pentecostalism, whether global or Latino. My analysis of the data from Latino Pentecostalism's first century, however, persuades me that even in the midst of calamity, what people may mean for evil is often used for good. Consider the borderlands Apostolic story.

Mexicans and Mexican Americans witnessed the very first perforation of Azusa Street's revivalism well in Los Angeles in 1906. Many others arrived to draw the waters in the ensuing months and years. A migrating people, they then carried Azusa's revivalism to the border zone, to several agricultural valleys and mining towns in the US Southwest and to points in northern Mexico and southern Texas.

---

[19] Solivan, *The Spirit, Pathos and Liberation*, p. 149.

The expansion took place precisely at a moment of extreme vulnerability. The history of the massive repatriation of Mexicans from the United States in the 1930s is not well known; but it remains instructive. As American political leaders cast about for blame and solutions to the Great Depression of 1929, they settled on a perennial scapegoat: Mexicans. Federal, state, county, and local authorities colluded in a massive campaign, starting with raids in Los Angeles – to leverage out by force or persuasion (what Mitt Romney now proposes as 'self-deportation') this now unwanted population. According to the historian Abraham Hoffman, nearly half a million (458,039) were pushed out of the country, including many children born in the US.[20] This represented a considerable demographic loss, about 35%, since the census of 1930 counted 1.3 million Mexicans in the US.[21] The social and political ramifications were incalculable. The 'exodus' also uprooted one out of every three Pentecostals.

As in the case of the earliest Christians fleeing Jerusalem for Antioch, however, the uprooting led to growth. When adversity struck in the form of forced return, many Pentecostals alighted upon and stretched webs of religious kinship, thereby expanding the movement's reach into new regions of Mexico, such as the western states of Sinaloa, Nayarit, and Jalisco and the Federal District. These Apostolic repatriates, together with their coreligionists who remained in the US, then set about weaving a transnational safety net out of both symbolic and material strands. The movement's transnational web proved supple in the face of prejudicial and favorable macro events. Within a decade-and-a-half of their forced return, Apostolic repatriates, together with their coreligionists in the United States, forged cross-border ecclesial agreements and structures that allowed

---

[20] Abraham Hoffman, *Unwanted Mexican Americans in the Great Depression: Repatriation Pressures, 1929-1939* (Tucson: University of Arizona Press, 1974), p. 32.

[21] <http://www.census.gov/apsd/wepeople/we-2r.pdf>. Historians Francisco Balderrama and Raymond Rodríguez argue for a number double that of Hoffman's. Francisco E. Balderrama and Raymond Rodríguez, *Decade of Betrayal: Mexican Repatriation in the 1930s* (Albuquerque: University of New Mexico Press, 1995), pp. 121-22. Historian Fernando Alanis has cautioned against the duo's methodology, arguing instead for Hoffman's more conservative number. Fernando Saúl Alanis Enciso, 'El impacto en la frontera México-Estados Unidos de la repatriación masiva de mexicanos durante la Gran Depresion, 1929-1934' (Paper Presented at the II Seminario sobre Transnacionalismo, Mexico-North Research Network, México, D.F., 7 August 2003). The ratio of repatriation remains significant, nevertheless.

their movement to ride the crest of migratory labor flows (Bracero program, 1942-64), endure perennial bouts of political xenophobia (Operation Wetback, 1954) in the US, and maximize the Immigration reforms of 1965 and 1986.

The robust historical agency of migratory and repatriated Apostolics can be gleaned from the movement's scattered records: transborder conclave documents; congregational, family, and life histories; congregational minutes and records; denominational records and periodicals; letters of recommendation carried by migrating workers; and hymnody. As noted, Alfaro discovered in the latter repertoire an artifact that allowed him to understand the movement's Christological vision. I wish to share one more.

The following song emerged on the eve of the newly intensified xenophobia of the early 1990s (its references to amnesty dates it around the time of the Immigration Reform and Control Act of 1983). It speaks to the ultimate questions of citizenship and belonging and to God's inscrutable ways beyond the intent of nation states and the powerful men that run them. In the corrido, 'Los Indocumentados', mariachi composer Ramón '*El Solitario*' González, who has at least sixteen recording projects to his credit, captures the complex motivations at play in transnational human movement. The ethical ambivalence concerning the matter of undocumented crossing and residency contrasts with the celebration of divine encounter in the wake of homesickness and disappointment with the fabled 'American Dream'. The prodigal son acquires heroic status as a converted migrant poised to return home to share his good news with kin. Whatever Pentecostal stories are told over the course of the movement's second century, they must surely include the ones from the underside of history, from the global South, from the borderlands.

Los Indocumentados
Author Ramón González

Dejé mi patria esperando encontrarme
Con una vida diferente a mi pasado
Y me introduje aquí en la union Americana
Sin pasaporte llegué bien indocumentado

Con ambición de conseguir ciudadanía
Traté de inmediato de que me dieran trabajo
Y como estaba ya a las puertas la amnistía
Conseguí cartas aunque todo fuera falso

Me habían dicho que en este país no hay hambre
Y que el dinero se conseguía en abundancia
Por esta causa abandoné yo a mis padres
Para acabar con la pobreza en que yo estaba

Y ahora me encuentro solo en un país extraño
Y les confieso que hasta veces he llorado
Cuando me acuerdo de mis seres tan queridos
Nomás mi Dios por puro amor me ha consolado

A tí, Señor, que cuidas del desamparado
Pido que nunca de tu gracia me abandones
Si en otro tiempo te ofendía en mi arrogancia
Arrepentido hoy te pido que me perdones

Al otro día por la noche yo buscaba
Una persona que de Dios me diera razón
Frente a una esquina una iglesia se encontraba
Pasar adentro me invitó mi corazón

Oí el mensaje que el ministro mencionaba
De una nación que Cristo había preparado
Donde no hay hambres ni dolores ni tristezas
Ese nación es la que siempre había soñado

Me convertí yo ilusionado al evangelio
Y espero un día compartirselo a mis padres
Cuando regrese yo a mi tierra espero verlos
De Jesucristo y de su amor yo quiero hablarles

Si a este país llegamos a buscar dinero
Y el evangelio de Jesús nos ha salvado
Salí ganando y de esto nunca me averguenzo
Nos ha pasado a muchos indocumentados

The Undocumented Ones
(translation mine)

I left my country hoping to find
A life different from my past one
And I slipped into the American Union (US)
Without a passport I arrived quite undocumented

Eager to obtain citizenship
I looked immediately for work
And since amnesty was just around the corner
I obtained documents, though all was false

I've been told there was no hunger in this land
And that money could be hand in abundance
For this reason I abandoned my parents
To end the poverty in which I lived

And now I find myself alone in a strange land
And I confess to you that sometimes I have cried
When I remember my very dear loved ones
Only my God out of pure love has consoled me

To you, Lord, who keeps the abandoned ones
I ask that your grace never leave me
If in other times I offended you in my arrogance
Repentant, today I ask for your pardon

The other day at nighttime I went searching
For someone to tell me about God
Across from the corner there was a church
My heart invited me to step inside

I heard the message where the preacher spoke
Of a country that Christ had prepared
Where there are no hungers, pains nor sadness
That was the land which I had always dreamed

Hopeful, I converted to the gospel
And I hope to share it one day with my parents
When I return to my land I hope to see them
And to tell them about Jesus Christ and his love

Although we come to this land seeking money
The gospel of Jesus has saved us
I came out ahead, and I'll never be ashamed
Of this, the story of many undocumented ones

13

'FOOLS AND FUNDAMENTALISTS': THE INSTITUTIONAL DILEMMAS OF AUSTRALIAN PENTECOSTALISM

MARK HUTCHINSON*

[*Image of alien creature on a mortuary slab. Laughter*]

Doug (UFO researcher): You don't expect to find one!

Lehmo: Well, Doug, if you do meet one, step 1, introduce your-self, and step 2, get a photo!

Carrie: And Doug, if you do find one, get me a photo too, be-cause I find it very hard to believe … But I am happy to be proven wrong.

Charlie: That said, Carrie does believe that a magical man in the sky created everything, and that his son died and rose again from the dead … So, we all believe strange things. Doug, thanks for joining us tonight.

Doug: Thank you.

---

* Mark Hutchinson (PhD, University of New South Wales) is Dean of Hu-manities and Academic Projects at The Scots College, Sydney, Australia. He has been University Historian and remains a core member of the Religion and Society Research Centre at the University of Western Sydney. His most recent books are Mark Hutchinson, *Iron in our Blood: A History of the Presbyterian Church in New South Wales, 1788-2001* (Sidney: Ferguson Publications and the Centre for the Study of Australian Christianity, 2001), Mark Hutchinson and John Wolffe, *A Short History of Global Evangelicalism* (Cambridge: Cambridge University Press, 2012), and Mark Hutchinson, *A University of the People: A History of the University of Western Sidney* (Sidney: Allen and Unwin, forthcoming).

Charlie: I am going to get a lot of complaints, I am going to get a lot of complaints for that …

Carrie: From my mother, too.

Charlie: All I am saying is that everything is a leap of faith, whether it is believing in UFOs or believing in (pointing to Carrie) superstitions.

Steve: Yeah, but you didn't need to say it twice. You did reiterate the point …

(*The Project*, Channel 10, July 23, 2012)

The Project is a panel format news and variety show filling a prime time commercial TV slot on one of Australia's national networks. It's design wraps 'serious' news in youthful comedy in order to overcome the growing public and generational resistance to claims to objectivity. The exchange quoted above is typical of the shift towards opinionated secular preaching in mass media, tailored to *homo ludens*. Simmel's understanding of the seriousness of playful discourse is everywhere applicable in the constant reference back to jocular experts arraigned to convince the audience to get aboard the Welfare State's latest campaign to reduce its problems in servicing the health sector, in relationships between subcultures, or in facilitating social democratic capitalism. In this context, the asides about religion and its plausibility can be seen for what they are – mechanisms of social control and secular ideology maintenance. For supernaturalist religions these mechanisms are everywhere evident in Australia, creating dilemmas for how they adopt institutional forms, frame their internal and external rhetorics, and how they express corporate citizenship. In multicultural Australia there is meaning in why the Panel's target was Christian supernaturalism and not, say, Muslim claims about Muhammad's prophetic status or the Buddha's transcendentalism. As Peter Berger noted with regard to Western intellectual elites more generally, any non-moribund form of Christianity in Australia is portrayed either as a paradise of fools or Fundamentalists.[1] The (post) [Modernist] Project, as we shall see, is well named.

---

[1] Peter Berger, Grace Davie, and Effie Fokas, *Religious America, Secular Europe? A Theme and Variations* (Burlington: Ashgate, 2008), p. 12.

Australia is a post-Christian, modernist secular state with a public square ideologically defined by the requirements of a pluralistic Welfare State. That ideology is propagated and defended by media, academia, and a two party majority system of government balanced between liberal democracy and economic liberalism, which filter out 'supernatural' religious content in the interest of maintaining policy settings which do not preference one or another of the major religious traditions which provide over half of the country's welfare services.[2] In the midst of this, supernaturalist religions find themselves in constant tension between participating in state recognized 'religious' functions as traditionally defined, on the one hand, and maintaining their spiritual self-identities and worldviews on the other. The growth of desecularizing movements – migrant Islam, Sydney evangelicalism, and globalizing Pentecostalism are examples – increases the tensions between the traditional state/church settlement as these energetic forms are 'schooled' in how to behave politely in the public square. One way of interrogating the dilemmas which arise is through a taxonomy, such as that provided by Thomas O'Dea's 'dilemmas of institutionalization'.[3] Progressively, these will be explained as dilemmas under the rubrics: Mixed Motivation, the Symbolic, Administrative order, Delimitation, and Power.

Mixed Motivation

O'Dea draws upon Weber's work to suggest that as religious institutions develop across time, across space, or in terms of entrenchment in a particular locality, the original motivations of the founding generation become diluted by other voices and aims. As a revivalist movement, Pentecostalism in Australia has been quite self-aware of this at such critical points as its turn away from American-style centralization in the 1950s. It has repeatedly renewed itself and attempted to avoid the problems of institutionalization through a series of 'restarts'. In its first generation, when it took the form of healing mission homes (Good News Hall, the Apostolic Mission

---

[2] See Stephen Judd and Ann Robinson, 'Christianity and Australia's Social Services', in S. Piggin (ed.), *Shaping the Good Society in Australia* (North Ryde: Macquarie University, 2006).

[3] Thomas F. O'Dea, 'Five Dilemmas in the Institutionalization of Religion', *Journal for the Scientific Study of Religion* 1.1 (Oct 1961), pp. 30-39.

House, West End Mission, Peoples' Mission, etc.), influenced by the Sunderland Revival in England and the various Irish revivals, the greatest dilemma was how to survive the first generation of founders, many of them women. Through the 1920s and 1930s, these healing missions remade themselves as denominations, energized by significant charismatic leaders from overseas (A.C. Valdez, F.B. Van Eyk, John Hewitt, etc.) who brought to bear the influences of Azusa Street and the Welsh Revival. Organizationally, they spawned magazines, annual conferences, defined roles and constitutions, Bible Schools, and initial conversations with the State. As these began to strike problems with generational renewal, a new generation of leaders absorbed the lessons of the Latter Rain Revival (1948) and the subsequent American Healing Revival and the Charismatic Renewal in order to generate a new crop of home-grown charismatic leaders and founders of large churches. Examples include Norm Armstrong at Penshurst, D.F. Cartledge at Townsville, Andrew Evans at Adelaide, Clark Taylor and Reg Klimionok at Brisbane. Through the 1960s and 1970s, this generation saw its role as to avoid the problems of the decaying Wesleyan Connexional form, which was externally 'liberalizing' and internally institutionalizing. The result was the rise of a dispersed large church form of congregational government, exerting regional influence through conferences and parachurch missions, youth, and social welfare agencies such as Youth Alive, held together by the denominational constitution and the biennial conference, in which the continuing value of tradition received occasional affirmation.

While the heavily Methodist origins of Australian Pentecostalism sensitized Australian Pentecostal leaders to the problems of institutionalization, in typical modernist form there has been a tendency to treat it as a problem which can be solved. A fourth generation of leaders institutionalized the lessons of the innovators of the 1970s, adding better organizational forms and an explicit address to what Arjun Appadurai refers to as the global *mediascape*. Brian Houston at Hillsong has been among these but also Edge Church in Adelaide, Planetshakers in Melbourne, and smaller variants on the urban fringes, such as Shirelive (Sutherland), Faith Church (Dandenong), and Inspire Church (Liverpool). The result was the growth of a megachurch-dominated congeries of sub-denominations, knit together by an approach to 'brand' (such as the 'Australian Christian

Churches' or their de-traditionalized names), culture and friendship circles among the chief leaders. 'Tradition' occurs in the parlance of such churches mainly as an extension of their marketing, having migrated through an earlier period when 'tradition' was equated with 'religiousness' and 'religiousness' equated with organizational death. Promotion occurs not on merit but on obedience and 'faithfulness', creating a widening expertise gap between internal church culture and the surrounding secular meritocracy and significant internal barriers to progression by the bright and the mobile. Frustration with the internal glass walls and ceilings leads to a large 'back door' and membership definitions which include 'acceptable rates of loss' as motivated people move on to find other opportunities for ministry expression. While this can – and does – lead to cultural emulation further afield, it also leads to burn out, disillusionment, and growing local cultural resistance to 'the brand'.

Efforts to 'solve' what is (according to O'Dea) the perpetual dilemma of mixed motivation, moreover, have provoked a series of crises in the fourth generation Pentecostal churches. The Global Financial Crisis (GFC), for instance, rapidly distinguished between those Churches which had created administrative structures of sufficient prudential strength and those which had not. At least one Pentecostal denomination, for example, teetered on the edge of financial ruin for some time, sparking a quiet turnover in leadership and shift in direction back towards a more broad-based appreciation of its constituency. (There are no particular signs that it changed approaches within the churches themselves.) In 2009, a megachurch-associated social welfare agency (Mercy Ministries) collapsed in a welter of accusations of 'widespread abuse' and financial irregularity.[4] The problem, again, was the assumption that what worked in the church worked in the world, because the church culture was absolutized as the *sine qua non* of success. The mixed motivations of those who sought to serve the large churches, however, meant that appropriate mechanisms were not put in place to assure that broader social expectations were met. The collapse of Mercy Ministries demonstrated the exposure that churches can become subjected to when they lack an intellectually-engaged professional

---

[4] Ruth Pollard, 'Mercy Ministries Home to Close', *Sydney Morning Herald* (hereinafter *SMH*) (October 28, 2009), <http://www.smh.com.au/national/mercy-ministries-home-to-close-20091027-hj2k.html> (accessed July 7, 2013).

tradition going in, and effective forms of public apologetics coming out. Leadership is not enough – mission-centered management, a sign that the institution has accepted that the dilemma cannot be solved but only managed, is also necessary. These crises indicate that Australian Pentecostalism is now perhaps seeking for a fifth generational organizational form.

The Dilemma of the Symbolic

In the dilemma of the Symbolic, O'Dea points to what he calls the 'central antinomy' of religion and particularly of a democratizing religion such as Pentecostalism. The faith is on the one hand sacred, transcendental, the domain of the unnamed God whose name is 'I Am'. On the other hand, to be effective, it needs to be consolidated in a material form, and distributed among the people. In Pentecostalism, this is an essentially democratizing function, where the Spirit becomes available to all. With the corporatization of the Australian Church in the 1980s, however, the engagement of the *mediascape* brought with it sharp constraints on the democracy of the Spirit. Consistent with the devaluation of tradition for institutional charisma, what the new generation deride as 'spiritual karaoke' or 'the crazies' of testimony from the church floor, or public utterance in tongues, is sharply constrained in a number of ways. Actively, the devaluation of tradition was a deliberate shift towards the contemporary: services are tightly controlled within the time limits set by contemporary music (limiting public engagement), within highly mediated spaces designed to create a sense of belonging (i.e. community) to groups of people drawn from scattered ex-urban settings who otherwise have no natural attachment. As Appadurai notes, in 'contemporary' (as opposed to 'modern') societies, the local is a matter of imaginative effort and constant maintenance. It imports the spatial as a factor rather than beginning with colocationality. They emphasize flows rather than fixtures. In other words, the 'contemporary church movement', as Australian Pentecostal churches now often refer to themselves, are linked to created, and perpetually recreated, local communities, in which traditional Pentecostal identifiers are repressed in order to allow for the constant in-breaking of 'the new'.[5] 'Passive limiters' also contribute to the decline of the democratic religion of the word: sound levels and the sheer size of churches drown out individual utterance in 'the spirituality of the mega'. More actively, moreover, 'ministry' is tightly concentrated in the hands of the few – usually the teaching pastorate and the worship team – who hold the mediatorial device, the microphone.

In part, this is a reaction to the declining 'effectiveness' of testimony and the prophetic as Pentecostal congregations aged, and successive generations sought to hold onto their children with a variety of compromises and cultural translations suited to the surrounding culture. To such people, the encouragement to transform the inspiration of God into prophetic words over time coopted the service and became 'ordinary' or 'boring'. The following generations sought novelty: the crisis in the 1950s was over healing practices, in the 1970s over dancing and exorcism. Again, it is a tension: the divine needs to be captured in terms which are understandable by people but are not rendered quotidian. One way of solving this in the fourth generational institutional church has been to isolate the charisma in the individuality of the pastor. This, however, runs the risk of stripping the rest of the organization and its activities of its sacred nature and of sacred participation by other people. The problem is one of objectifying the original charismatic moment in stable forms and procedures without routinization and 'a consequent superficiality of participation'.[6] When that occurs, objectification will have resulted in alienation. The fourth generation dismissal of older forms of spiritual expression for ritualized engagement with the mediascape has proved highly effective – many Australian megachurches (Hillsong in particular) have a significant footprint around the region and even globally, and numbers of them – such as the Christian Outreach Centres and Christian City Churches – have founded expansive, global denominations. By the mid-2000s, however, the generational issues again began to catch up with numbers of these, requiring team changes and new forms.

---

[5] *Perspecta*, 'The Illusion of Permanence: An Interview with Arjun Appadurai', *Perspecta* 34 (2003), p. 46.

[6] James A. Mathisen, 'Thomas O'Dea's Dilemmas of Institutionalization: A Case Study and Re-Evaluation after Twenty-five years', *Sociological Analysis* 47.4 (Winter, 1987), p. 304.

In 2010, for instance, *Ministry Today* magazine covered the story of Mark and Darlene Zschech moving from Hillsong to the NSW central coast in order to 'build' and 'lead' their own church. Zschech 'whose songs "Shout to the Lord," "The Potter's Hand" and numerous others over the last decade made the name of Hillsong Church in Sydney synonymous with modern worship music worldwide'[7] had been seeking alternatives for some time. Why? O'Dea points to the problem: as Houston had long held, Hillsong was named after its worship culture but was not defined by it. The music ambience and the convention form had already, in a sense, become the 'daily' fare of all churches and no longer distinguished the megachurch as such. One indicator that the mediascape engagement of the 1990s was no longer quite as capable of suspending belief, of bypassing the critical function, came with the repeated successes of megachurch-based Christian singers in secular competitions such as 'Australian Idol'. A form of TV yellow journalism called 'Today Tonight' went to air accusing Hillsong Church of 'rigging' a competition, rapidly finding itself under fire when it turned out that none of the contestants were in fact from Hillsong, though five of them were from other Pentecostal churches, as was previous winner Guy Sebastian.[8] The ignorance of the TV reporters was constructed – plucking at the powerful secularist strain in Australian culture, while suppressing knowledge of the importance of churches for the ethnic and local communities among whom music is so important. Also missed was the fact that, with its small market, Australian charts are naturally bent by *any* large, coherent church or movement. Hillsong's previous innovations were now owned by all of the larger churches, with natural consequences for the quality and quantity of music in the Pentecostal constituency and its impact on the likewise corporatizing music scene in Australia. The sudden visibility of the two mutually entangled cultures – one of which depended on round the clock visibility, the other which depended on a certain continued mystery – did neither of them any good with the

---

[7] 'Darlene Zschech Leaving Hillsong to Co-Pastor Church', *Ministry Today* (November 1, 2010) <http://ministrytodaymag.com/index.php/ministry-news/18988-darlene-zschech-leaving-hillsong-to-co-pastor-church>.

[8] Fiona Connolly, 'Hillsong church may sue over Idol vote-rigging claims', *Daily Telegraph* (October 13, 2007), <http://www.dailytelegraph.com.au/news/sydney-news/church-sue-bid-on-idol-nonsense/story-e6freuzi-1111114630875>.

public for the affections of which both were contesting. On the one hand, the myth of the democratic 'reality genre' was pricked, and shown to be manipulated by the media corporations; on the other, the 'mystery' of worship music was brought into the public gaze and debated for its financial value.

By the time Zschech left, moreover, Churches such as Hillsong were already making the shift towards social engagement and programmatic teaching in order to catch the ear of a new generation of followers. The old symbolic fabric that had been woven to catch the youth of the 1990s was, 25 years later, threadbare and needed changing. The shift to social engagement, however, carries its own dangers. It has seen much closer relationships with the major NGOs, such as Compassion and World Vision, implying a form of cultural incorporation which – as the Mercy Ministries crisis pointed out – many Pentecostal churches may not be equipped to deal with. Meanwhile, at the lower level, the emergence of churches such as the 'Sydney Worship Centre' and defections from the Assemblies of God by revivalist congregations such as the Mount Annan congregation, indicate that vacating the spiritual basement for society's living room is merely an invitation for others to occupy the space that traditional Pentecostalism has always claimed for its own. As Martin notes, this is the secret to the long charismatic moment which is Pentecostalism. Liberalization and class movement results in a 'downward mobilisation' of the Spirit – repression of prophecy and testimony in one setting leads not to its extinction but to its relocation into other settings.

The Dilemma of Administrative Order

O'Dea proposes that religious organizations need to maintain a balance between their pursuit of *effectiveness* (often measured around 'fit to mission') and their need to bring their congregations with them (*elaboration*). In a sense, the emphasis on the 'new' in contemporary churches provides a ready tool for maintaining this balance, undermining continuities, and placing the cultural controls in the hands of the managing elite. On the other hand, as Appadurai notes, 'The modern is a project, while the contemporary is a condition'. Launching a church onto the waves of the contemporary removes the ready legitimacy of many of the normal mechanisms by which religious organizations are managed. It is no longer possible for such organizations to require their members to do things simply because 'the priest' tells them or 'because it is in the constitution' (in Weberian terms 'traditional' or 'rational-legal' forms of authority) – contemporary church members need to be convinced that they should do so because it is in their own best interests (a form of 'affective social action'). When the personal interests of leaders emerges from under the cover of religious self-sacrifice, however, burnout among members is not unknown.[9] The delicacy of the balancing act may be seen in the 'blessing' theology which is common among larger churches. In Australia, as Shane Clifton has shown, this has been caricatured as 'prosperity theology',[10] though in fact it has stronger genealogical links to Yonggi Cho and Oral Roberts than it does to Kenneth Hagin or E.W. Kenyon. While the latter was strong in some independent megachurches such Riverview (Perth) in its early days, it only began to emerge strongly in AOG churches in the 1990s. By the early 2000s, however, it was already 'not contemporary', and sacrificial themes began to reemerge in 'blessing' circles as the larger churches began to establish social welfare and overseas aid connections. In other words, non-native traditions can be absorbed, and then discarded as their effectiveness as generators of locality, mission-alignment, and 'passion' waxed and waned with broader social trends. As post-Gen X motivators became important for youth cultures, however, the amount of energy required to 'elaborate' the convoluted psycho-theology of prosperity doctrine for the churches' target group began to act as a drag upon their effectiveness.[11] It was quietly sidelined as a personal option in the spiritual buffet of the contemporary Church: believe it, buy the DVDs if you like, but it will rarely now be heard from the front.

Other forms of the dilemma of administrative order have been seen in a series of high profile discipline cases which have emerged from prominent Australian churches. While, as noted above, administrative effectiveness has often failed at supra-congregational levels

---

[9] For the reflections on this by a current, contemporary church leader, see Mark Connor, 'Pentecostalism', <http://markconner.typepad.com/catch_the_wind/2009/10/pentecostalism-pt3.html>.

[10] Shane Clifton, *Pentecostal Churches in Transition: Analysing the Developing Ecclesiology of the Assemblies of God in Australia* (Leiden: Brill, 2009), p. 163.

[11] Ruth Powell, 'Gen X Missing in Christian Cross-section', *Macquarie University News* 317 (Mar 2000), p. 8.

due to the hollowing out of meritocratic and rational-legal bureau-cratic cultures through the articulation of institutional charisma in the pastoral oligarchy, moral failure in the pastorate produces some-times startling results. In the case of Frank Houston, de-certification followed distant accusations of child abuse which threatened the continuity of those churches which had been found-ed under his headship.[12] The collapse of Pat Mesiti's ministry in 2001, likewise, produced action.[13] Again, de-certification followed, this time with a restoration period in another megachurch, in part to protect Hillsong from attacks in the secular press. Notably, while Mesiti was restored from 'sexual addiction', his former boss Antho-ny Venn-Brown (who resigned from ministry in 1991 prior to 'com-ing out' as a gay man) has never been restored to ministry. He ex-presses the tension between 'fit to mission' and the effort required to elaborate on his personal sexuality in terms of authenticity: 'I feel I've had my ministry. When I came back to God I felt like I had the essence of what it was all about. What I have now is real. I have learned to live non-judgementally, to live with integrity and I didn't have that as a preacher.'[14]

What all three of the preceding cases shared was the need to re-solve the tension between being swallowed in a transcendent (and relatively unforgiving) mission, the 'performance' requirements of ministry, and the shaping norms of religious organizations. The same analysis can be applied to other cases, both those equally spec-tacular,[15] and those less well known.[16] In each case, the 'administra-tive order' normally invisible under the imagined contemporary community became visible, though only when a significant threat appeared imminent.

---

[12] One result of this was a fusion of campuses which set Hillsong along the pathway of becoming a network Church.

[13] 'The Interview: Pat Mesiti, *Sight Magazine* (May 8, 2006), <http://www. sightmagazine.com.au/stories/Features/mesiti8.5.06.php>.

[14] 'Anthony Venn Brown: Mr Charismatic Gay Australia', *Out In Perth* (Febru-ary 15, 2007) (accessed April 9, 2012.

[15] Elissa Lawrence, 'Disgraced Pastor Michael Guglielmucci a Porn Addict', *Sunday Mail* (SA) (August 24, 2008), <http://www.theaustralian.com.au/fraud-pastor-a-porn-addict-says-shocked-dad/story-e6frfkx9-1111117284239>.

[16] Ian G. Clark, *Pentecost at the Ends of the Earth: The History of the Assemblies of God in New Zealand (1927-2003)* (Detroit: Christian Road Ministries, 2007), p. 186.

Delimitation

O'Dea suggests that the fourth dilemma is that of 'delimitation', where a balance needs to be held between concrete definition and the transformation of the 'Spirit' into 'the letter that kills'. As was recently the case with an American snake-handling pastor, the letter can literally kill,[17] though such literalism is vanishingly rare among Australian Pentecostals. Rather, typological and elliptical interpretations of the text are more common, depending on the social location of the message. 'Materialization' is central to all religions – somehow, each makes 'the divine' present to the believers, be it in the form of possession/embodiment, sacrifice, or even the measured tones of 'the Word among us' of a Reformed sermon. The 'presence', the materialization of the divine, is boxed within an agreed set of definitions which permit the tension between the Spirit and the Law, the numinous and the imminent, to be maintained. In its earliest manifestation as 'mission' or 'healing homes', Australian Pentecostal materialization was literally *embodied* in accounts of physical healing and semiotically demonstrated by the crutches and other now unnecessary aids fixed around the walls of meeting halls.[18] There was also the physical presence of texts taken from the King James Bible and the materializations of the end times in tongues, reported visions, and encounters of touch with the Holy Spirit and with angels. With many members of Good News Hall emerging from the Salvation Army, the bonnet, the sash, the tambourine, and the badge (with mottos such as 'Christ for me' and 'Jesus is coming soon' replacing their former organization's 'Blood and Fire')[19] were worn during the physically present street meeting pointing towards the ultimate materialization to come, the physical return of Jesus Christ.

---

[17] 'Serpent-handling Pastor Profiled Earlier in Washington Post Dies from Rattlesnake Bite', *Washington Post* (May 30), <http://www.washingtonpost.com/lifestyle/style/serpent-handling-pastor-profiled-earlier-in-washington-post-dies-from-rattlesnake-bite/2012/05/29/gJQAJef5zU_story.html> (accessed September 5, 2012).

[18] J. Lancaster, 'Behold He cometh', *Good News* 20.1 (January 1929), p. 7.

[19] See for instance, *Good News* 20.11 (November 1929), p. 20, <http://webjournals.ac.edu.au/ media/ pdf/ GN/gn-vol20-no11-nov-1929/GN1929.11_web .pdf>.

These forms of materialization, however, shifted with the forms of Church. In the early period of denominational formation during the 1920s, materialization shifted from healing and the street meeting to the form of the apostolic figure, striking a pose on a stage. Major figures such as Aimee Semple Macpherson, A.C. Valdez, Smith Wigglesworth, and F.B. Van Eyk presented extremely physical forms of enactment, which opened up spaces for indigenous characters such as C.L. Greenwood and the Enticknap brothers. This was a new way of being Pentecostal, importing a performance style that displaced the motherly mission home leaders and materialized the faith in the big black Bible in the performance of spirituality in a particular Pentecostal dialect, attitude, and 'strut'. The displacement was not unintentional – verbal spats delimiting Pentecostal orthodoxy became the normal order of relationship between the old and new forms, with the casual biblical immediacy and individual culture of interpretation of the first generation replaced by the dogmatic insistence of the inspired preacher. Statements such as 'Jesus was coming back' served different functions– in the former generation, it was an inspiration to action, in the latter a way of insisting on instant conversion. In the delimitation wars of the 1920s, the 'Spirit' was applied to the emerging denominations, while 'the Letter that kills' was applied to the opposition. Not surprisingly, the cost of the latter was a shift from behavioral prohibitions (don't dance, don't drink, don't wear make-up, don't go to the movies, etc.) as a form of cleansing of the body's temple in *preparation* for the indwelling of the Spirit, to a form of legalism linked to that *sine qua non* of the denominational form, church 'membership'. Unholiness now no longer simply separated one from God; it threatened shunning and separation from ministry and the local Church.

The key problem was that not all believers could become spiritual masters of the apostolic type. Subtly through the 1930s, the founding apostolic embodiment in the inspired preacher was traded for the inspired *teacher*, as figures such as Kelso Glover, Donald Gee, Howard Carter, H.E. Wiggins, and James Wallace became the embodiment of Pentecostal leadership. Their role was to more specifically moderate the 'Letter that Kills' so that a longer term, sustainable Pentecostal life became possible for those in the pews. Gee in particular pointed to the lessons of Acts in order to create a sustainable revival: 'There are many of our problems that are Spiritual problems and they can only be solved by spiritual remedies. Beware lest we organize beyond the point of necessity'.[20] All of them had a common theological problem, approached through a common ecclesiological mechanism. The problem was the delay of the *parousia*: if the ultimate materialization, the return of Jesus, is delayed, what does that mean about how Pentecostals live in the meantime? Their common ecclesiological mechanism was the Bible college, which effectively detached apostolic formation from quotidian spirituality, allowing the formation of ministers and preachers to run parallel to, but institutionally detached from, the daily life of churches. The short term 3 week or 3 month program gave way to the one, two, and then three year program. Inevitably, this meant that the people of the Spirit (the whole Church) became distinguished from the persons of the Spirit (the embodied, apostolic figures in Bible college alumni lists), the Letter for the one being distinguished by a bifurcation of 'calling' from the Letter for the other. Readers of Weber will recognize in this division of spheres and labor the incipient centralization and bureaucratization typical of religious institutionalization.[21] For Australian Pentecostalism, it also laid the roots for a series of crises of delimitation and materialization.

Taking the Assemblies of God as an example, Gee's warning about organization pointed to the first of these. By the mid-1950s, partially through the influx of Methodists and the expansion of the pastorate by those who were specifically *not* apostolic in their intrinsic gifts, 'the Conference' began to seek for dominance not only over national affairs but over such local and regional affairs as the selection of visiting ministries, theological definitions (such as with regard to British Israelism), and the right to operate in conjunction with interdenominational ministries.[22] From the presence of old grey heads such as Maxwell Armstrong, who 'held an honourable place among the brethren for age, courtesy and loyalty to Confer-

---

[20] D. Gee, 'Can this Pentecostal Revival be Maintained', *Australian Evangel* (March 1938), p. 3. <http://webjournals.ac.edu.au/journals/AEGTM/1938-march/can-this-pentecostal-revival-be-maintained/>.

[21] See Sebastiaan P. Tijsterman and Patrick Overeem, 'Escaping the Iron Cage: Weber and Hegel on Bureaucracy and Freedom,' *Administrative Theory & Praxis* 30.1 (March 2008), pp. 71-91.

[22] S. Clifton, 'An Analysis of the Developing Ecclesiology of the Assemblies of God in Australia' (PhD, ACU, 2005), p. 200.

ence',[23] it sustained its place by transforming individual charisma into institutional charisma. Under this order, in Shils's words,

> What the 'subject' responds to is not just the specific declaration or order of the incumbent of the role – as the definition of rational-legal authority would have it – but the incumbent enveloped in the vague and powerful nimbus of the authority of the entire institution. It is a legitimacy constituted by sharing in the properties of the 'organization as a whole' epitomized or symbolized in the powers concentrated (or thought to be concentrated) at the peak.[24]

It did not reach this height without struggles. Regional fights broke out over the balance of power between the national convention and the state presbytery. The 1951 Conference was a special conference called by NSW and Victoria in order to discuss State representation and the threat of Queensland secession. At that conference, Pastor Alex Davidson (a former businessman) was appointed General Superintendent (1951-1955; he would be Vice Chair to Bible College Principal James Wallace, 1957-1959, and Chairman again 1959-1969), precisely because the movement needed a cool administrative head and a uniting alternative in a difficult time.[25] Under the influence of the American push into the world, the administrative pendulum arced even more towards a centralized, Presbyterian model. Davidson was funded to become the movement's first fulltime chairman. While he remained in the position, his personal gifts kept the national boat on an even keel.

> The appointment of a full-time chairman derived largely from the American example and, in 1967, the AGA decided to send Davidson to the Assemblies of God head office in Springfield. It was hoped that he could learn more about the organisation and structure of the American movement, and return to Australia with recommendations for emulating its success. At the follow-

---

[23] D.A. Simmons, 'Commonwealth Conference', *Australian Evangel and Glad Tidings Messenger* 13.7 (June 1947), p. 11.

[24] Edward Shils, 'Charisma, Order, and Status', in S.N. Eisenstadt (ed.), *Political Sociology: A Reader* (New York: Basic Books), 1971, p. 67.

[25] Mark Hutchinson, 'Davidson, Alexander Thomas (1902-1987)', *Australasian Dictionary of Pentecostal and Charismatic Movements*, <http://webjournals.ac.edu.au/journals/ADPCM/a-to-d/davidson-alexander-thomas-1902-1987/> (accessed September 6, 2012).

ing conference in 1969, the executive presented a new draft of the AGA constitution which, among other things, delegated additional responsibilities to state presbyteries, implemented new controls and procedures over ordination, and changed the title of 'chairman' to 'General Superintendent'. This latter change was the title given to the leader of the AGUSA, and was symbolic of the transition from chairing a conference to leading a movement. The American example also gave rise to the desire to set-up an AGA head office that would facilitate the ever-increasing responsibilities of the AGA and its home and foreign missionary departments.[26]

In short, the organization itself became the materialization of the Kingdom, the 'Conference' the voice of God. As Clifton points out, however, when his successor (Ralph Read) took office, the anti-institutionalism of the charismatic renewal threatened to blow the movement apart.

The new generation emerging from James Wallace's Bible College emerged to find their carefully nurtured sense of calling fanned by the rhetoric of inspiration and 'mega' results from personalities such as Oral Roberts, T.L. Osborn, and later Yonggi Cho.[27] The 'new crop of home-grown charismatic leaders and founders of large churches' mentioned above moved steadily into conflict with their denominations. In the AGA, the conflict broke out over charismatic phenomena such as dancing and spirit possession, though fundamentally it was a conflict between two charismas: the centralizing institutional charisma of Conference on the one hand and that of the charismatic leaders of rapidly growing regional churches on the other. This broke into the open in 1975 and was resolved at the 1977 conference with the election of elements of the latter to senior positions on the national executive. Within the Christian Revival Crusade, crisis came in the same year with the death of the founding father of the movement, Leo Harris. Peter Vacca's Bethesda church was already in conflict with Harris's centralist Crusade Hall on Sturt Street, Adelaide, over denial of the younger church's desire

---

[26] Clifton, 'An Analysis', p. 199.
[27] Mark Hutchinson, 'Cartledge, David Frederick (1940-2005)', in *Australasian Dictionary of Pentecostal and Charismatic Movements*, <http://webjournals.ac.edu.au/journals/ADPCM/a-to-d/cartledge-david-frederick-1940-2005> (accessed September 6, 2012).

to establish an independent bookshop and training school.[28] New denominations and independent megachurches popped up progressively through the late 1970s and the 1980s, their emphasis shifting charisma to the leader, for whom the materialization was now the church assembled, the 'mega' experience of worship.[29] In time, the largest example of this became the massive Hillsong Conference and, as a result, the Hillsong Church. Capturing the energy of the now fading interdenominational conferences, it spawned many imitators – Planetshakers Conference, CCC's Presence Conference, and many others besides. In each, the materialization is the worship experience, reaffirmed by the appearance of leading speakers from around the globe, whose own 'success' reflects back the sense of global 'presence' captured by the individual believer in the midst of the masses. So, locality is created, and connected to similar glocalities elsewhere to project an image of the materialized Kingdom of God. In Goh's words:

> There is a fundamental underlying quality in the very nature of the megachurch, inhering in its spatial logic, the performativity and semiotics of its typical liturgy and other related aspects, which constructs charismatic Protestantism's version of materiality. We might call this the 'performance of the mega'.[30]

Its importance for our present argument is that this synthesis is clearly a solution developed to solve the problems of 'delimitation' experienced by the older, 'Conference' ecclesial model defined by the 'national church'. In turn, suggests O'Dea, the dilemma will emerge for the megachurch solution as well – and indeed, the literature on 'church excellence' suggests that this is already beginning to occur.[31]

---

[28] L.C. McMaster, 'The Founding of a New Christian Denomination: The Bethesda Movement of South Australia' (MA (RS), UNISA, 2002), p. 32.

[29] See Robbie B.H. Goh, 'Hillsong and "megachurch" Practice: Semiotics, Spatial Logic and the Embodiment of Contemporary Evangelical Protestantism', *Material Religion* 4.3, pp. 284-305.

[30] Goh, 'Hillsong and "megachurch" Practice', p. 288.

[31] For a discussion of this see M. Hutchinson and J. Wolffe, *A Short History of Global Evangelicalism* (Cambridge: Cambridge University Press, 2012), pp. 265-70.

Power

O'Dea draws on religious history to note that the growth of a movement brings entanglement with secular powers. A consequence has been a 'weakening voluntary adherence and thereby diluting the religious ethos and substituting external pressures for interior conviction'.[32] While this is unlikely to occur in Australia, it is certainly possible in migrant populations which come to the country, especially those from Africa and the Pacific. There is also a noticeable drift in *local* and *regional* secular entanglement among Pentecostal churches. For most churches, the dilemma of power entanglement commences at the local level. Norman Armstrong, in talking about the planting of Revival Life Centre in 1972, for example, moved from itinerant evangelist to local church pastor through his involvement in the charismatic movement. Through the Full Gospel Businessmen (FGBMI) he came into contact with a leading engineer from large building company, Civil and Civic, and through Intercessors Australia the leading charismatic church Architect, Noel Bell. This pool of 'connected' talent enabled the building of a Pentecostal church in Penshurst. As such local churches grew, they came – through their institutional presence – to have a significant influence on their local councils, facilitating their ability to leverage cooperation. A number of major shifts in the Australian political scene rendered this of increasing importance through the 1980s. At the same time as Pentecostal churches – attracted by cheaper land and large numbers of younger people settling in mobile new suburbs without pre-empting cultural institutions – were growing on the metropolitan periphery, those same new electorates gave their constituents a voice in governments increasingly sensitive to the rise of the lobbyist society. Inevitably, as the support base of mainline political parties began to fragment with the rise of independents and limited-range issue parties, politicians began to target these 'aspirational' fringes for their 'swinging' votes.[33] When they got there, however, what they often found was that Pentecostal churches were

---

[32] O'Dea, 'Five Dilemmas', p. 37.

[33] As John Robinson has pointed out, the term 'aspirational' is a retrospective term pointed at political mobilization rather than a category describing a quantitatively demonstrable social phenomenon. 'The Aspirational Class: Social Class or Ideological Category?' (Paper Presented to TASA Conference 2005, University of Tasmania, December 6-8, 2005).

among the few large coordinating institutions *in situ*. As Maxine McKew, a reporter who used her public notoriety to defeat John Howard in her own run for public office, noted, 'Winning the hearts and minds of these so-called aspirational voters is the door to government'.[34] Scenes of conservative Prime Minister John Howard opening Hillsong Church, or his Labor counterparts (such as NSW Premier Bob Carr) ill at ease on the Hillsong conference platform, were regular events in the 1990s.[35] Some politicians – such as Louise Markus and Alan Cadman – found the association more comfortable than others. All, however, had to deal with the fact that the ideologues who rule the Australian public square now had to do more than simply dismiss religion as unimportant. The federal Australian Labor Party, indeed, attempted to de-ideologize its public stance in order to enable the social conscience of evangelical churches more latitude than their social conservatism. Kevin Rudd, a publicly-religious figure well known at Brisbane's largest megachurch, Christian Outreach Centre, declared Australia to now be in a post-ideological age,[36] and successfully attracted Pentecostal votes leftwards. His failure to hold the middle ground in the face of the factions in his own Party, however, and incursions from the Green left, saw him removed as Prime Minister by Labor powerbrokers in a move which pushed many Pentecostals back onto their socially conservative mores. Perhaps the age was not as post-ideological as he had hoped.

Certainly, the ideology of secularism was alive and well and camping in the Australian public square – the period needs to be counted as one in which there was a hardening of secularism against the rise of public religion. Not only was Australia involved in two wars, and dealing with an influx of boat-born refugees from Asia, but there were concerted attempts to push back against what were seen as increasingly strong religious lobbies and to increase secularity in the delivery of government services.[37] In the midst of this,

---

[34] 'God and Politics Mix at Hillsong', <http://www.abc.net.au/7.30/content/2004/s1154131.htm>.

[35] Jana Wendt, 'Hillsong: Songs of praise – and politics', <http://sgp1.paddington.ninemsn.com.au/sunday/cover_stories/transcript_1811.asp>.

[36] Oliver Hartwich, 'Say it like you mean it, we love a bold leader', *Sydney Morning Herald* (August 7, 2009), p. 13.

[37] See among which, Max Wallace, *The Purple Economy: Supernatural Charities, Tax and the State* (Elsternwick: Australian National Secular Association, 2007); and

megachurches often became 'whipping boys' for broader public debates, Hillsong in particular receiving criticism for its political footprint. Marion Maddox, among others, has put forward the case that this was a form of threatening Fundamentalism impacting on an existing Australian secular norm, an imported form of the American religious right.[38] There is indeed evidence of such elements present in the Australian body politic: the same charismatic movement which facilitated the entanglement of previously separationist Pentecostals in the 1960s and 1970s imported (through organizations such as Howard Carter's Logos Foundation) a different understanding of the 'righteous nation' and the role of the church in its destiny. Organization such as Saltshakers, the Parliamentary Prayer Breakfast, etc. *are* visible in Canberra. The analysis ignores, however, that there has been a general rise in factional lobby culture in Australian political life from *all* sectors due to the global engagement of the society chosen by Australian politicians themselves. Bipartisan family reunion policies, for instance, have ensured the rapid growth of previously marginal religious groups in Australia (Islam, Buddhism, Hinduism, Orthodoxy, etc.), all of which have been wooed by politicians of various stripes.[39] The world from which they came is a much more religious place than secularists would prefer to admit. The fact that Christian groups also engage in vocal representation of their interests should not be surprising when the variants of the modernist project create conditions which require citizenship to be energetically constructed by self-aware communities. As the conscription debates, the living wage, the eight hour week campaign, and the Split of the 1950s attest, moreover, religious politics have always been an element in Australian life.[40] As Peter Berger has noted, one might say that secularists 'protesting

---

see Philip Rieff, *My Life among the Deathworks: Illustrations of the Aesthetics of Authority* (Charlottesville: University of Virginia Press, 2006).

[38] Viz. Marion Maddox, *God under Howard: The Rise of the Religious Right in Australian Politics* (Crows Nest: Allen & Unwin, 2005).

[39] 'Ted Baillieu and Gary Singer applaud "Greece is Macedonia" chant', *Vexnews* (November 11, 2008), <http://www.vexnews.com/2008/11/oops-ted-baillieu-and-gary-singer-applaud-greece-is-macedonia-chant/>; Kais Al-Momani, Nour Dados, Marion Maddox, and Amanda Wise, 'The Political Participation of Muslims in Australia, June 2010, <http://www.immi.gov.au/media/publications /multicultural/pdf_doc/political-participation-muslims.pdf>.

[40] This case is made by Patrick O'Farrell in his 'Spurious Divorce, Religion and Australian Culture', *Journal of Religious History* 15.4 (1989), pp. 519-24.

too much' is a result not of a 'new Fundamentalism' but of disappointment that the 'hard secularization' assumptions of many modernist disciplines are not progressing in as unilinear a fashion as the underlying theory would project.[41]

Berger's observations – about contesting secularization and desecularizing forces – brings us back to O'Dea's concept of a core dilemma affecting the presence of Pentecostal churches in the Australian public sphere. While 'visible' due to their local presence and size, Australian Pentecostals are neither as passively united by class as, say Muslims, nor as actively united by intrinsic political theology or overarching community groups. Nor do Pentecostals have the protective insulation from public critique provided by ethnicity or migrant status given to Buddhists or Confucians. At the same time that the murder of Nigerian Christians by Boko Haram groups was being covered in the Australian press, for example, social commentator and 'activist' Eva Cox sat at one end of a nationally televised panel beside Muslim academic Susan Carland and launched criticisms of Nigerian Pentecostal 'Fundamentalists' and their politics at a Pentecostal academic at the other end of the panel.[42] She seemed utterly unaware of the ironies of her position, speaking as she was of global realities while unreflectingly cloaked within her armor of old Modernist ideology. The reason was simply because 'tolerance' in Australia's public square is extended to minorities within the modernist project whenever they remain minorities, within defined communal walls, and do not belong to that traditional enemy of Western 'deathwatch' disciplines, public Christianity. Religion is permissible whenever it is ethnicity, and so social and 'quaint', but not when it claims its own status as specifically religious, i.e. supernatural. At this point it becomes considered 'ridiculous' or 'dangerous'.[43] It was another ABC journalist, James Valentine, who humorously defined 'Christians' and 'Hillsong' alongside the 'fiery

---

[41] Vyacheslav Karpov, 'Desecularization: A Conceptual Framework', *Journal of Church and State* 52.2 (July 2010), p. 232.

[42] ABC Q&A, televised July 18, 2011.

[43] See for instance, the ironic tie made by Richard Glover between the Sydney Anglican position on women in leadership and their 'completely coincidental … long history of believing in miracles'. R. Glover, 'For a Happy Marriage, Try the Submissionary Position', *SMH* (September 1, 2012), <http://www.smh.com.au/opinion/society-and-culture/for-a-happy-marriage-try-the-submissionary-postion-20120830-251ih.html#ixzz25puqrCeI>

redheads', 'stupid blondes', and 'bottom-feeder lawyers' who could be legitimate targets of Australian public bigotry.[44]

The only substantive attempt to project a Pentecostal presence into politics (apart from the generic support given to the broad, socially-conservative positions of the Australian Christian Lobby) was the emergence of the Family First Party. The party began in 2001 as a result of what the father and son team, Andrew and Ashleigh Evans from Paradise Church in South Australia, felt was an inspiration from God to attempt to forestall what they saw as the flood of bad legislation which was coming through the South Australian Parliament. His original model was not church based at all, but the single issue 'No Pokies' party established by lawyer Nick Xenophon formed to bring about change in gambling legislation. Indeed, it was Xenophon who had suggested to Andrew Evans that he establish his own party.

> The significance of that was that when we ran federally, and looked like we were going to win some seats, the media kept painting us as a right wing Fundamentalist religious American party in light of George Bush. I replied, 'look, guys, I have never met these guys that you're talking about. I've got no money from them, and it was Xenophon that suggested that I start, so you go and talk to Xenophon.' He confirmed that that was what he had said. That really took the heat off that American thing [at least in South Australia]. It gave us more credibility.[45]

Nor was this a 'church' party. While the party's constitution mentioned Judaeo-Christian values, Evans had seen how the 'Christian' label had marginalized the so-called Christian Democratic party in New South Wales. Due to the lack of media interest, and later its outright hostility, however, Evans needed to address his constituency directly. Church mailing lists and interchurch relationships through organizations such as the 'Heads of Churches' therefore became important. And while the national AG executive was dubious with regard to Evans's political campaigning, this past AG General Superintendent rapidly found support in Catholic, Greek

---

[44] Quoted in M. Hutchinson, 'Trust and Jest: Evangelicalism in Australia, 2011', *Evangelical Studies Bulletin* 79 (Fall 2011), p. 11.

[45] Interview, Andrew Evans, July 23, 2011, Pentecostal Heritage Centre, Alphacrucis College.

Orthodox, and even Spiritualist and Mormon churches. Evans also had a significant personal following amongst older holiness Pentecostals, many of whom turned out to work on polling booths. Ultimately, the party was less successful in terms of correctly returning candidates than in its ability to barter preference votes for sympathetic legislation. The media storm which resulted, however, demonstrated that breaking the rules of the secular public sphere was not without cost. Pentecostal churches paid in many ways for the brief successes in the South Australian and Federal Parliament. While the first Muslim member of Federal Parliament, Labor's Ed Husic, was welcomed as a symbol of multicultural success,[46] the surprise election of Family First's Steven Fielding to the Australian Senate in 2004, in a political climate which briefly enabled him to hold the balance of power with only 2% of the vote, saw him branded (according to the modernist 'ridiculous/dangerous' antinomy) as naive and foolish.[47] Entangled in their localities, Pentecostals suddenly found themselves to be political targets without effective assets in political theory or rhetoric, individual citizens but corporate pariahs.

Conclusions

The dilemmas of Australian Pentecostalism are, as with all forms of religious institutionalization, the result of increasingly self-aware sub-cultures encountering secular norms. Traditionally, the churches have dealt with mechanisms of social control through a combination of flexibility (shifting form, and the locus of charismatic authority) and self-renewal through periodic crises. Just as Pentecostals did not make the ground rules for the Australian public square, it is unlikely that they will be able to change them. What they can do, however, is develop the sort of internal conversation which allows for intelligent identification and management of the dilemmas, and public skills and rhetoric which engage Australians on their own terms. Its indigenous movements have shown remarkable adaptability, often in the face of public ideological harassment,

---

[46] <http://www.abc.net.au/7.30/content/2010/s2994694.htm>.

[47] Mark Davis, 'Mr 2%: Why Steve Fielding Bothers', *SMH* (September 26, 2008), <http://www.smh.com.au/news/national/mr-2-why-steve-fielding-bothe rs/2008/09/25/1222217430711.html>.

spreading across the nation and engaging globalization with an alacrity which has seen the movement emerge as the second largest Christian denomination by attendance in the country. While numbers hesitate at the term 'Fundamentalist', the constant jibing of the culture's gatekeepers has been taken with remarkable good humor, even a willingness to be counted among Paul's 'fools for Christ'. Developing an intentionality around its proven ability to throw up charismatic solutions to institutional problems will, however, be one of the movement's challenges going forward.

14

ANGLICANS, PENTECOSTALS, AND ECUMENICAL THEOLOGY

DAVID HILBORN*

Introduction

This essay suggests theological grounds for enhanced ecumenical dialogue between Anglicans and Pentecostals. In doing so, it highlights key themes identified in a research project supported by the Council for Christian Unity of the Church of England – a project which recently saw the launch of bilateral talks between English Anglicans and representatives of various English and UK-wide Pentecostal churches and networks.[1] From this more specific national context, several themes will emerge as relevant to global ecumenical interaction between these two church traditions.

Over the past 40 years Pentecostals have engaged in either regional or international dialogue with Roman Catholic, Reformed, Lutheran, and other major church bodies. By contrast, Anglican–

---

* David Hilborn (PhD, Nottingham University) is Principal of St John's College, Nottingham, England. Prior to that he was Assistant Dean of St Mellitus College in London, which he helped to establish in partnership with the School of Theology at Holy Trinity, Brompton. From 1997-2006 he was Head of Theology at the Evangelical Alliance UK. He has been an Associate Research Fellow at the London School of Theology and is currently a member of the Faith and Order Commission of the Church of England and the Society for Pentecostal Studies. His several books include David Hilborn, *'Toronto' in Perspective: Papers on the New Charismatic Wave of the Mid-1990's* (Milton Keynes: Paternoster, 2001), and Ian M. Randall and David Hilborn, *One Body in Christ* (Milton Keynes: Paternoster, 2001).

[1] The first meeting of this bilateral process took place at Church House, Westminster on April 19, 2013. Further meetings are planned.

Pentecostal theological exchange has rarely progressed in a structured ecumenical framework beyond recorded intentions or preliminary explorations.[2] This is especially surprising given that it was an Anglican priest who acted as a key conduit for the inflow of Pentecostalism to Britain over a century ago. One of the first European Christian leaders affected by the Azusa Street Revival, the Norwegian Thomas Ball Barratt (1862-1940), was visited soon after he had made an exploratory trip to America by Alexander Boddy (1854-1930), Rector of the Church of England parish of All Saints Monkwearmouth, in Sunderland. Boddy was deeply touched by Barratt's ministry and on his return All Saints became a focus for those pursuing baptism in the Spirit from all over the British Isles.[3] Baptism in the spirit and glossolalia became prominent features of this ministry, even as Boddy himself stressed that divine love and exaltation

---

[2] At the Lambeth Conference of 1988, a resolution was passed by the Bishops resolving to seek dialogue between the Anglican Communion and classical Pentecostal denominations: 'This Conference notes the rapid growth of Pentecostal Churches in many parts of the world, and encourages where possible the initiation of personal contact and theological dialogue with Pentecostal Churches especially at the local level' (Resolution 11). At the next Lambeth Conference in 1998, a further resolution (IV.21) invited the Inter-Anglican Standing Commission on Ecumenical Relations (IASCER) to explore the possibility of conversations 'between the Anglican Communion and the Pentecostal churches, at an appropriate level'. At the same conference, a complementary resolution (IV.25) was also passed resolving to improve understanding and encounter with 'New Churches and Independent Christian Groups' – specifically Neocharismatic networks such as the Vineyard, which had no 'ecclesial connection with an historic denomination or alliance'. Whereas the resolution on Anglican–Pentecostal dialogue was taken forward on the global Anglican level by IASCER, this second resolution was at first progressed more specifically through the Church of England, in the form of an 'open-textured' group chaired by the then Bishop of Ely, the Rt Revd Prof Stephen Sykes. Two 'pre-dialogue' meetings of this group were held in January and May 1999, but Bishop Stephen Sykes's move to become Principal of St John's College, Durham soon after this meant that was no longer able to chair the Ely group, and it appears from the archive that no suitable or willing replacement for him could be found. Certainly, there were no more meetings of the group after the second one of May 1999. As for IASCER and the ACC, the subject of Pentecostal and New Churches continued to feature as a topic of discussion in meetings and conferences until 2003, as it did in the Inter-Anglican Standing Commission on Mission and Evangelism (IASCOME), but it seems to have faded from focus thereafter.

[3] Gavin Wakefield, *The First Pentecostal Anglican: The Life and Legacy of Alexander Boddy* (Cambridge: Grove Books, 2001). See also Wakefield's more in-depth study, *Alexander Boddy: Pentecostal Anglican Pioneer* (Milton Keynes: Paternoster, 2007).

of Christ were more important than speaking tongues.[4] This so-called Sunderland Revival bore significant fruit – both directly in terms of initiatives led by Boddy himself and indirectly in terms of those touched by his ministry who would go on to pioneer their own more distinctively Pentecostal churches and networks – among them Donald Gee, Howard Carter, and Smith Wigglesworth, the last of whom went on to partner George Jeffreys, founder of the Elim Alliance. After the First World War, however, Boddy's part in the story began to fade from view, and it would be another four decades, with the rise of the neo-Pentecostal or Charismatic movement in Anglican and other churches, that the two traditions would once again converge in a significant way.[5]

Now, almost a century after the Sunderland Revival and half a century after the rise of the Charismatic movement in Anglicanism, the Council for Christian Unity has identified Anglican–Pentecostal ecumenical relations as a priority for the Church of England, along-side the Anglican–Methodist Covenant and the ongoing Anglican–Roman Catholic conversations in England and worldwide (ARCIC). It should be clear from what follows that this initiative is long over-due. It should also become clear that whereas the more classically ecumenical concern with 'faith and order' that has preoccupied so many Anglican theologians has registered far less prominently in Pentecostal theology, there is now a genuine flowering of Pentecostal ecclesiology which promises to make theological dialogue between the two traditions more substantial and more mutually enriching than it might have been even 10 years ago. Although more specific treatment of them belongs to another paper, the various anatomies of Pentecostal ecclesiology offered in recent years by, among others, Simon Chan, Wolfgang Vondey, Frank Macchia, Amos Yong, and Veli-Matti Kärkkäinen promise greater ecumenical methodological congruity with Anglicanism than ever before, even if significant differences of focus and emphasis might remain.[6] In-

---

4 Wakefield, *Alexander Boddy*, p. 7.

5 For a thorough history of this convergence see Peter Hocken, *Streams of Renewal: The Origins and Early Development of the Charismatic Movement in Great Britain* (Carlisle: Paternoster, 2nd edn, 1997).

6 Simon Chan, *Pentecostal Ecclesiology: An Essay on the Development of Doctrine* (JPTSup 38; Dorset: Deo Publishers, 2011); Wolfgang Vondey, *Beyond Pentecostalism: The Crisis of Global Christianity and the Renewal of the Theological Agenda* (Grand Rapids: Eerdmans, 2010), pp. 141-70; Frank D. Macchia, *Baptized in the Spirit: A*

deed, confirmation of this is provided by the fact that among the most sophisticated such Pentecostal ecclesiologies is that recently published by an Anglican priest and scholar: Andy Lord's *Network Church: A Pentecostal Ecclesiology Shaped by Mission.*[7]

Pentecostalism and the Changing Shape of Ecumenism

Whether Pentecostals are numbered around 300 or 600 million, their reshaping of the world Christian map has, in Allan Anderson's phrase, 'enormous ecumenical implications'.[8] Yet as noted above, the Church of England and the Anglican Communion have taken far longer than other Christian traditions to realise this – or at least, to respond to it in programmatic ecumenical terms. Given this neglect, there is much that Anglicans can gain by studying past and present dialogues between other historic churches and Pentecostals. In particular, the distinctive history and theological complexion of Anglicanism as a church 'both catholic and Reformed' means that Pentecostal dialogues in recent times with Roman Catholics, Presbyterians, and Lutherans are likely to prove the most pertinent.

Pointers from Pentecostal dialogues with other traditions

Roman Catholic–Pentecostal dialogue

From 1972 onwards the Vatican Secretariat for Promoting Christian Unity sponsored a series of dialogues with 'Leaders of Some Pentecostal Churches' – a process which has continued in one form or another to the present and which has produced four brief but helpful reports and a fifth much longer document.[9] This encounter is

---

Global Pentecostal Theology (Grand Rapids: Zondervan, 2006), pp. 155-256; Amos Yong, *The Spirit Poured Out on All Flesh: Pentecostalism and the Possibility of Global Theology* (Grand Rapids: Baker Academic, 2005); Veli-Matti Kärkkäinen, *Toward a Pneumatological Theology: Pentecostal and Ecumenical Perspectives on Ecclesiology, Soteriology and Theology of Mission* (Lanham, MD: University Press of America, 2002), pp. 81-146.

[7] Andy Lord, *Network Church: A Pentecostal Ecclesiology Shaped by Mission* (Leiden: Brill, 2012).

[8] Allan Anderson, *An Introduction to Pentecostalism: Global Charismatic Christianity* (Cambridge: Cambridge University Press, 2004), p. 15.

[9] Jeffrey Gros, Harding Meyer, and William G. Rusch (eds.), *Growth in Agreement II: Reports and Agreed Statements of Ecumenical Conversations on a World Level, 1982-1998* (Grand Rapids: Eerdmans, 2001), Ch. XXVI – 'Pentecostal-Roman

significant from an Anglican point of view because many of the topics it has covered over the past 40 years resonate with issues that Anglicans would be likely to highlight in ecumenical discussion with Pentecostals – e.g. Christian initiation, charismata in public worship, the relative authority of experience, tradition and Scripture, the nature and exercise of healing, orders and functions of ministry, apostolicity and episcopacy, church, koinonia and Christian unity, the communion of saints, the Spirit and the Church, mission, evangelization, proselytism and religious freedom, and conversion and discipleship. Also worth noting here, however, is the fact that this process initially involved Charismatic participants from Protestant churches with whom Rome was in dialogue, as well as Catholics and Pentecostals. Among these additional contributors was Michael Harper (1931-2010), a pioneer of neo-Pentecostal theology and spirituality in the Church of England who had led the influential ecumenical charismatic network known as the Fountain Trust. However, just as the Pentecostals taking part were doing so as committed individuals rather than as 'delegates' of their denominations or networks, so Harper was invited on the basis of his parachurch role rather than as a spokesman for the Church of England or the Anglican Communion.[10] Even so, Harper's main contributions to the process reflected characteristic 'catholic' Anglican concerns for church and liturgy: in the third round of the first dialogue he contributed a paper entitled 'The Holy Spirit Acts in the Church, its Structure, its Sacramentality, its Worship and Sacraments', and in the fourth round he gave a further paper on 'Principles of Congregational Worship'.[11]

As with other ecumenical dialogues in which Pentecostals would be involved, it soon became clear after some preliminary meetings between the Pontifical Council and Pentecostals in 1970-71 that traditional 'faith and order' approaches would need to be modified in this context. As the report on the first Quinquennial phase of the

---

Catholic Dialogue', pp. 713-79. For the text of the report on the fifth dialogue, which took place between 1998 and 2006, see the website of the Pontifical Council at <http://www.vatican.va/roman_curia/pontifical_councils/chrstuni/eccl-comm-docs / rc_pc_chrstuni_doc_20060101_becoming-a-christian_en.html> (accessed August 10, 2013).

[10] Jerry L. Sandidge, *Roman Catholic/Pentecostal Dialogue (1977-1982): A Study in Developing Ecumenism* (Frankfurt am Main: Peter Lang, 1987), pp. 79, 98.

[11] Sandidge, *Roman Catholic/Pentecostal Dialogue*, p. 90.

dialogue proper notes, 'before it began it was made clear that its immediate scope was not "to concern itself with the problems of imminent structural union" ... Its purpose has been that "prayer, spirituality and theological reflection be a shared concern at the international level".'[12] Although by the second Dialogue (1977-82) non-Roman and non-Pentecostal input had been phased out in order to bring 'clearer focus' to the interaction,[13] this less formal, more relational ethos has continued down to the present, sixth stage of the process. Furthermore, it established an important template for other bilaterals that would follow – a template that will surely need to be maintained as Anglican–Pentecostal dialogue develops in England and beyond.

Pentecostal-Reformed Dialogue

For all its claims to continuity with medieval Catholicism, the Church of England is at least as much if not more defined by its distinctive constitution as a Protestant church in the Reformation period as by its more general pre-existence as a Catholic 'English Church', or by more recent attempts to reassert that Catholic past.[14] Given this Reformation background, any putative Anglican–Pentecostal dialogue would benefit from taking note of the ecumenical exchanges that have taken place in the past twenty years or so between Pentecostals, Reformed, and Lutheran traditions.

Between 1996 and 2000, the informal tenor of the Roman Catholic–Pentecostal process was echoed in a wide-ranging dialogue between the World Alliance of Reformed Churches (WARC) and 'leaders from some classical Pentecostal churches'.[15] Once more here, an 'asymmetry' was acknowledged in that Pentecostal representatives were largely participating as respected individuals within their own church contexts but had no global body such as WARC to mandate them or to which they were officially accountable. A

---

[12] 'Final Report: Dialogue between the Secretariat for Promoting Christian Unity and Leaders of Some Pentecostal Churches and Participants in the Charismatic Movements within Protestant and Anglican Churches', in Gros, Meyer, and Rusch, *Growth in Agreement II*, p. 713.

[13] Gros, Meyer, and Rusch, *Growth in Agreement II*, p. 722.

[14] Diarmaid MacCulloch, 'The Myth of the English Reformation', *Journal of British Studies* 30.1 (January, 1991), pp. 10-14.

[15] 'Word and Spirit, Church and World: Pentecostal–Reformed Dialogue, 1996-2000'. Available at <http://www.warc.ch/dt/erl1/20.html> (accessed August 10, 2013). Also published in *Pneuma* 23.1 (Spring, 2001), pp. 9-43.

second round of dialogue commenced in 2001 on the subject of 'Experience in Christian Faith and Life' and was recently concluded, with WARC having changed its name part-way through to the World Communion of Reformed Churches.[16] Here, due to constraints of space and because it established core themes on which the second dialogue elaborated, I will focus on the first of these two processes.

The 1996-2000 dialogue began by concentrating on spirituality, and this was deliberate – a recognition of the fact that Pentecostalism characteristically construes theology through prayer and worship.[17] By contrast, the Reformed tradition has typically seen doctrine as framing and defining worship and on this basis has allowed liturgy to be varied and extemporised within loose, non-prescriptive frameworks as long as it is 'orthodox' and specifically as long as it accords with various dogmatic confessions of faith.[18] This, in essence, was the aspiration of the Puritan party within the Church of England, but since the reintroduction of the *Book of Common Prayer* after the Restoration under Charles II, Anglicanism's attachment to authorised liturgical texts has led even its most Calvinistic constituencies to acknowledge liturgy as embodying and delineating the faith of the Church, in accordance with the ancient formula *lex orandi lex credendi*.[19] Likewise, Pentecostals may eschew the prescribed liturgies of Anglicanism, but their characteristic construal of theology as fundamentally doxological should find an echo in Anglicanism which was, perhaps, less apparent in the WARC process.

Under the subsequent heading 'Spirit and Word', both parties in the WARC–Pentecostal dialogue agreed that their respective historic emphases on the ministries of the Spirit (Pentecostal) and the Word (Reformed) should be subjected to more thoroughly Trinitar-

---

[16] Full text available at <http://www.pctii.org/cyberj/cyberj21/WARC_ 201 1d.html> (accessed August 10, 2013).

[17] 'Word and Spirit, Church and World', pp. 9-14.

[18] Nicholas Wolterstorff, 'The Reformed Liturgy', in Donald K. McKim (ed.), *Major Themes in the Reformed Tradition* (Grand Rapids: Eerdmans, 1992), pp. 273-304; Hughes Oliphant Old, *Themes and Variations for a Christian Doxology: Some Thoughts on the Theology of Worship* (Grand Rapids: Eerdmans, 1992), pp. 1-16. John H. Leith, *Introduction to the Reformed Tradition* (Atlanta: John Knox, rev. edn, 1981), pp. 174-97.

[19] Cf. D.E.W. Harrison & Michael C. Sansom, *Worship in the Church of England* (London: SPCK, 1982); Kenneth Stevenson, Kenneth Spinks, and Bryan Spinks (eds.), *The Identity of Anglican Worship* (London: Mowbray, 1991).

ian examination. While for the Reformed this would mean a reappraisal of the role of charismata in worship, Pentecostals recognised that there would be value in taking account of the generally greater Reformed emphasis on the life of the Trinity in relation to creation – an emphasis which had historically informed a more distinct social and political heritage.[20] To some extent this mutual re-emphasis on the Trinity reflects a broader 'Trinitarian turn' in doctrinal theology, and ecumenical theology in particular, since the 1960s.[21] Anglican theologians like Rowan Williams, Daniel Hardy, Paul Avis, and Tim Bradshaw have made their own valuable contributions to this turn, and with its unique blend of Catholic, Reformed, and Lutheran influences, the Anglican contribution to prospective Anglican–Pentecostal dialogue is well set to enhance the good work already done in this area by the WARC–Pentecostal report.[22]

In a later section of the WARC–Pentecostal document entitled 'The Holy Spirit and the Church', both parties affirmed that the Church is the creature of the Word and Spirit, that it is the community of the Spirit's leading and of the Spirit's gifts, and that it is in but not of the world. However, whereas the Reformed tradition's characteristic stress on 'covenant' as a key descriptor of God's initiative in forming the Church had led to a strongly corporate and sacramental ecclesiology, Pentecostals had tended towards a pneumatocentric ecclesiology in which the Church is 'formed by the outpouring of the Spirit and shaped by the Spirit's gifts', but in which the role of sacraments or ordinances may not be so obviously linked with the building up of the body. In similar vein, whereas corporately agreed confessions had gone a long way towards defining the faith, life, and mission of the Church in the Reformed tradition, Pentecostals were likely to place greater stress on the accumulation of personal testimonies as authenticators of rightness with God.[23] While Anglicanism might not have relied as distinctively on

---

20 'Word and Spirit, Church and World', pp. 15-21.

21 World Council of Churches, *The Nature and Mission of the Church* (Faith and Order Paper 198; Geneva: WCC, 2005), esp. pp. 13-28.

22 Rowan Williams, *On Christian Theology* (Oxford: Blackwell, 2000), esp. pp. 129-80; Daniel W. Hardy, *Finding the Church: The Dynamic Truth of Anglicanism* (London: SCM, 2001); Paul Avis, *Reshaping Ecumenical Theology: The Church Made Whole?* (London: T&T Clark, 2010); Tim Bradshaw, *The Olive Branch: An Evangelical Anglican Doctrine of the Church* (Carlisle: Paternoster, 1992), esp. pp. 239-301.

23 'Word and Spirit, Church and World', pp. 21-28.

covenant theology, its indebtedness to the Reformed tradition is reflected in a similarly sacramental ecclesiology which is, if anything, intensified by its simultaneous self-definition as a 'Catholic' church.[24] This should again complement and extend the insights gained in the WARC–Pentecostal exchange.

Under the heading of 'The Holy Spirit and Mission' both parties in the WARC–Pentecostal conversations recognised the centrality of the *Missio Dei* for their understanding of the Church's witness in the world. While the specific *empowerment* of the Church for mission is construed more distinctively by Pentecostals in relation to baptism in the Holy Spirit, both parties agreed on the importance of the prevenient work of the Spirit in the missional task – namely that 'the Spirit of Christ goes ahead of the Church to prepare the ground for the reception of the gospel'. While Reformed churches tend to view this prevenient work more positively than Pentecostals in relation to culture and non-Christian religions, both agreed that 'witness to the gospel should be embodied in culture' and that more attention should be paid to how such embodiment might best take place.[25] Pursuing this theme in a final section of the report headed 'Spirit and Kingdom', characteristic Reformed postmillennialism and Pentecostal premillennialism were frankly acknowledged as tending towards different emphases in social and civic engagement. Whereas Reformed Christians may naturally view themselves as 'stewards of the rich gifts of God' in the whole of creation, and might on this basis organise actively to oppose 'social injustices, economic exploitation and ecological destruction', Pentecostals were more likely to view structural and systemic sin in terms of 'spiritual warfare', and to take a more personalised and incremental view of social transformation.[26]

Evangelicals and Charismatics within the Anglican tradition have typically shared Pentecostalism's historic prioritization of evangelism over social concern, but ongoing interaction with more Catholic, liberal, and radical streams within their own tradition, as well as more developed hermeneutical understandings of mission on their own account, have seen Anglican Evangelicals and Charismatics

---

[24] Williams, *On Christian Theology,* pp. 197-221; Bradshaw, *Olive Branch,* pp. 129-95, Hardy, *Finding the Church,* pp. 77-114.

[25] 'Word and Spirit, Church and World', pp. 28-31.

[26] 'Word and Spirit, Church and World', pp. 32-37.

more recently endorsing and promoting broader definitions such as the 'Five Marks of Mission' developed by the Anglican Consultative Council between 1984 and 1990 ('to proclaim the Good News of the Kingdom; to teach, baptise and nurture new believers; to respond to human need by loving service; to seek to transform unjust structures of society, and to strive to safeguard the integrity of creation and sustain and renew the life of the earth').[27] At the same time, the growth and relative strength of Charismatics within Anglicanism in recent decades has been reflected in denominational reports such as *Mission-Shaped Church* (2004), which make traditional 'Pentecostal' concerns with evangelism and church planting central.[28] Thus as with the WARC–Pentecostal process, ecumenical dialogue between Anglicans and Pentecostals has the potential to enrich the nascent Pentecostal political theologies charted in more recent years by Douglas Petersen, Donald Miller, Tetsuanao Yamamori, and others,[29] even while reminding Anglicans in a post-Christendom context of their continuing evangelistic obligations.

Lutheran–Pentecostal Dialogues

With the success of the WARC–Pentecostal dialogue in mind, representatives of the Lutheran World Federation embarked in 2004 on an open dialogue with selected Pentecostal leaders. Conscious of the need to allow Pentecostals authentically to 'speak a Pentecostal language', the initial phase of this process focused on the question 'How do we encounter Christ?' Further phases of the dialogue are anticipated, but the report on this first round of conversations was published in 2010.[30] This established clear respective emphases in each of the traditions on justification (Lutheran) and sanctification

---

[27] <http://www.anglicancommunion.org /ministry /mission/fivemarks.cfm> (accessed August 10, 2013).

[28] *Church of England Mission and Public Affairs Council, Mission-Shaped Church: Church Planting and Fresh Expressions of Church in a Changing Context* (London: Church House, 2004).

[29] Douglas Petersen, *Not by Might nor by Power: Pentecostal Theology of Social Concern in Latin America* (Carlisle: Paternoster, 1996); Donald E. Miller & Tetsuanao Yamamori, *Global Pentecostalism: The New Face of Christian Social Engagement* (Berkeley: University of California Press, 2007); Ruth Marshall, *Political Spiritualities: The Pentecostal Revolution in Nigeria* (Chicago: University of Chicago Press, 2009).

[30] Institute for Ecumenical Research, David Du Plessis Center For Christian Spirituality & European Pentecostal Charismatic Research Association, *Lutherans and Pentecostals in Dialogue* (Strasbourg; Pasadena; Zurich: Institute for Ecumenical Research, 2010).

(Pentecostal), on formal and extemporary public worship, on *charismata,* on orders of ministry, and on sacraments.

These themes mirrored several concerns that, as we have seen, had already featured prominently in the Roman Catholic and Reformed–Pentecostal dialogues. However, their re-occurrence in this context bears particular significance for Anglican–Pentecostal interaction. This is because of all those engaged ecumenically by Anglicans, Lutherans are the ones with whom most progress towards unity has been achieved. *The Porvoo Common Statement* (1992) ensured full visible communion between British and Irish Anglican churches and Baltic and Nordic Lutheran churches, while the *Reuilly Common Statement* (1999) brought British and Irish Anglicans into closer unity with French Lutheran and Reformed churches. As the Anglican bishops noted at their Lambeth Conference of 1998, 'Anglicans and Lutherans are rediscovering substantial doctrinal agreement and, sometimes with surprise, a similarity in worship, mission and ministry. We have a familial likeness'.[31] On one level this is not surprising: after all, Luther's retention of bishops and formalized liturgy, together with his relative conservatism compared with other Reformers on questions of Church and state, mean that it is his theology and ecclesiology, more than Calvin's or Zwingli's, which has come more durably to influence the Church of England.[32]

As with the Roman Catholic and WARC dialogues, the problem of Pentecostal representation was acknowledged in this exchange with the Lutheran World Federation, as was the lack of any Pentecostal equivalent to the Lutheran Augsburg Confession (1530) – that is, to a core statement or code of doctrine which might be said to define the movement. Even so, the common Pentecostal formulation of the 'full gospel', in which Christ exercises a five-fold office as Justifier, Sanctifier, Baptizer in the Spirit, Healer, and Soon-Coming King, was seen as fertile ground for more convergent understanding of the faith, as was each tradition's commitment to the

---

[31] Sarah Rowland Jones (ed.), *The Vision Before Us: The Kyoto Report of the Inter-Anglican Standing Commission on Ecumenical Relations, 2000-2008* (London: Anglican Communion Office, 2009), p. 156.

[32] C.R. Trueman, *Luther's Legacy: Salvation and the English Reformers 1525-1556* (Oxford: Clarendon, 1994).

supremacy of Scripture.[33] These starting-points will no doubt also prove fruitful in any future Anglican–Pentecostal discussions.

World Council of Churches Joint Consultative Group on Pentecostalism (JCGP)

Since 2000, a sustained process of dialogue between World Council of Churches and Pentecostal representatives has developed in a Joint Consultative Group (JCGP).[34] The initial report of the JCGP acknowledged the 'fears, stereotypes and apprehensions' which participants carried into the meetings, but constructively addressed key divergences over proselytism, sacraments, discernment of the Spirit, and the nature of the Church.[35] As it completes its second term, the JCGP is currently preparing a report of its discussions on the marks of the Church.[36]

While non-Pentecostals on the JCGP range from backgrounds as diverse as Methodism, Presbyterianism, Russian Orthodoxy, Baptist, and Lutheran church communities, it is striking that no one has served on the group as an Anglican representative, despite the fact that Anglican churches have been full members of the WCC since its inception in 1948. Even so, Anglicans have been actively involved in the WCC-sponsored Global Christian Forum (GCF) and the Conference of Secretaries of Christian World Communions (CSCWC). These are loosely-constituted relational organizations which provide space for interaction between Pentecostal leaders and representatives of other Christian traditions.[37] The GCF was conceived by the then WCC General Secretary Konrad Raiser in 1999 as a non-affiliated body designed specifically to enfranchise Pentecostals and Independent Evangelicals, among others. As an Anglican contributor Sarah Rowland Jones describes it, the GCF

> aims to bring together the widest possible range of Christians. Rather than focusing on questions of faith and order, its meetings begin with personal encounter through sharing faith jour-

---

[33] Institute for Ecumenical Research *et al.*, *Lutherans and Pentecostals in Dialogue.*

[34] World Council of Churches, 'Joint Consultative Group WCC–Pentecostals (JCPG) 2000-2005: Excerpts from the Report to the Ninth Assembly', in *Programme Book: Ninth Assembly, Porto Allegre* (WCC; Geneva, 2005), pp. 169-73.

[35] World Council of Churches, 'WCC–Pentecostals', pp. 171-72.

[36] <http://www.oikoumene.org /who-are-we /organization-structure /joint-bodies/with-pentecostal-churches.html> (accessed January 10, 2013).

[37] Rowland Jones, *The Vision Before Us*, pp. 202-204.

neys and exploring shared challenges faced by Christians … The Anglican Communion actively supports this 'affective' or 'spiritual' ecumenism, as a means of complementing and strengthening more traditional ecumenical approaches.[38]

Continuing this more flexible approach, a second Global Gathering of the GCF took place in Manado, Indonesia in September 2011. The Archbishop of Canterbury sent formal greetings to it, and the current author was privileged to represent the Church of England and to read the Archbishop's message there.

Although these trends indicate that greater partnership and cooperation is taking place between Pentecostals and a wide range of other church traditions, it remains the case that more focused bilateral ecumenical dialogue between Pentecostal and Anglican communities is still significantly under-developed – even if it is to move in the more 'affective' or 'spiritual' direction described by Rowland Jones. Hence the final section of this paper proposes a more detailed rationale for theological, and more specifically ecclesiological, understanding between Pentecostals and Anglicans.

Theological and Ecclesiological Considerations

Many of the theological concerns raised in the Roman Catholic-Pentecostal, WARC–Pentecostal, Lutheran–Pentecostal, and WCC–JCGP bilateral reports are likely to recur in Anglican–Pentecostal dialogue. Pneumatology in general and the understanding and expression of charismata in particular, the process of spiritual discernment and models of biblical authority and hermeneutics, the nature of the church and criteria for Christian unity or *koinonia*, the 'prosperity gospel' and demonology and deliverance ministry – all these issues will surely command attention. However, certain concerns are likely to arise more specifically from the Anglican–Pentecostal dynamic and not least from the expression of that dynamic in the English Anglican context.

Protestant and non-Protestant identities

As we have seen, the Church of England's self-understanding has often been marked by attempts to mediate between its Reformation

---

[38] Rowland Jones, *The Vision Before Us,* p. 198.

formularies and its pre-Reformation or 'Catholic' roots. Like Anglicans, Pentecostals differ on the debt they owe to the Reformation and the extent to which they might claim a 'Protestant' or 'Evangelical' identity in addition to their particular claims to 'apostolic' authenticity.[39] A dedicated Anglican–Pentecostal dialogue could helpfully relate these self-understandings to practical ecumenical alignments between Anglicans and Pentecostals, and between Anglicans, Pentecostals, and others.

Christian Initiation

Important questions arise at the Anglican–Pentecostal interface with respect to Christian Initiation. Since Pentecostal churches are gathered 'believers' churches' overwhelmingly practising adult baptism by immersion, Pentecostals can find the Church of England's commitment to infant baptism, and more particularly its undertaking to baptize all parishioners who come or are brought for baptism, challenging. If the issues at stake here are similar to those raised in recent Baptist–Anglican dialogues, a more distinctive question concerns the relationship, if any, between the Anglican practice of confirmation and the key Pentecostal doctrine of 'baptism in the Spirit'. The same NT texts (e.g. Acts 8.14-17; 19.1-7) are typically cited in apologetics for each, but for the most part Pentecostalism does not practise or recognise confirmation. Anglican–Pentecostal dialogue could thus usefully explore continuities and discontinuities between Anglican understandings of confirmation and Pentecostal models of conversion and baptism in and/or filling with the Spirit. This in turn would have implications for Anglican Charismatics, who are obliged by canon to hold confirmation and Spirit baptism in creative theological relationship. Possible rapprochement here is suggested by Laurence W. Wood, who construes 'holiness' emphases on Christian perfection in certain forms of Wesleyan and Pentecostal soteriology as a reinterpretation of Roman Catholic and Anglican rites of confirmation.[40] Hence Anglican and Catholic confirmation, like Wesley's concept of perfection or 'entire sanctification', is 'a second definitive work of grace in the life of the Christian be-

---

[39] Amos Yong, 'The Word and the Spirit or the Spirit and the Word: Exploring the Boundaries of Evangelicalism in Relationship to Modern Pentecostalism', *Trinity Journal* 23.2 (Fall 2002), pp. 235-52.

[40] Laurence W. Wood, *Pentecostal Grace* (Grand Rapids: Francis Asbury, 1980), pp. 240-57.

liever', even if the Wesleyan doctrine of entire sanctification 'does not absolutize the concepts of crisis and subsequency' quite in the way that much Pentecostal soteriology tends to do.[41] More practically, the questions posed to Anglicans and Pentecostals by Martin Davie on this subject will be well worth addressing:

> [Anglican and other] churches that practise confirmation might want to ask the Pentecostals what prevents them from recognizing the rite of confirmation as providing an occasion for people to receive the power and presence of the Holy Spirit in their lives in a new way ... On the other hand, the Pentecostals might want to ask those churches that practise confirmation for evidence that those who are confirmed really do receive the gift of the Spirit. Where, they might ask, are those supernatural signs of the Spirit's presence that are present in the New Testament accounts of the life of the early church and have been a key part of Pentecostal experience?[42]

The experience and legacy of John Wesley

This presentation of Wesley as a 'bridge figure' between Anglican and proto-Pentecostal theologies of confirmation may be extended into other areas of theological dialogue between the two traditions. The rootedness of many Pentecostal churches in Wesleyan Holiness spirituality is significant here as is the fact that despite his founding of Methodism, Wesley maintained a lifelong commitment to the Church of England.[43] Wesley's development of a theology of experience and of experience complementing Scripture, reason, and tradition as sources of theology has been deeply influential on both Pentecostals and Anglicans. In a 2002 article for *Pneuma,* the journal of the Society for Pentecostal Studies, Edmund Rybarczyk comments on this Wesleyan link but then makes a suggestive further connection, *via* Wesley, between Anglicanism, Pentecostalism, and Eastern Orthodoxy:

> Pentecostals built upon and reprocessed Wesley's own experiential foundations, foundations that were themselves modifi-

---

[41] Wood, *Pentecostal Grace*, p. 242.

[42] Martin Davie, 'Confirmation and Christian Unity', in Paul Avis (ed.), *The Journey of Christian Initiation: Theological and Pastoral Perspectives* (London: Church House, 2011), p. 88.

[43] William K. Kay, *Pentecostalism* (London: SCM, 2009), pp. 25-32.

cations of the implications of Greek patristic theology. Through Wesley, Anglicanism provides some historical connection between Pentecostalism and Orthodoxy. Because it severed its ties from Rome but continued to maintain the latter's ... ecclesial system, Anglicanism understands itself to be a *via media* between Catholicism and Protestantism. [In turn] I think Pentecostalism can be viewed as a kind of mystical *via media* between Orthodoxy and more rational branches of Protestantism [44]

The significance of 'the Anglican Wesley' in this sense should not be lost amidst the fast-growing interest of Pentecostal scholars and leaders in the 'Methodist', 'Holiness', and 'Perfectionist' Wesley as a precursor to their own tradition – an interest demonstrated very clearly by the fact that the 2013 conference of the Society for Pentecostal Studies took place in conjunction with the Wesleyan Theological Society at the Methodist-founded Seattle Pacific University and focused on the theme of Holiness. This is a subject which bears considerable further exploration at the Anglican–Pentecostal interface.

Sacraments

Given the emphasis of many classical Pentecostals on believers' baptism, baptism in the Spirit as a 'second blessing', and speaking in tongues as 'initial evidence' of such Spirit-baptism, it might strike more sacramentally-minded Anglicans as strange that the Lord's Supper has so relatively low a profile in most modern-day Pentecostal churches. Building on the substantial work done on this area by the Catholic, Reformed, and Lutheran dialogues mentioned above, Anglican–Pentecostal dialogue will need to explore the two traditions' respective understandings of sacraments and sacramental life and offer guidelines for mutual reception of the Lord's Supper in each tradition. In doing so, it may well pursue John Christopher Thomas' suggestion that although many Pentecostals prefer to present sacraments in terms of 'ordinances', Pentecostal 'sacramentality' might be seen as having been reconfigured into a five-fold pattern of water baptism, footwashing, glossolalia, and anointing

---

[44] Edmund J. Rybarczyk, 'Spiritualities Old and New: Similarities between Eastern Orthodoxy and Classical Pentecostalism', *Pneuma* 24.1 (Spring, 2002), p. 23.

with oil, alongside the Lord's Supper understood mainly in terms of Christ the Coming King.[45]

Ministry, Apostolicity, and Episcopacy

Ecumenical dialogues between Anglicans and others have been significantly shaped by Anglicans' insistence on the three-fold order of Deacons, Priests, and Bishops as a key mark of their ecclesial identity.[46] Certain Pentecostal churches appoint their leaders as 'Bishops', but others do not. Even those who do so, however, typically apply a pragmatic approach related to function rather than any more 'catholic' notion of 'apostolic succession' linked to episcopal orders. As one leader of the English New Testament Assemblies has put it, 'In the Sixties we called them Superintendents; in the Seventies we changed the name to Overseers; more recently we have been calling them Bishops'.[47] Most Pentecostal churches term their ministers 'Pastors' rather than 'Priests', and Deacons are rarer. Some ordain women as Pastors and Bishops; others do not. Some do not ordain church leaders at all, whereas others ordain pastors and non-pastors alike to a wide range of offices and tasks, defined not least in relation to the 'five-fold' pattern of Eph. 4.11 (apostle, prophet, evangelist, pastor, and teacher). Anglican–Pentecostal dialogue would benefit from exploring lines of rapprochement and divergence on such models of ministry and leadership, and could suggest ways in which orders and offices might be mutually recognized across the two traditions.

More specifically, it will be worth noting that the concept of apostolicity has been radically reapplied in certain Pentecostal and Charismatic communities as a designation merited by those who plant churches, oversee church networks, or otherwise lead significant numbers of Christians, regardless of whether or how they might have been ordained.[48] Once again this apparently functional, mission-driven approach presents challenges to more institutional-

---

[45] John Christopher Thomas, 'Pentecostal Theology in the Twenty-First Century', *Pneuma* 20.1 (1998), pp. 18-19.

[46] See especially the Meissen Agreement, 1988; the Porvoo Common Statement, 1995. Available at <http://www.anglicancommunion.org /ministry / ecumenical/dialogues/index.cfm> (accessed August 10, 2013).

[47] Interview conducted by the author with Nezlin Sterling of the New Testament Assemblies (January 27, 2011).

[48] Keith Warrington, *Pentecostal Theology: A Theology of Encounter* (London: Continuum, 2008), pp. 138-42.

ized understandings of apostolicity linked to episcopacy – challenges that have already been recognized and addressed in some depth by the Roman Catholic–Pentecostal dialogue but which could benefit from fruitful re-examination in the distinct but related context of Anglican–Pentecostal interaction.[49]

Mission, Social Action, and Proselytism
Dialogues between 'magisterial' Christian traditions and Pentecostals have characteristically revealed differences of theology and practice with respect to mission. Whereas churches shaped by a 'Christendom' paradigm have tended to relate mission to inculturation of the gospel within societies and nation states and have developed missiologies and public theologies to match, Pentecostals have typically promulgated a 'believers' church' ethos in which mission is understood principally in terms of evangelism, or what the Elim scholar Keith Warrington more precisely calls 'enlargement of the Church' – that is, in terms of personal conversion, immersion baptism, and incorporation into the local congregation. Although as noted above, some are now developing distinctive Pentecostal theologies and missiologies of social concern, Warrington still reports 'limited social involvement' as a trait of Pentecostal mission,[50] and we have already noted how the WARC–Pentecostal dialogue in particular highlighted the need for Pentecostals to develop a more holistic 'extra-ecclesial' pneumatology in which the gifts of the Spirit are seen to be applied in the service of the common good and in which the prophetic racial and gender inclusiveness of Azusa Street is recovered and reasserted.[51] As we have also noted, recent moves by Anglican Evangelicals and Charismatics to promote more holistic paradigms such as the 'Five Marks of Mission' mean that creative Anglican–Pentecostal engagement on social action should be possible.[52]

---

[49] Gros, Meyer, and Rusch, *Growth in Agreement II*, pp. 731-33; 747-48. Cf. Terry Virgo, leader of the Neo-Charismatic network New Frontiers International, who argues for apostleship as a modern-day designation of church planting as well as a description of those directly appointed by Christ or privy to his resurrection. At <www.terryvirgo.org> (accessed August 10, 2013).

[50] Warrington, *Pentecostal Theology*, p. 263.

[51] 'Word and Spirit, Church and World', p. 6.

[52] <http://www.anglicancommunion.org/ministry/mission/fivemarks.cfm> (accessed August 10, 2013).

Liturgiology and Doxology

As Ann Dyer notes, Pentecostal worship is distinguished by its preference for 'freedom of expression and extempore prayer'. While this might appear to contrast with an Anglican polity defined to a significant degree by its attachment to canonical liturgical texts like the *Book of Common Prayer* and *Common Worship*, Dyer echoes a number of linguistic and theological studies when she suggests that 'there is often an underlying oral liturgy in Pentecostal services'. The seminal work of Bruce A. Rosenberg and subsequent studies by Daniel Albrecht and James Steven bear this out.[53] Although Anglican–Pentecostal dialogue will no doubt highlight significant differences of approach in this area, the more general instinct towards 'structuring' and 'ordering' worship, even when it is not codified in writing, will be worth exploring.

Having said this, Anglican Charismatic worship, at least, often sits quite lightly to the canonical liturgies of its *own* denominational tradition and typically more resembles the ethos of Pentecostal worship. By the same token, fieldwork undertaken on ten Pentecostal and neo-Pentecostal services in preparation for the current Church of England–Pentecostal dialogue reveals the emergence of a more generic version of 'free worship', distinct in certain respects from the ethos of classical Pentecostalism. For example, whereas the open exercise of *charismata* is typically taken to be a defining mark of Pentecostalism, not one of the services studied in this survey featured a prophecy, word of knowledge, tongue, or interpretation from within the congregation. Nor was 'ministry' to individuals conducted within the service itself; rather, it was offered as a separate event after the service proper had concluded with a blessing or dismissal. Likewise, whereas regular celebration of the Lord's Supper has been identified as a mark of earlier classical Pentecostal

---

[53] Ann Dyer, 'Worship: Introduction', in William K. Kay & Anne E. Dyer (eds.), *Pentecostal and Charismatic Studies: A Reader* (London: SCM Press, 2004), p. 144; Bruce A. Rosenberg, *The Art of the American Folk Preacher* (Cambridge: Cambridge University Press, 1970); Daniel E. Albrecht, *Rites in the Spirit: A Ritual Approach to Pentecostal/Charismatic Spirituality* (JPTSup 17; Sheffield: Sheffield Academic Press, 1999); James H.S. Steven, *Worship in the Spirit: Charismatic Worship in the Church of England* (Carlisle: Paternoster, 2003).

worship,[54] Communion was celebrated in only one of these ten services.[55]

This apparent shift of approach to public worship resonates with a key trend highlighted by Dyer – namely the rise of the 'music leader' and 'the music group', whose playing of extended 'praise songs' has become a common feature of worship in these contexts. Such songs, indeed, seem now to offer the main opportunity for ecstatic congregational expression in these settings, with the exercise of charismata by 'the people' becoming relatively less prominent. Calvin Johansson has also noted these trends and assesses them critically as seemingly spontaneous but in fact 'highly scripted' and 'carefully orchestrated', on the basis that 'orders of songs, numbers of repetitions, keys, and decibel levels require pre-planning and rehearsal.[56] Indeed, for Johansson, Pentecostal worship has 'maintained its subjective and emotional approach but ... to a considerable extent it has dropped true congregational spontaneity and a good share of congregational participation for the appearance of spontaneity which is highly planned and dominated by worship leaders'.[57]

Perhaps this pattern was reinforced in the generally larger congregations featured in the CCU survey, where the ability of all to hear a prophecy, word of knowledge, or tongue was limited, and where the imperatives of starting, finishing, and even broadcasting successive services on time made for a more programmatic and controlled style, driven 'from the front'. Anglican–Pentecostal dialogue could helpfully explore the development of this new 'common order', and assess what has been lost and gained by it in relation to more established approaches in each tradition and in relation to the implicit pneumatology being mediated in each case.

---

[54] Walter Hollenweger, *The Pentecostals* (London: SCM, 1972), pp. 385-90.

[55] Survey of public worship services conducted between January and March 2011. Churches surveyed: Jesus House, Brent – 1/16/11; Kingsway International Christian Centre, Walthamstow – 1/23/11; Kensington Temple (London City Church), Notting Hill – 2/6/11; Tower Hamlets Community Church, Bow – 2/27/11; City Chapel, Beckton – 3/5/11; Glory House, Plaistow – 3/20/11; City Gates, Ilford – 3/27/11; Spring Harvest Big Top Celebrations – 4/20/11 – 4/22/11 inclusive.

[56] Calvin Johansson, 'Pentecostal Worship', in *New SCM Dictionary of Liturgy and Worship* (London: SCM, 2002), pp. 370.

[57] Johansson, 'Pentecostal Worship', p. 371.

Continuing the 'Harper Legacy'

As the dialogue outlined above is developed, it will owe much to Michael Harper. Although he later left the Church of England to become a priest and then Archpriest in the Antiochian Orthodox Church, there can be little doubt that apart, perhaps, from Boddy, he was the most influential ecumenical partner to Pentecostals that Anglicanism has yet produced.

Shortly before he died in 2010, Harper gave an address at an event held to mark the centenary of the Sunderland Revival.[58] Among other things, the address is a passionate call to Pentecostals and Charismatics to engage with Eastern Orthodox theology and spirituality, and Harper would be glad to know of recent attempts by Harold Hunter and others to take forward the interaction between these traditions that he fostered towards the end of his life.[59] Warming to his theme, Harper rejoiced in the increased openness of Pentecostals to historic ecumenical concerns with 'the Church itself, her sacraments, liturgy and authority'. Yet he also rejoiced in the successive 'waves of the Spirit' that had refreshed and energised that same church in revival, Pentecostal outpouring, and Charismatic renewal. 'Let us weigh all things carefully, let us test the spirits', he concluded, 'but let us then welcome the new waves as they come in, and bathe ourselves in them'.[60] It is sincerely to be hoped that this judicious blend of discernment, openness, and enthusiasm will mark the Anglican–Pentecostal dialogue that has been mapped out here.

---

[58] Michael Harper, *The Waves Keep Coming In: The Evangelical, Charismatic, Orthodox Axis* (Cambridge: Target, 2008).

[59] His All Holiness Ecumenical Patriarch Bartholomew I met a Pentecostal team including Harold D. Hunter in Istanbul on October 3-7, 2010 for informal talks. Talks are continuing at the time of this writing.

[60] Harper, *The Waves Keep Coming In*, p. 21.

15

A NEVER ENDING CANADIAN PENTECOSTAL CHALLENGE: WHAT TO DO WITH THE WOMEN

PAMELA HOLMES*

Introduction

The Women

Within the early years of Canadian Pentecostalism, whether or not one was qualified to minister, it was the Holy Spirit who was understood to be the One who gifts people for ministry within the church. As the Spirit could gift whomever the Spirit pleased, leadership was on the basis of giftings. 'Individuals were to be honored for their God-given gifts and not their pedigree, natural talents or education'.[1] When it came to women, 'in the early Pentecostal movement, having the "anointing" was far more important than one's sex'[2] or being part of an organization. Women as well as men

---

* Pamela M.S. Holmes (PhD, University of St Michael's College) is Assistant Professor at Queen's School of Religion, Queen's University, Kingston, Ontario, where she directs the Field Education program and coordinates the Flora Jane Baker Clergy Sabbatical Fellowship. An ordained Pentecostal pastor with the Fellowship of Christian Assemblies, she is currently a Minister-at-Large with Quinte Community Christian Church Belleville and the FCA representative on board of the Ontario Multi-Faith Council.

[1] Randal Holm, 'Organizational Blues: The Struggle of One Pentecostal Denomination with the Bugbear of Institutionalism' (Paper presented at 24th Annual Meeting of the Society for Pentecostal Studies, Wheaton, Illinois, November 10-12, 1994), p. 2.

[2] Edith L. Blumhofer, *The Assemblies of God: A Popular History* (Springfield, MO: Gospel Publishing House, 1985), p. 137.

were free (in fact had an obligation) to follow the call to preach the gospel.[3] As R.E. McAlister writes in the Pentecostal Assemblies of Canada's (PAOC) periodical in October 1921, 'It is the privilege of every Minister of the Gospel – of every Christian man and woman, boy and girl, to be a soul-winner'.[4]

Such soul-winning was urgent due to the belief in the imminent return of Christ. As an article in 1922 explains it, 'We are a missionary people because we believe in the Second Coming of Jesus'.[5] However, when Christ did not return as soon as expected, the original impulse towards viewing everyone as soul-winners was seriously undermined. This particularly affected women, who found themselves sidelined as the movement set about organizing itself for a longer stay in this world. As long as the movement remained relatively unorganized, questions of male headship and/or female submission could play themselves out on individual and local levels, remaining relatively hidden. Yet, once the Pentecostal Assemblies of Canada was organized, a dominating assumption of male only leadership emerged in regards to the exercise of corporate authority and how it might function.[6] At the same time, while warning women not to overstep their bounds and attempt to usurp authority over men, the role of women within the home was being idealized. As the mothers of men, women were told that they had a 'grander sphere' of responsibility and privilege.[7]

---

[3] Women's obligation to be obedient can be seen in the words of Blanche A. Appleby when she signs her correspondence regarding her work in South China, reported in the December 1922 issue of the *Canadian Pentecostal Testimony*, 'Yours in His bonds', which implies that she was a slave for God with no choice but to do the Master's will. *Canadian Pentecostal Testimony* 2.12 (December 1922), p. 1.

[4] R.E. McAlister, 'Soul Winner', *Canadian Pentecostal Testimony* 9 (October 1921), p. 2.

[5] Walter McAllister, 'Do You Love the Lord's Appearing', *Canadian Pentecostal Testimony* 2.2 (February 1922), p. 1.

[6] See my articles 'Ministering Women in the Pentecostal Assemblies of Canada: A Feminist Exploration', in Michael Wilkinson (ed.), *Canadian Pentecostals* (Montreal, Quebec, Kingston, Ontario: McGill-Queens University Press, 2009), pp. 171-94, and 'The "Place" of Women in Pentecostal/Charismatic Ministry Since the Azusa Street Revival', in Harold D. Hunter and Cecil M. Robeck, Jr. (eds.), *The Azusa Street Revival and Its Legacy* (Eugene: Wipf & Stock, 2009), pp. 297-315, for further analyses of this process.

[7] D.N. Buntain, 'The Christian Wife', *The Pentecostal Testimony* (December 15, 1940), p. 3.

Evangelicalism and Fundamentalism

Soon after Pentecostalism's emergence within Canada, the various Pentecostal fellowships sought to be accepted and recognized by other Christian groups. Evangelicalism, of which Fundamentalist is a small subset, was the one, and pretty much the only Christian group that tentatively recognized Pentecostalism's existence in its infancy.[8] The PAOC was eager to maintain a good reputation with Evangelicals even though it recognized that it was different from them. For example, Gloria Kulbeck mentions that Evangelicals criticized the Pentecostal movement within Canada as unscriptural due to the fact that 'many of the outstanding evangelists, missionaries, teachers and pastors ... have been women'.[9] In response to the criticism, Kulbeck explained that the PAOC position was similar to that of the Assemblies of God as understood by Carl Brumback, whom she quotes, 'Perhaps the present-day Pentecostal Movement has been somewhat lenient in its enforcement of I Corinthians 14:34, 38'. She continues citing Brumback,

> This leniency may be due to a reaction against the extremely legal attitude of other groups; or it may be that we have been influenced by the Twentieth Century idea about women's rights or it may be that we have emphasized the Scriptural exception rather than the rule. Nevertheless, we do feel that the spirit of the rule is in effect in our midst. On the whole, women are not given undue prominence in the movement; they represent a very small percentage of the ministry; and they are virtually silent with respect to doctrinal and governmental questions ... in some instances, women may speak in the church without violating their subjection to men.[10]

However, Kulbeck also highlights women's active involvement. The ambiguity is obvious. Although women were actively involved in ministry during the early years of the PAOC's formation, their

---

[8] Edith L. Blumhofer, *Restoring the Faith: The Assemblies of God, Pentecostalism and American Culture* (Urbana and Chicago: University of Illinois Press, 1993), p. 185.

[9] Gloria Grace Kulbeck, *What God Hath Wrought: A History of The Pentecostal Assemblies of Canada* (Toronto: The Pentecostal Assemblies of Canada, 1958), p. 13.

[10] Kulbeck, *What God Hath Wrought*, p. 14, citing Carl Brumback, *What Meaneth This?* (London: Elim Publishing Company Limited, 1946), pp. 314-15.

participation in ministry was accepted but limited, affirmed but re-stricted. A 'place' may have been created for women in public min-istry, but women's involvements seemed to require a defence or an explanation.

During this period of seeking acceptance, the Assemblies of God considered themselves 'Fundamentalists with a difference' in that they were in basic agreement with the 'fundamentals of the faith'. Nonetheless, Fundamentalists would have nothing to do with Pentecostals and officially opposed the movement in 1928.[11] This is understandable in that Fundamentalists tend to be rational and text-directed in their practice. As such, they view the Bible as the author-itative, verbally inspired, literal and inerrant, written Word of God.[12] The 'letter of the law' is very important to them. Pentecostals, in comparison, are experiential and believe themselves to be Spirit di-rected in their practice. While Pentecostals have a high view of the Scriptures, they tend to approach them in a less literal and rational sense. The 'Spirit of the law' is important to Pentecostals.[13] Funda-mentalists tend to be suspicious of the Pentecostal emphasis on the immediate experience of the Spirit. Therefore, Fundamentalists tend to be anti-Pentecostal and anti-charismatic. Many Pentecostals consider it at least an uninformed overgeneralization if not an out-right insult when they are labelled Fundamentalists. This distinction between Pentecostals and Fundamentalist is important in that it holds out the promise of the development of hermeneutical ap-proaches within Pentecostalism that are not held hostage to a mis-placed historicism or debates regarding 'inerrancy' or false choices between 'Fundamentalist' or 'liberal' methods of interpretation. Pentecostal approaches provide examples of other ways to handle the biblical texts to which they assign authority. Fundamentalists consider the Scriptures inerrant. Evangelicals consider them suffi-

---

[11] Blumhofer, *Restoring the Faith*, pp. 5, 6, 159.

[12] See, Kenneth J. Archer, *A Pentecostal Hermeneutic for the Twenty-First Century: Spirit, Scripture and Community* (JPTSup 28; London, New York: T & T Clark In-ternational, 2004), pp. 35-62.

[13] Timothy B. Cargal, 'Beyond the Fundamentalist-Modernist Controversy: Pentecostals and Hermeneutics in a Postmodern Age' (Paper Presented to the 21st Annual Meeting of the Society for Pentecostal Studies, Lakeland, Florida, 7-9 November 1991), pp. 1, 5-6, later published in *Pneuma* 15 (Fall 1993), pp. 163-87).

cient and authoritative. Pentecostals consider them inspired and illumined.[14]

The identification of Pentecostalism with Fundamentalism even among Pentecostals is far from settled. As one Pentecostal, Timothy Cargal, explained the situation within the United States:

> Pentecostal biblical interpreters in the United States have become increasingly entangled in debates originating in the Fundamentalist–Modernist controversy of the early twentieth century ... Modernism finds its epistemological roots (and some would say its defining characteristic) in the Enlightenment ideal of 'objectivity'. Its basic presupposition is that reality is objectively knowable, and (by implication) only that which is objectively knowable is real. This objectivist/positivist presupposition is then brought into the service of a historicist view of meaning; history becomes the 'field encompassing field' which gives significance and meaning to the knowledge about 'objective reality' ... Fundamentalists sought to maintain their beliefs within the confines of the modernist philosophical paradigm by comparing and contrasting their approach to the Bible with that of their modernist opponents. For the modernists, the meaningfulness of the Bible for twentieth century Christians was found in the 'kernels' discovered by critical, objective historical reconstruction and in the very process of historical development itself; for Fundamentalists, already committed to the belief that the bible is true and meaningful, biblical interpretation demonstrates that the Bible is objectively and historically true ... What both Fundamentalists and modernists have in common is a philosophical presupposition that only what is historically and objectively true is meaningful.[15]

This has had serious repercussions when it comes to the women in its midst. When Scriptures are granted the status of some sort of 'final authority', they are often used in a literalistic, prescriptive

---

[14] Cargal, 'Beyond the Fundamentalist-Modernist Controversy', pp. 1-3, pp. 6-7.

[15] Cargal, 'Beyond the Fundamentalist-Modernist Controversy', pp. 1, 5-6. See also Archer, *A Pentecostal Hermeneutic,* for an ongoing discussion of this controversy along with a suggestion for a particularly Pentecostal approach.

sense. Within Pentecostalism, such a use of Scriptures is common, stemming from and feeding into its Fundamentalistic leanings.

EDITED However, a primarily rationalistic approach, whether that is expressed in Fundamentalism, or even liberalism, is incongruent with Pentecostalism's experientialist practices.[16] As well, a Fundamentalist approach tends to be hierarchical and exclusive, which is in direct conflict with Pentecostalism's original egalitarian impulse and inclusive ethos. While in the early years, Pentecostals were not in the position to be involved in this controversy due to their small size, loosely organized structures, lower class backgrounds, and dismissal by the larger, dominant churches,[17] they indiscriminately went along with the larger evangelical community that sided with Fundamentalism. Now that Pentecostals are finally seeing the need to determine their own identities and decide their own loyalties, this Fundamentalistic stance can be critically rethought.[18] As Allan Anderson, a scholar of Pentecostalism has argued, 'Pentecostalism ... predated Fundamentalism and is essentially different from it'. In addition, Pentecostalism 'brought a new *experience* rather than an argument against theological liberalism'. As a 'harsh critic' of Pentecostalism, Fundamentalism is 'better seen as the "fraternal twin" of liberalism and its "logical end"'[19] than as interchangeable and synonymous with Pentecostalism.

---

[16] Harvey Cox discusses this tendency, describing it as a conflict between 'fundamentalists' and 'experientialists' evident globally in all religious groups in his book *Fire from Heaven: The Rise of Pentecostal Spirituality and the Reshaping of Religion in the Twentieth-First Century* (Reading, MA: Addison-Wesley, 1995), pp. 299-321. Cox sees experientialist family resemblances between Pentecostals, liberationists, and feminists.

[17] Gerry Sheppard, using an insight from James Washington, labelled Pentecostalism a 'submodern' movement in that, while it emerged within modernity, it nevertheless was 'not invited as equal partners into the modernist debate'. Gerald T. Sheppard, 'Biblical Interpretation After Gadamer,' *Pneuma* 16.1 (1994), pp. 121-41 (127).

[18] A careful reading of Theodor Adorno's *The Psychological Technique of Martin Luther Thomas' Radio Addresses*, while dated, could assist in this critical rethinking, particularly Adorno's discussion of 'emotional release' religion as having a 'good old time', following a leader, maintaining 'unity', the 'last hour' approach, 'speaking with tongues' in a decidedly non-Pentecostal understanding of the practice, 'anti-institutionalism', appeal to the 'faith of our fathers', and 'communism'. See Theodor Adorno, *The Psychological Technique of Martin Luther Thomas' Radio Addresses* (Stanford, California: Stanford University Press, 2000).

[19] Allan Anderson, *An Introduction to Pentecostalism* (Cambridge, UK: Cambridge University Press, 2004, 2006), p. 259.

Identifying Pentecostals with Fundamentalism is not only false but also potentially harmful when it comes to the liberation of women within its midst. As Elisabeth Schüssler Fiorenza notes, Fundamentalist groups in the various religions, including Christianity, 'are a political-religious response to the struggle of democratic movements', including feminist ones 'around the globe'. Within Christianity, not only does the 'political-religious right' claim 'the power to name and to define the true nature of biblical religions against liberation theologies of all colors and geographical locations', their 'well-financed think tanks ... supported by reactionary political and financial institutions ... seek to defend kyriarchal capitalism'. In the process, they continue to 'debate ... women's place and role' even as they portray liberated 'women as signifiers of Western decadence or of modern atheistic secularism' and 'masculine power as the expression of divine power'. While they use 'modern media technologies', 'modern technological science', 'modern industrialism and nationalism', they denounce 'many of the political and ethical values espoused by modern democracy'. These political and ethical values include

> basic individual rights, pluralism, freedom of speech, the right to housing, health care, and work, equal compensation for equal work, social market measures, a democratic ethos, the sharing of power and political responsibility, and especially equal rights for women.[20]

The Bible

Significant when it comes to the liberation of women within Pentecostalism, Fundamentalists use the Scriptures to attack women, as Schüssler Fiorenza suggests,

> Not only in the last century but also today patriarchal right-wing forces in society lace their attacks against women's rights and freedoms in the political, economic, reproductive, intellectual, and religious arenas with biblical quotations and appeals to scriptural authority. In countless pulpits and Fundamentalist TV pro-

---

[20] Elisabeth Schüssler Fiorenza, *Jesus: Miriam's Child, Sophia's Prophet: Critical Issues in Feminist Christology* (New York: Continuum, 1994, 1995), p. 8.

grams, such patriarchal attacks are proclaimed as the Word of God while the feminist struggle for women's liberation is denounced as 'godless humanism' that undermines the 'American family'.[21]

However, the Bible has been used by others to authorize and legitimate women who seek liberation from exploitation and enslavement. It has 'inspired' many women to 'speak out and to struggle against injustice, exploitation, and stereotyping' providing them with a 'vision of freedom and wholeness' and empowering them 'to struggle against poverty, unfreedom, and denigration'. At the same time, these same Scriptures, both in the past and currently, have been used to exploit and enslave women, children, and non-elite men. As Schüssler Fiorenza claims,

> the political right does not simply misquote or misuse the Bible as a Christian feminist apologetics seeks to argue. It can utilize certain Scriptural texts because they are patriarchal in their original function and intentions … Certain texts of the Bible can be used in the argument against women's struggle for liberation not only because they are patriarchally misinterpreted but because they are patriarchal texts and therefore can serve to legitimate women's subordinate role and secondary status in patriarchal society and church.[22]

Therefore, feminists advocate the use of a 'hermeneutics of suspicion' when seeking to interpret both 'contemporary androcentric interpretations of the Bible and the biblical texts themselves'.[23] The 'critical dialectical mode' of interpretation Schüssler Fiorenza promotes is her own 'critical feminist hermeneutic of liberation' which both recognizes the ambiguities of the Scriptures when it comes to women and non-elites while drawing out its potential to 'end relations of domination and exploitation'.[24]

Therefore, Schüssler Fiorenza recasts biblical studies in rhetorical terms in the hopes of displacing supposed objective and non-political approaches presently gaining ground even within some

---

[21] Elisabeth Schüssler Fiorenza, *Bread Not Stone: The Challenge of Feminist Biblical Interpretation* (Boston: Beacon Press, 1984), p. xii.

[22] Schüssler Fiorenza, *Bread Not Stone*, p. xiii.

[23] Schüssler Fiorenza, *Bread Not Stone*, p. xii.

[24] Schüssler Fiorenza, *Bread Not Stone*, p. xiii.

women's studies.[25] She argues that biblical interpretations are not disinterested but rather have a political context and content and tend to reinforce society's status quo.[26] Therefore, she stresses that biblical interpretation be recognized as 'the site of competing discursive practices'.[27] As she explains it, the current paradigm functioning even within the academy, which stresses supposedly impassive, detached, objective, value-free, non-ideological, non-political scholarly research and discourse, is in reality an exercise in self and institutional deception.[28] This is because everyone brings his or her experiences and preunderstandings to any task including that of interpretation. As a result, she would most likely *not accuse* but rather *assume* that Pentecostals 'eisegete', that is, read their preunderstandings into the Bible like everybody else. Still, she would also probably insist that Pentecostals, like everyone else, must *take responsibility* for the effects of their interpretations of biblical texts. It is not enough to recognize that eisegesis is occurring. Those often unconscious preunderstandings that are brought to the biblical text must be critically examined and evaluated to determine how they are influencing the interpretative process and people.

In addition, Schüssler Fiorenza views the Bible as an 'historical prototype' rather than a 'mythic archetype'. When viewed as a mythic archetype, the historical assumptions of the contexts within which the Bible was formulated including androcentrism, patriarchy and kyriarchy, are posited as normative and authoritative. In contrast, when viewed as an historical prototype, the Bible is recognized as being written and read from within particular historical and ideological contexts. Therefore, it can be critically examined to discern those portions that appear to legitimate oppression from those which are liberating.[29] In her view, the Bible becomes, at the very most, a source, or even only a resource, for women's struggles for liberation.[30]

---

[25] Schüssler Fiorenza, *Bread Not Stone*, p. xiii.

[26] Schüssler Fiorenza, *Bread Not Stone*, p. 3.

[27] Schüssler Fiorenza, *Bread Not Stone*, p. 152.

[28] Elisabeth Schüssler Fiorenza, *Sharing Her Word: Feminist Biblical Interpretation in Context* (Boston: Beacon Press, 1998), pp. 40-46.

[29] Schüssler Fiorenza, *Bread Not Stone*, pp. 10-14.

[30] Schüssler Fiorenza, *Bread Not Stone*, p. 14. Earlier she had claimed that the New Testament is both a source of revelatory truth and a resource for patriarchal practices. Elisabeth Schüssler Fiorenza, *In Memory of Her: A Feminist Theological*

For many Pentecostal women and men, viewing the Bible as only a resource is insufficient. While a variety of different hermeneutical approaches have been and still are used by different Pentecostals,[31] for many of them the Scriptures are understood as a place, among others, where God encounters people. The goal of interpretation for Pentecostals is not simply to discern what the text may have originally meant or even what it still means today. Rather, in their reading, studying, and preaching of the Scriptures, Pentecostals seek to know and be known by God in a transformative and ongoing experiential fashion. Pentecostals view the Scriptures as much more than a resource. Yet, the Scriptures do tend to be read as a type of 'archetypal' document. When coupled with a lack of awareness of preunderstandings influencing interpretation and with an assumption of 'objectivity' derived from the larger societal 'norm', the Bible becomes a site of contradiction and conflict for all Canadian Pentecostals, particularly ministering women as can be illustrated by referencing the PAOC's history.

The Spirit and Experience

Pentecostals insist that the Spirit's involvement is a major factor in understanding the Bible as the Word of God; there is significance to the biblical text that goes beyond its function as a work of literature that can only be perceived with the aid of the Spirit. The assumption is that the Bible can be read by a non-Christian without anything of spiritual value being gained. Non-Christians are thought to be blind to the reality of God's revelation in Scripture unless the Spirit opens their eyes. It is only when the Spirit illumines the Bible that it becomes spiritually meaningful for readers. In this sense, the language and grammatical aspects of the text are not what makes

---

Reconstruction of Christian Origin (New York: Crossroad, Tenth Anniversary Edition with a New Introduction, 1998), p. 30. With the use that she makes of the Bible in deriving norms such as the 'Spirit', 'Sophia', 'divine Presence', 'discipleship of equals', and 'reign of God' from it, the Bible seems to be functioning as a significant source in her work. In spite of this discrepancy, Schüssler Fiorenza insists that her approach is in keeping with the statements of the Second Vatican Council that affirmed that the Bible is without error in what matters 'for the sake of our salvation' (Schüssler Fiorenza, *Bread Not Stone*, p. 14).

[31] Discussions of these various approaches have appeared, for instance, in *Pneuma*, Society of Pentecostal Studies annual meeting papers, and *The Journal of Pentecostal Theology* in recent years. However, no consensus has been reached.

the writings the Word of God but God's use of them. As the Word of God, the Spirit-illumined Scriptures are understood to possess transformative power and authority. This strong emphasis on the Holy Spirit in interpreting the Bible is derived by Pentecostals from the Scriptures themselves that emphasize the role of the Spirit in revealing God and God's will.[32]

Pentecostals also stress the role of the Spirit in inspiring both the original writers and the current readers. While a distinction is made between the original Spirit *inspired* authors – resulting in the text being granted ultimate authority – and the current Spirit *illuminated* interpreter – resulting in a less binding appropriation – 'within a Pentecostal setting these "illuminated" meanings exercise far more power over Pentecostal believers since they are perceived as carrying divine sanction and authority'.[33] As it is the same Spirit guiding and assisting both the original authors and the modern interpreters, the historical gap between past and present is assumed to be bridged.[34] Expressions such as 'the Spirit showed me' or 'the Holy Spirit revealed to me' are commonly heard from both the pulpit and the pew regarding the interpretation and possible applications of Scripture. Multiple meanings of the biblical text are understood to apply to various situations as they arise – situations that never occurred to the original author(s). Obviously, the potential for abuse exists in such practices. In spite of this, acknowledging that there are several interpretations of a text is not the same as saying that all interpretations are correct. Any text can be misinterpreted.

Regardless, within Pentecostalism, limiting the text's meaning to what the original author(s) thought is considered too restrictive.[35] As Roger Stronstad explains,

---

[32] For examples, such passages as Jn 14.26; 16.13; 1 Cor. 2.10.

[33] See Cargal, 'Beyond the Fundamentalist-Modernist Controversy', pp. 10-12, and French L. Arrington, 'The Use of the Bible by Pentecostals', *Pneuma* 16.1 (1994), pp. 101-107 (101).

[34] See Roger Stronstad, 'Pentecostalism, Experiential Presuppositions and Hermeneutics' (Paper Presented to 20th Annual Meeting of Society for Pentecostal Studies, Dallas, Texas, 8-10 November 1990), pp. 1-24, and Arrington, 'The Use of the Bible by Pentecostals', p. 101.

[35] Such as Evangelical exegesis does. See for example, Gordon Fee's *New Testament Exegesis: A Handbook for Students and Pastors* (Westminster: John Knox Press, 2002).

understanding involves the creative capacity of the interpreter to open up new insights which transcend the time-bound situation of the original author and the original audience. It is at this juncture where creative transcendence is needed, where the Spirit may indeed teach us and lead us into all truth.[36]

Interpretation is thought to be both an art and a technique that involves the Word and the Spirit. Faithfulness to the text as an 'archetypal' document, which provides a relatively 'objective' control, along with inspired creativity, which allows God to move and causes the Scriptures to function more as an 'historical prototype', are both important in the interpretative process.

While this emphasis on the Spirit allows for a certain amount of fluidity when interpreting the Scriptures, it does not take into account the influence of preunderstandings in the process. Such preunderstandings have an experiential basis. Pentecostals are concerned about 'religious experience'. This is significant in that 'Pentecostals said yes to both the authority of Scripture and the authority of experience' thereby putting the two concepts 'into a creative dialectical tension'.[37] As one Pentecostal explains, echoing the thinking of Schüssler Fiorenza, this approach is significant:

> The Pentecostal hermeneutic that allows experience to inform interpretation brings into focus the issue of subjectivity versus objectivity. The assumption is that if the biblical text is approached from the stance of human experience, then the interpretation is more subjective; but if approached on the basis of logic and reason, the interpretation is more objective. Logic and reason occur within the human mind and, therefore, are subjective to some degree. The restriction of the hermeneutical process to reason and logic is to try to take a broader sweep of human experience and to encounter a stranger's point of view ... Objectivity and subjectivity have been thought of as opposites. Both need to be seen as two sides of the same coin, and both need to be seen as falling in the sphere of the experience of faith that has been ignited by the Word of God and the Holy Spirit. From this perspective the hermeneutical process can be viewed as dialogi-

---

[36] Stronstad, 'Pentecostalism, Experiential Presuppositions and Hermeneutics', pp. 1-24.
[37] Archer, *A Pentecostal Hermeneutic*, p. 63.

276 The Many Voices of Global Pentecostalism

cal rather than linear, so that, at every point, experience informs the process of interpretation and the fruit of interpretation informs experience. So Pentecostals admit that their praxis informs what they find in Scripture, and they go on to acknowledge that what they find in Scripture informs their Pentecostal praxis.[38]

Pentecostals tend to move from their experience of God to the Bible.[39] If their experiences are not supported by Scripture, they are suspect.[40] As one Pentecostal explains, such an approach has advantages in that the authority of Scripture is not founded upon a 'bedrock of doctrine' but rather doctrine rests on the experience of encountering God as Spirit. Therefore these doctrinal positions, various practices, and even unexamined assumptions about how things should be or are (such as patriarchy) can be challenged and corrected without doing damage to the core of Pentecostal faith, i.e. an encounter with God as Spirit and the outworkings of that encounter. Pentecostals are not likely to enter into a 'fight to the death' in defence of rational, doctrinal statements and the potential is there to think critically about their practices and positions.[41] Moreover, authority itself is fluid, not embedded or grounded in the above-mentioned 'bedrock of doctrine' but understood to reside within human experiences of the Spirit.

---

[38] Arrington, 'The Use of the Bible by Pentecostals', pp. 105-106.

[39] Hermeneutically, a common criticism of Pentecostals, particularly by evangelicals, is that they 'eisegete their experience into the text'. However, many Pentecostals feel no need to defend their approach. See for example Roger Stronstad, 'Pentecostal Experience and Hermeneutics', *Paraclete* 26.1 (Winter 1992), pp. 14-30.

[40] Kenneth J. Archer, 'Pentecostal Hermeneutics: Retrospect and Prospect', *Journal of Pentecostal Theology* 8 (1996), pp. 63-81 (77-78), citing M. McLean, 'Toward a Pentecostal Hermeneutic,' *Pneuma* 6.2 (1984), p. 38.

[41] The exception, of course, is those Pentecostal groups that have aligned themselves with the more fundamentalistic evangelicals. As well, this is not to suggest that doctrines are unimportant to Pentecostals. Doctrines are very important. However 'Pentecostals base their faith *first* on the God that they have met and know in relationship' (Scott A. Ellington, 'Pentecostalism and the Authority of Scripture', *Journal of Pentecostal Theology* 9 [1996], pp. 16-38 [17-18]).

The Community

For Schüssler Fiorenza, reflection and analysis of experience are carried on within the *ekklesia* of wo/men.[42] Within this *ekklesia* of wo/men, feminist discourses seek 'to persuade the democratic assembly and to adjudicate arguments in order to make decisions for the sake of everyone's welfare'.[43] As she describes it, wo/men church is not a 'site of competing confessional discourses'. Rather, it is a 'rhetorical space from where to assert women's theological authority to determine the interpretation of Christian scriptures, tradition, theology, and community' where 'the divine breath of life' invigorates 'all and everyone' and authority is derived from the 'experience of G-d's[44] liberating presence in today's struggles to end patriarchal domination'[45] and historical and kyriarchal contexts.[46] She argues that the 'authority of inspiration' is not limited to only certain people or even texts but is given to the whole church as comprised of people who are 'enlivened and empowered by the life-giving breath of Sophia-Spirit'.[47] She declares, 'inspiration must not

---

[42] Schüssler Fiorenza writes 'women' as 'wo/men' 'in order to destabilize the essentialist notions of woman and indicate that from the perspective and positionality of wo/men who are multiply oppressed, the term is also inclusive of disenfranchised men'. Schüssler Fiorenza, 'Introduction: Feminist Liberation Theology as Critical Sophialogy', in *Power of Naming: A Concilium Reader in Feminist Liberation Theology* (Maryknoll, New York: Orbis Books, 1996), pp. xiii-xxxix, p. xxxv, n. 1.

[43] Schüssler Fiorenza, *But She Said*, p. 131.

[44] In recognition that language is 'not capable of adequately expressing the Divine', Schüssler Fiorenza first used this manner of spelling God and later 'G*d'. Elisabeth Schüssler Fiorenza, 'Cartography of Struggle', *Discipleship of Equals: A Critical Feminist Ekklesia-logy of Liberation* (New York: Crossroads, 1993, 1994), pp. 1-12, p. 10 n. 13. In her book, *Jesus: Miriam's Child, Sophia's Prophet*, Schüssler Fiorenza 'switched from the orthodox Jewish writing of G-d which she had adopted in *But She Said* and *Discipleship of Equals* in order to indicate the brokenness and inadequacy of human language to name the Divine to this spelling of G*d, which seeks to avoid the conservative maelstrom association which the writing of G-d has for Jewish feminists'. Schüssler Fiorenza, 'Introduction: Feminist Liberation Theology as Critical Sophialogy', in *Power of Naming: A Concilium Reader in Feminist Liberation Theology* (Maryknoll, New York: Orbis Books, 1996), pp. xiii-xxxix, p. xxxv, n. 4.

[45] Schüssler Fiorenza, *But She Said*, p. 152.

[46] Schüssler Fiorenza, *Bread Not Stone*, p. 10-14.

[47] Schüssler Fiorenza, *But She Said*, p. 156.

be understood as a reified given in biblical texts but as inherent in the practices of a critical interpretation for liberation'.[48]

Furthermore, Schüssler Fiorenza claims that 'inspiration' as 'the life-giving breath and power of Sophia-Spirit' did not cease once canonization occurred. The Spirit remains active today. She calls for a return to the 'practice of "discerning the spirit" as a deliberative rhetorical spiritual practice',[49] not only in everything the church does but also more specifically within 'the people of Sophia-G-d who are women', who are 'sisters of the Spirit'. To Schüssler Fiorenza's words could be added 'brothers', as through the ages such sisters and brothers of the Spirit have proclaimed the gospel in the authority of the Spirit, thereby overcoming racial and gender prejudices along with social and educational disadvantages.[50] While 'discerning the Spirit' is supposedly a regular practice in Pentecostal circles, rarely has anyone dared to ask what 'spirit' is being manifested in a community where androcentric assumptions and kyriarchal practices continue to silence and restrict Spirit gifted and called women and men. Moreover, what 'spirit' is being manifested when Scriptures are appealed to in order to undermine the Spirit's authority to blow where She will?[51]

While Schüssler Fiorenza's location of inspiration primarily in the practices of the *ekklesia* of wo/men is debatable, her point that inspiration is a result of the breath and power of the Spirit and is, therefore, not to be located in the Bible alone, is valid. For Pentecostals, inspiration, with its inherent authority, resides with the Spirit, Who continues to gift and empower people and to illumine the Scriptures. Therefore, experiences and the Scriptures can be critically examined to discern those portions that appear to legitimate oppression from those which are liberating.[52] The influence that experience exerts within Pentecostalism is both strength and a weakness.

In early Pentecostalism, the Spirit-inspired and Spirit-illumined Scriptures were understood to be authoritative. As the *Apostolic*

---

[48] Schüssler Fiorenza, *But She Said*, p. 163.

[49] Schüssler Fiorenza, *Sharing Her Word*, p. 88.

[50] Schüssler Fiorenza, *But She Said*, pp. 156-157.

[51] 'She' is my preferred pronoun for referring to the Spirit, rather than the more commonly used 'he' or 'it'. Part of my reason for doing so is to raise awareness about the use of 'he' commonly used within Pentecostalism and how it feeds into the assumption that God is male.

[52] Schüssler Fiorenza, *Bread Not Stone*, pp. 10-14.

Faith declares , 'We are feeding upon the Word which is revealed by the Holy Ghost – the whole Word and nothing but the Word,' even though certain portions of that Word, such as the above mentioned 'Slaves, be obedient to them that are your masters', were not expounded.[53] Yet, the Spirit was also understood to be empowering people to speak with authority. As *The Apostolic Faith* explains, '"He will guide you into all truth." We ought to take the Holy Ghost before any other teacher. We should have no teacher between us and the Holy Ghost.'[54] Authority was also being exercised through people telling and retelling their stories of how the Spirit was at work in their lives, thereby examining and re-examining the interpretations of the Bible in the light of the insights of all Spirit filled believers.[55] Intentional effort was made to allow all to contribute, including non-elite men and women regardless of race or social class.

Part of the living out of the gospel for Pentecostals includes paying attention to context, discerning the Spirit at work in the world drawing the world toward God, while at the same time noting the evil that must be confronted and challenged. This involves paying attention to voices, to perspectives, which they may not be eager to hear, prophetically calling the movement to account for how it is living out the gospel in the power of the Spirit.

Experiences and Scriptures are being used as sources within Pentecostalism along with reason and Pentecostal communal tradition. Due to the lack of acknowledgement of the direction of this movement – from experiences to the Scriptures – confusion and conflict arise. Recognition of the direction of this movement could help resolve this confusion and conflict when it comes to the 'women question' as well as other issues. Once the direction of the movement is acknowledged, experiences can be critically analyzed using reason and Pentecostal communal tradition in order to decide which experiences are in keeping with the good news of the gospel for *all* people. Pentecostalism's Fundamentalistic tendencies, even when they attempt to function as a counter balance, are incongruent with their experientialist practices. Pentecostals understand themselves to have experienced the Spirit Who empowers them to live out the ramifications of that experience. Pentecostals are constantly

---

[53] *The Apostolic Faith* 1.7 (April 1907), p. 2.
[54] *The Apostolic Faith* 1.6 (February-March 1907), p. 3.
[55] *The Apostolic Faith* is full of such stories, testimonies, sermons, etc.

seeking to discern and experience the Spirit. There are no clear guidelines as to what experiences should be considered, as everything and anything has the potential to be considered an experience of the Spirit. Experiences are considered of primary importance in that they are what are used to make sense of and make up lives. Pentecostals start with what they consider to be experiences of the Spirit and then reflect on them.

Even so, when it comes to the liberation of women, Schüssler Fiorenza cautions that the methodological starting point for hermeneutics cannot be a 'commonsense' type of experience alone. Experiences along with values and mind-sets can be critically reflected upon and analyzed.[56]

Conscientization

Convinced that 'wo/men have internalized and are shaped by kyriarchal "commonsense" mind-sets and values', Schüssler Fiorenza maintains, 'the hermeneutical starting point of critical feminist interpretation can only be wo/men's experience of injustice as it has been critically explored by a hermeneutics of suspicion in the process of "conscientization"'. According to Schüssler Fiorenza, a feminist critical process of conscientization 'strives to create critical consciousness and has as its goal both a praxis of solidarity and a commitment to feminist struggles that seek to transform patriarchal relations of subordination and expression'. Accompanied by cognitive dissonance, conscientization includes "'breakthrough" and "disclosure" experiences which bring into question the "commonsense" character of patriarchal reality'.[57]

Within the Pentecostal community, women can be heard. Even so, before they speak, they must become aware of their own internalization of patriarchal assumptions. Otherwise, their speech will simply reinforce their own subordinate positions and undervalued contributions. Pentecostal women can become self-aware – have their 'consciousness raised' – and then act. Perhaps a place to begin is with the recovery of their own somewhat egalitarian history and

---

[56] Schüssler Fiorenza, *Bread Not Stone*, p. 81.
[57] Schüssler Fiorenza, *Sharing Her Word*, p. 82.

hermeneutic that involves experiences and community as discussed above.

Schüssler Fiorenza points out that feminist approaches, being explicitly committed to the struggle to change patriarchal structures, 'must disentangle the ideological (religious-theological) functions of biblical texts for inculcating and legitimating the patriarchal order'.[58] Within the Pentecostal community, this would include the ideology of male headship reinforced by patriarchal interpretations of Scripture. As mentioned earlier, Schüssler Fiorenza also notes that 'there is no place outside ideology from which one can critique ideology. One can only critique an ideology by locating oneself in another one, or by using the contradictions within a single ideology to uncover its disjunctures and opposing relations.'[59] Although a difficult position to be in, being both explicitly Pentecostal and feminist could prove fruitful.

The Possibilities of a Self Reflective Exercise of Authority

Schüssler Fiorenza emphasizes that many hermeneutical discussions revolve around the issue of authority. The Pentecostal community is caught up in this conversation, the debate concerning the role of women within the church being a case in point. Still, her concern regarding the issue of authority tends to overlook the fact that in any relationship, power and authority is being exercised, for example, her own as an 'expert' in feminist theology including her concept of 'women church' as a democracy of equals. Schüssler Fiorenza also seems to assume that authority is always exercised in dominating ways. It, of course, can be, but does not necessarily have to be. Relocating authority from the biblical text to a woman affirming community inspired by the Spirit may not correct the problem of the misuse of authority. Even a woman affirming community is comprised of women and women identified men who have been saturated with patriarchal assumptions from which it is difficult to disentangle themselves. There is a very real danger of reproducing oppressions of various types. As well, the biblical text has always been interpreted by a community, Spirit inspired or not.

---

[58] Schüssler Fiorenza, *But She Said*, p. 41.
[59] Schüssler Fiorenza, *But She Said*, p. 113.

Within Pentecostalism, which was Spirit focused and woman affirming (as well as racially and socially inclusive) in its beginning, patriarchy/kyriarchy still eventually became the unquestioned model of relationships. Conscientization might help. Yet, even that involves interaction with and interpretation of the biblical text. The problem is not so much to dismiss, ignore, or argue against the authority of Scripture as much as to exercise that authority in a healthier way.

A method that honours the Bible, recognizing that it has the potential to speak and influence in non-dominating ways, is preferable. Schüssler Fiorenza and Pentecostals are not primarily concerned with the historical facts of the biblical text (although historical questions do enter into the interpretative process). Instead both focus on the symbolic meaning of the text, ascertaining that meaning through 'imaginative reconstruction' (Schüssler Fiorenza) or 'Spirit illumination' coupled with various evangelical methodologies (Pentecostals). The meaning of the text applies then today as 'women church' (Schüssler Fiorenza)' or 'Spirit-filled believers' (Pentecostals). The possibilities and potentialities of this dialectical model that brings together the role of Bible and the role of the community linked by the Spirit in the process of interpretation deserve exploration. Within this dialectic the Bible acts as a meta-narrative or a 'historical prototype' as Schüssler Fiorenza calls it, in the sense of being a significant resource of stories and teachings illustrating how the Spirit of God has acted within the lives of people in the past. As within Pentecostalism it is assumed that the self-same Spirit inspired the recording of this material and continues to illumine its interpretation, it then becomes a significant source of inspiration for Pentecostals' ongoing lives together. As such, the Bible would provide the consistency for the ongoing living out of the biblical narrative in a creative fashion acting as an authoritative text that can be constantly re-examined to determine whether its interpretation is promoting abundant life for all, in accordance with the Spirit, or only for a privileged few. In addition, 'that we may have life, and have it more abundantly' (Jn 10.10) is an often repeated phrase within Pentecostal congregations. Within Canadian Pentecostal worship contexts, one of the reasons for being filled with the Spirit is so that people might receive the power or be empowered to experience life in all its fullness and abundance.

The Possibilities of Pentecostal Particularities

The Pentecostal community's attempt to continue to live out the implications of its Christian commitment in creative ways consistent with its context would be the other side of the dialectical relationship. Pentecostals often speak of being an 'Acts 29 people', indicating that they consider the story of the Bible to be ongoing. The attempt can be regularly examined to see how it continues the story of the Bible. As the Bible is considered not essentially a doctrinal treatise, but a 'record of testimonies, a story of the relationship between God and his creation', it witnesses to the 'diverse ways in which the biblical authors *experienced* the revelation of God'.[60] This lends itself to the attempt at continuing to experience the revelation of God.

It is the Spirit's bringing the various aspect of the biblical text to life that the community would then recognize as relevant and authoritative, compelling and enabling them to apply these insights to particular continuing contexts in the power of the Spirit. The Spirit-illuminated Scriptures serve as judge and corrector of experiences while at the same time pushing towards the possibilities of new realities being recognized and realized. While Spirit-illuminated Scripture may be the final authority, such authority does not become concretized in doctrinal positions. Such an approach should be conducive to the conscientization process because all voices are being heard and considered.

Conclusion

In order to be considered humane, any thinking, including theological thinking, must remain intentionally self-reflective and critical in order to identify and analyze those aspects of a movement or tradition which hold emancipatory potential and those aspects which are oppressive. Within Pentecostalism, a move away from dogmatic, biblical text and theology with its apologetic and polemical attitudes toward doctrines and articles of faith can be undertaken. As American Pentecostal scholar, Frank Macchia has explained in a work dealing with global Pentecostalism,

---

[60] Ellington, 'Pentecostalism and the Authority of Scripture', pp. 29-31.

within Anglo-American Pentecostalism with its concern to remain acceptable to Christian Evangelicals and Fundamentalists, systematic theology has been equated with scripturally supported doctrines which summarize Pentecostal beliefs. As a result, dialogical, contextual, critical and creative reflection on those beliefs and their implications for social and cultural issues has been lacking and needs to be encouraged.[61]

Nevertheless, Macchia continues,

Afro-American, marginalized Pentecostals in the United States and Two Thirds World Pentecostals have focused on 'experience' validated only by the 'text of Scriptures and the experience of the Spirit in the daily lives of those searching to be faithful to Jesus Christ'. As a result, some 'theological creativity' has emerged and is reflected in preaching, various publications and 'non-official expressions of church life'.[62]

According to Macchia, a 'paradigm shift' is occurring within Pentecostal theology from a theology of 'Bible doctrines' to the 'rise of critical theology' which is prophetically concerned for personal and social liberation. As Macchia highlights,

If Pentecostal spirituality is to become identified with liberating praxis, an ongoing discernment of the forces of deception and their ideological defences utilized by corporate power to maintain the status quo will need to be utilized by Pentecostal communities of faith.[63]

Although overcoming kyriarchal attitudes and practices within Pentecostalism will not be easy, it is possible. Pentecostals are intensely interested in liberation, in life abundant for *all*. There is an underlying, emancipatory impulse in Pentecostalism dating from its origins. Its continuing growth among oppressed, marginalized peoples continues to be fertile ground for this liberative lens. Today

---

[61] Frank Macchia, 'The Struggle for Global Witness: Shifting Paradigms in Pentecostal Theology', in Murray W. Dempster, Byron D. Klaus, and Douglas Petersen (eds.), *The Globalization of Pentecostalism: A Religion Made to Travel* (Carlisle, California: Regnum Books, 1999), pp. 8-29 (8-9).

[62] Macchia draws on the work of another Pentecostal scholar, Russ Spittler. See Macchia, 'The Struggle for Global Witness', pp. 10-11.

[63] Macchia, 'The Struggle for Global Witness', pp. 8-13.

Pentecostalism is in a position to reclaim its liberative stance and explicitly and intentionally reapply such a stance to all those within its own midst who are experiencing oppression, not only at the hands of others, but also as a result of its unacknowledged harmful, ideological presuppositions and its incongruent hermeneutical practices. Pentecostal people will hopefully once again recognize that life experiences, including experiences of the Spirit, are influencing how Scriptures are read and appropriated. These experiences, if critically discerned and evaluated, will assist in interpreting and appropriating the Scriptures in a fashion that is liberative rather than oppressive. This will require Pentecostalism to re-emphasize its natural tendency to move from experiences to the Scriptures and resist pressures to reverse this tendency. Pentecostals can read Scriptures and examine diverse experiences more discerningly and intentionally in ways which move 'beyond exegetical and historical dialogues' while also retaining 'an emphasis on the role and authority of experience'.[64] These include insights gleaned from the experiences of women and those of other oppressed groups within its midst in order to recognize and to interpret passages with kyriarchal frameworks in a fashion which truly makes the gospel 'good news' for all. As Pentecostal Christians, both experiences of the Spirit and the Scriptures can be acknowledged as possessing authority by virtue of the fact that they are 'of the Spirit'. It is the Spirit as God who is, and who grants, authority. As the Spirit is understood to be constantly moving, different people and biblical texts are constantly being authorized and empowered. Authority shifts as the Spirit moves. To statically locate authority within one book, office, or person is to undermine the Spirit's authority and independent agency. The Spirit blows where She wills.

---

[64] Macchia, 'The Struggle for Global Witness', p. 10.

Index of Biblical and other Ancient References

Index of Authors

Made in the USA
Middletown, DE
25 November 2015